LEFT-BRAIN FINANCE for RIGHT-BRAIN PEOPLE

A MONEY GUIDE FOR THE CREATIVELY INCLINED

2nd Edition

Paula Ann Monroe

Sourcebooks, Inc.
Naperville, IL

Published by Sourcebooks, Inc., P.O. Box 372, Naperville, Illinois 60566
(630) 961-3900 FAX: (630) 961-2168

Library of Congress Cataloging-in-Publication Data
Monroe, Paula Ann.
  Left-brain finance for right-brain people, 2nd ed. : a money guide for the creatively inclined / Paula Ann Monroe.
       p. cm.
  ISBN 1-57071-340-5 (alk. paper)
  1. Finance, Personal. 2. Investments. 3. Insurance 4. Estate planning. I. Title.
HG179.M5978   1998
332.024—dc21   98-13241
                                                                 CIP

Printed and bound in the United States of America
10 9 8 7 6 5 4 3 2 1

Contents

PART 2: How Money Disappears

PART 3: How Money Grows

PART 4: Protection

PART 5: The Self-Employed

PART 6: Financial Planning

Tables and Charts

Mindmap of Left-Brain Finance for Right-Brain People

Part 5
The Self-Employed, p. 195

To TWO SPECIAL PEOPLE IN MY LIFE:

My intelligent, sensitive husband, **John Farrell Fay**, an accomplished trial attorney and author of his own book on arbitration, who completed his education in excellent institutions with a business major, but who was never taught the important principles found in this book. Sweetheart, you have mastered well the first thing you can do with a dollar: spend it. My hope is that you will now master the other two things you can do with that same dollar: save and invest it.

AND

To my sister **Louise Willoughby**, a wonderful first grade teacher, who inspired the idea behind this book when she put down my original manuscript and announced, "I don't read anything that doesn't have pictures!"

Acknowledgments

I AM GRATEFUL to the following people for their support and help with this book:

John Farrell Fay, my husband, for his encouragement, his logical thinking skills, and the many hours he spent helping me get more specific.

Jean Lenton, my sister and her husband **Dennis Lenton** for their editorial skills and helpful comments.

John Borsos, Esq., for his comments and encouragement.

Ron Karasiczkiewcz, CPA, for his comments on the tax chapter.

Susan Rylander, EA, a friend and colleague for her comments on "The Self-Employed."

Scott Wingett, CFP, who ran tons of proposals to convince me that variable life and universal life can be wise investments.

To all of my wonderful neighbors in Park City, Utah, who have given their continued support and friendship.

Introduction

LEFT-BRAIN FINANCE FOR RIGHT-BRAIN PEOPLE is a basic money book with an innovative approach. It is specifically written for creative individuals who find the standard books about personal finance boring. Typically, such readers become overwhelmed reading page after page of print with no visual references.

Right-brain people think differently, and this book complements their style. It does not have to be read from beginning to end to make sense; many different sequences will work. Overviews introduce each part, and key phrases summarize the main points. This makes it easy to skip around or review particular topics of interest. In addition, the graphs, tables, pictures, anecdotes, and stories aid comprehension for those who learn best by using these means.

The Left Brain vs. the Right Brain

Our bodies are bilateral, and the brain is no exception. It has two identical hemispheres joined by nerve fibers. Just as people are left- or right-handed, they are also left- or right-brained. "Left-brain" people have dominant left hemispheres, while "right-brain" people have dominant right hemispheres. We don't know why some people develop the right side of their brain more than the left or vice-versa. The

Our Brain Has Two Sides: Left and Right EVERY PERSON HAS A DOMINANT SIDE

THE LEFT SIDE: Logic, Reason, Literal, Thinks Part to Whole

THE RIGHT SIDE: Holistic, Imaginative, Figurative, Thinks Whole to Part

development could be hereditary, or it could be preference. The fact remains, however, that for most people, one side is dominant.

Each hemisphere excels at different skills with the dominant hemisphere influencing a person's general thinking patterns. The left side is logical; the right side is holistic. The left side comprehends through reasoning, the right side comprehends through images. While the left side listens to the literal meanings of words, the right side listens to tone of voice, body language, and voice inflection. The left side works with the smaller parts leading to the whole, but the right side previews the whole first, then works with the parts. Left-brain thinkers can put a jigsaw puzzle together by studying the individual pieces. But, the right-brain thinker wants to see the picture on the box cover before the pieces make sense.

Left-brain thinkers approach the world in a linear fashion. Compare them to a straight line. Their minds naturally move in sequence from point "A" to point "B" then to point "C". They remember details easily, follow directions without difficulty, and often have good vocabularies. After reading several pages, they can accurately summarize the main points. Describing and labeling are effortless because their minds move naturally from **part** to **whole.**

In contrast, right-brain people rarely start at the beginning and move in sequence from "A" to "B". Instead, they jump around from point to point: "M" to "C" to "A". Compare them to a curved line. Visualization, intuition, and artistic expression are their strong points. They associate ideas with pictures, colors, and textures. Frequently, right-brain people do not remember a stranger's name, but they do remember his general appearance and if they liked him. Right-brain thinkers start with the **whole** then move to the **parts.** Only when their trial and error methods fail do they resort to reading directions.

Some people naturally work better with numbers and formulas, while others work better with people and ideas. Most likely, if this book caught your eye, you are the latter. You are a "do-it-yourself" personality, directed by your visions. You probably excel at counseling, composing, teaching, creating, or building, not at following budgets, figuring taxes, balancing checkbooks, or calculating gains and losses.

This book is written for people who tend to be more right- than left-brained. It starts with the basics and builds a foundation that will help creative thinkers better understand themselves and how they use their money. This book does not assume its readers know how to figure net worth, or know the difference between income and growth investments. Moreover, it is the first practical guide on personal finance written especially for those who find the "money world" complex and boring.

This book has six sections.
1. The Big Picture
2. How Money Disappears
3. How Money Grows
4. Protection
5. The Self-Employed
6. Financial Planning

Each section has an overview because right-brain thinkers want to see the "whole" before they work with the parts or details. A mindmap outlines the material presented in the chapters. Mindmaps are graphic outlines that serve as a quick, easy way to find needed information.

A mindmap of the book, plus mindmaps of each part are located at the front of the book after the standard table of contents. Since a mindmap is a visual reference tool, your right brain may prefer it to the table of contents. Both are included to give you a choice.

This book is designed so you can easily find information and skip around to read the parts that interest you. Few right-brain people would attempt to read a book on finance. This book is different because you can skim through it and learn. The section overviews, the highlighted text, the pictures, margin quotes, and the charts make skimming easy. Then when you want to learn more, just read the regular text. **Key sentences and ideas have been set off in bold text. By glancing at the key ideas and margin quotes, you will learn the main points and know where to find needed information.** Most people are not interested in a financial topic until it affects them. Use this book to read about information when it is meaningful to you.

By using this text as a reference, you can stay on top of your finances. It won't turn you into a financial whiz (unless you already are one), but it will give you a working foundation of knowledge. This foundation will aid your continued learning because you will recognize where previously ignored "pieces" fit into the total financial puzzle.

RIGHT BRAINED INDIVIDUALS NEED A MONEY BOOK THAT HAS Graphs, Pictures, Stories, Summaries, Overviews

Most People Are Not Interested in a Financial Topic until It Affects Them

Part 1
The Big Picture

THE BIG PICTURE comes from taking an objective view of your finances. Part 1 covers:

- Money Talk
- Prosperity Attitude
- Basic Money Rules

Money Talk looks at what money can and cannot do for you. You will look at your spending and saving habits to see if they are in line with what you want out of life. Your Prosperity Attitude touches on your self-worth and the idea that you must feel deserving in order to get and keep more money. Basic Money Rules explores some interesting and well-known concepts about different ways that money grows over time.

If you take a ride in a hot air balloon, the higher you rise, the smaller the landscape becomes. As you journey upwards, the horizon expands to show more of the surrounding area and to give you a broader view. The chapters in part 1 help you gain this broader view toward your finances.

1
Money Talk

What Money Can and Cannot Do

THOUSANDS of books and magazines focus on how people can get more money, how they can invest to make their money grow, or how they can reduce expenses and cut taxes so they keep more of their money. Money can pay for an education, buy works of art, fine paintings, or luxury automobiles. It can fund travel to new cities, visits to famous libraries and museums, or attendance to local and international sporting events. The list is endless.

The more money we have, the more we can spend, travel, or play. Being wealthy and having money can give us the freedom to work less and play more. Having more money can make us important in the lives of others. We can contribute more to our church, to our community, or to special causes.

Money can be a means to an end, whether it be education, travel, fine clothes, or giving to others. Be aware that money creates an illusion. It is too often seen as the end instead of the means. Money cannot buy friendship, it cannot buy love, it cannot buy peace or happiness. It can fund an education or many experiences, but it cannot buy knowledge. The important values that give meaning to our lives—it cannot buy.

The Best Things in Life Are Not Things

So be clear right from the start on what you want to achieve with your money. How does its presence, its lack, or its mismanagement affect you? How could having more money improve your life? **What is important about money to you?** What are you willing to do or give up (if anything) in order to have more money, now and in the future?

The wise use of money is a skill that anyone can learn. During our working years, we need to provide for that time when we won't be working. Also, we need to have a good balance between saving and spending, to be investors as well as consumers. Finally, we need to learn the money rules so we can invest wisely. This book will help you develop the skills you need to manage your money. A good place to start is looking at your values and your financial goals, or what you want to accomplish with your money.

Values and Ambitions

You make decisions based on what you value. Therefore, financial goals cannot be separated from these values. Take the time to know what you value and what you want to accomplish.
Look at:

- What is important to you
- What makes you happy
- What you want to experience during your lifetime
- What skills you want to develop
- How much money you want to have
- How you want to spend your money
- What you want to contribute to others

Answers to the above questions reveal your values and your ambitions. Both give your life direction and purpose. Without a destination, any road will do. While traveling on "any" road, an obstacle can easily stop your progress. When you know your destination, however, you travel on a specific route instead of "any" road. **With direction and purpose, obstacles may slow you down, but they won't stop you from moving forward.**

Focused direction has power. Many streams meandering through the woods have little force, but once joined upon a single course, they become the mighty rivers that provide the energy that runs cities. **Define your values so you know what is important to you. Then, define your**

What Is Important about Money to You

You Make Decisions Based on What You Value

Without a Destination, Any Road Will Do

Focused Direction Has Power

ambitions so you know what you want to accomplish. List both on paper until they become clear and specific. Clear values and ambitions are necessary to formulate your financial dreams.

Financial Goals

Define Your Priorities

The foundation for financial success is money at work. Many people, however, never find the "right" time to put some dollars away. In their twenties, these people feel that ample time exists later to begin saving, so spending money on recreation receives the higher priority. Then, in their thirties and forties, they find funds tight because they are buying a home or raising and educating children. So, they enter their fifties to discover time only has a few years to work until they retire. Unfortunately for many, it takes too much money at this late date to build an adequate nest egg. As a result, maintaining a comfortable lifestyle in retirement is difficult. In this predicament, they regret that they didn't find a way to start saving and investing when they were younger. Don't let this happen to you! **Think about your future prosperity, and start now to plan for all your tomorrows.**

Start Now to Plan for All Your Tomorrows

Those who don't set financial priorities probably won't increase their net worth. Their expenses grow with their income. After paying the bills, they seldom have money left to put to work for them. **Many people reach middle age with empty bank accounts and unfulfilled dreams because they haven't given what they really wanted a priority.** While time passed, they didn't focus on their goals. At this late date, they launch new careers, begin to exercise, and because retirement is near, finally start to save. Now they need to make drastic changes to make up for losing so much time.

Those Who Don't Set Financial Priorities Probably Won't Increase Their Net Worth

Know what you want to attain with your money. If you do not take charge of how you spend your money, you allow circumstances to direct your spending. When you don't give money an objective, it will get used up on whatever comes along.

Planning your finances is similar to building a house. The design comes first, then selection of the proper materials. A single board contributes a small but important part to the structure of the house. It takes many boards nailed together to build a frame. **With financial goals,** consistency and time are important "building materials." Money put aside from one paycheck contributes a small part. It takes many weeks, or even years, of consistent saving to reach a financial goal.

A blueprint directs the building of a house. It shows how to construct a strong foundation, what materials to use, and when and where to place them so they will fit. Without a blueprint, building is haphazard, hit-and-miss. **Similarly, financial goals direct how you spend your money.** They help you establish a strong financial base. From this base, you then have many options available to meet different financial objectives. A good plan sets up spending priorities that will help you achieve your goals. **A vision of tomorrow gives today direction.**

Whatever your ambitions, you will never regret increasing your net worth through saving and investing. **The more you save and invest, the more you increase your options, your confidence, and your security.**

The earlier you start thinking about financial goals, the more time you have on your side. With more time, your accomplishments can be greater. **TIME** also compensates for not having much "extra money."

Be Specific

Lack of progress is often due to vague goals. You need to get specific about what you want. Some ways to do this are: 1) through writing, 2) through using pictures, or 3) through talking to another person.

The best way to make your ambitions specific is to write them. **Undefined thoughts require no commitment. Clear, specific details about what you want lead to committed action.** In clarifying your goals through writing, you may uncover subconscious doubts or forgotten encouragements. **Writing helps you be more objective so you think over merits or problems apart from your emotions.** Writing also helps you look beyond other people's biases. Being specific in writing helps you make new discoveries. Maybe what you thought you wanted, you realize you don't; or, you may find you want to develop a completely new interest.

If you don't like to write, you can get specific by using pictures. **Either draw your goal or find pictures in magazines that express what you want.** Come up with one picture for each goal. You might want to use these pictures to make a scrapbook or collage. Take time in drawing or selecting your pictures. Make sure the details fit your goal exactly. If they do not, you may be sorry. Being specific is a powerful tool; you could end up with what is in the picture instead of your goal if they are not the same.

You Will Never Regret Increasing Your Net Worth by Saving and Investing

Lack of Progress Is Often Due to Vague Goals

Express Your Goals in Writing

Express Your Goals with Pictures

Expressing your thoughts to someone close to you is the least effective way to become specific. The person may judge your ideas or put a damper on them before you get the chance to define them clearly. Additionally, by merely expressing your thoughts, you have no visual reference.

Refine your goals at least three times, each time becoming more specific. The answers to "how" questions lead the way. Forget "why" questions. You do not need to justify your ambitions to anyone. **Concentrate on "how" and "what".** If you do not readily know an answer, ponder the question for a few days, with **"how"** directing your thoughts.

State Your Goals

Example: I want to be wealthy.

Comment: Be more specific, Consider what wealth means to you. Does wealth mean: A large bank account? Many investments? Having your own company? A larger home? A better car? More exotic travel?

Write Several Sentences That Better Define Your Goal

Examples: I would like to retire early and not have to worry about money. I would like to start my own company by the time I am thirty years old. I would like to live in a large house.

Comment: Be more specific. What age would you like to retire? How much money would you need? What kind of company would you run? Would anyone work for you? Who are your customers? What do you sell or service? How large of a home? What does it look like? Where is it located?

Make Your Round Two Statements Even More Specific

Examples: I own a four bedroom home. It is on one level and has a spacious backyard with a swimming pool. It has a large, sunny kitchen. It is located in a hillside subdivision twenty miles from the city. (Name all of the features that are important to you.)

I have investments and savings worth $825,000 at age sixty-five. I accomplished this by saving $100 a week for the past __ years. I invest my money in various mutual funds that have an average 12% compound rate of return.

Take the time to come up with clear statements of what you want to achieve with your money. Once you have a specific statement, you will be able to find the information you need to turn these desires into reality. Chapter 3, **Basic Money Rules;** chapter 8, **Investments;** and, chapter 20, **Planning** will help you identify how much you need to save or invest and where to open an account. **Clearly defined goals help you to stop thinking about what you wish you had and show you what needs to be done to get what you want.**

Focused Energy Gets Results

Identify the Conflicts

Identify the conflicts between important goals. For instance, maybe you do not have enough money to save for a down payment on a home and also to take a European vacation. Perhaps you want to start a new career and also spend more time with your family, but learning the new career will take you away from home even more. When conflicts exist, it is often necessary to select the highest priority and be willing to put the second or third priority "on hold."

Prioritizing is never easy, but it is necessary for making wise decisions. Greater accomplishments often require giving up something or making concessions. Such negotiations are easier when you know that what you give up is only temporarily surrendered and will eventually take a higher priority position.

Greater Accomplishments Often Require Giving Up Something

Devise a Plan of Action

Each specific goal needs an action plan. You need to work out, step by step, what it will take to reach that goal. Your financial goals require specific knowledge about many money rules, e.g., how much you must save and for how long you must save to reach a certain sum. You need to know the best places to put your money. Also, it is important to evaluate the risks, rewards, and earnings of different investments. You need to know about tax planning, estate planning, and insurance because they all help to preserve your assets.

This book addresses all of these topics, and more, to arm you with the knowledge you need to devise a plan of action. **The first step, knowing what you want and defining it in detail, is more difficult than working through how to attain it.** Many say they can't or don't know how but have never resolved the real issue of what they want.

Many Say They Can't or Don't Know How but Have Never Resolved the Real Issue of What They Want

Assess Your Progress

Reassess your goals often. Through this assessment, weed out what is unimportant, then reconfirm what is important. Continually prioritize the important, and concentrate on your top priorities.

Try to learn from what didn't work out as planned. Above all, don't forget to compliment yourself on your progress. Concentrate on your accomplishments, both great and small. **Look at what went right, and use it as a springboard to advance. Build on your successes.**

Face Your Challenges

Some people don't take action because they fear failure. Others fear success. Many fear losing face with friends and family. A few choose to be in the background so others will make their decisions. They prefer comfort to challenge.

Most people face criticism, discouragement, and setbacks before they experience success. These feelings are not failures, but tests of determination. Ask any person who has attained a goal that took several years if they were criticized or got discouraged. Overwhelmingly, their answer will be "yes."

Successful people find ways to work through obstacles. They step back, reassess the situation, and continue forward with a new approach. **They know that disappointments are only detours slowing their progress, not barriers blocking them from their destination.**

All achievements have their challenges, and you must have the stamina to face them. **The greater the challenge, the greater the accompanying obstacles.** The wind can bend a fragile tree, but a tree firmly rooted becomes stronger after surviving the wind's resistance. Give current stumbling blocks a proper perspective by centering on your objective. **Today's inconveniences, such as studying, exercising, and doing without to save money, all help to create tomorrow's success.**

Attaining a goal takes commitment and a belief in what you are doing. **If you are making progress, you will face adversity.** Adversity, however, contains seeds of hope. Focus on the sunlight that will help these seeds to surface. They are your new beginnings.

*Greater Challenges
Invite Greater
Obstacles*

*All Adversity Contains
Seeds of Hope*

2
Prosperity Attitude

Self-Worth and Net Worth

YOUR PROSPERITY attitude is a part of "The Big Picture." To build a large nest egg, a positive self-image is as important as financial goals. The amount of money you feel necessary to your lifestyle influences the sum you will receive. Self-made wealthy men and women would readily confirm that self-concept and attitude play an important part in financial success. The mind needs to accept higher levels of prosperity before it can implement them.

Expectations

Some people live under more promising circumstances than others. Some have more talents or better training. Favorable conditions, however, only play a part in determining financial success. An often overlooked factor is our expectations. **Expectations can hold us back or move us to greater heights.** Take note of how Hazel, Samuel, and Jonathan all fulfilled their expectations.

Hazel

Hazel, age sixty, dreamed for seven years of going on a cruise. Hazel lived on social security and had little extra money but decided to save for her vacation. So, for seven years, she put money away until she had enough to finally purchase her ticket.

From the time she boarded the ship, Hazel loved the carefree atmosphere. She immediately met new friends and spent most of her days with them on the upper deck relaxing in the sunshine and enjoying the sea breeze.

The only discomfort Hazel faced was at mealtime. She would make excuses to her new friends that she didn't feel well so she could go to her cabin. Tears would fill Hazel's eyes as she watched while her friends went to the dining room, laughing and joking.

Hazel boarded the ship with her private stockpile of food, which she had carefully planned and prepared at home. So, during the entire cruise, she went alone to her cabin at mealtime, where she ate sandwiches, cheese, and fruit because she knew she couldn't afford to dine with the others. Hazel's vacation ended without her discovering that **all meals had been included in the price of the ticket!**

Hazel never considered that the meals were prepaid, and the travel agent never told her because he assumed Hazel knew. Sadly enough, Hazel experienced what she expected and turned down a paid benefit. We all have some "Hazel" in us, often letting expectations blind new experiences or opportunities. **Don't settle for cookies when you can have baked Alaska!**

Believe in Your Right to Abundance

Samuel and Jonathan

A parable tells about two men from separate villages who travel to the same marketplace in a nearby city to trade their wares. The first man, Samuel, met an old man resting under a tree when he arrived at the city gates.

Samuel said, "Tell me, sir, what is your city like? This is my first visit, and I want to make sure I get a high price for my merchandise."

"Before I answer, tell me what it is like where you live," replied the old man.

"My people are sneaky and dishonest," answered Samuel, "They cannot be trusted. I work and then must watch over my fields so others won't steal my crops or trample my vines. It is a miserable world."

"I'm sorry to report that the people in this city are similar to those in your village. They also will rob you blind," warned the old man. With that warning, Samuel entered the city.

The second visitor, Jonathan, arrived shortly after Samuel. Jonathan saw the same old man under the tree and asked him what the people were like in his city. Before replying, the old man again asked what the people were like in Jonathan's village.

Jonathan said, "My people are friendly, honest, and fair. We help each other as much as possible. Several times in my life I have had bad luck, but with the help of neighbors and friends, I pulled through. Today I am trading goods for a newcomer to our village who has a broken leg. I would like to see him get a fair profit."

"You will find the people in our city much like those in your village. They are friendly, helpful, and trustworthy. They will be good to you," the old man answered. Jonathan thanked him and continued his journey.

That evening when Samuel left the city, the old man was still under the tree. As he passed by in his wagon, the old man shouted, "Tell me sir, how did the people in our city treat you?"

"I had a horrible day," Samuel replied. "Your people are as disagreeable as mine. Several tried to cheat me. The rest wouldn't pay a decent price for my goods. They are a wretched sort, and because of them, I barely broke even. I hope to never return." With head bowed, Samuel left for his long, difficult journey home.

Jonathan followed behind Samuel. The old man also asked him about his day. With a smile, Jonathan replied, "The people were first-rate, just like you said. A strange lady helped me find a good spot. I gave one man a good price, and he brought all his relatives over to make purchases. I am leaving with a healthy profit for myself and my friend. The people in your city are wonderful, and I look forward to my return."

Expectations are magnetic. Whether conscious or unconscious, they will rule your behavior. **What you expect, you fulfill.** Therefore, assume you will have wealth (or more wealth), and you will see moneymaking opportunities. What you expect usually happens.

Your Expectations Are Magnetic. They Repel or Attract Your Dreams

Attitude

A person with a positive outlook views a closed door as an opportunity to change direction. That person will find fertility in a desert, seeing animal life under shaded rocks and noticing plants and wildflowers living in rocky crevices where they can take advantage of the precious moisture.

Similarly, a person with a negative outlook will see an open door as a threat to personal security. That person will see barrenness in a rain forest abundant with life. Being concerned the dampness might bring on a cold, the person doesn't notice the lush foliage. Instead, fears that an insect might bite or that a poisonous plant is just around the corner shadow the beauty of the forest. The colorful, tropical birds sing to mute ears.

Your Attitude Influences Your Reactions

Attitude decides an experience of abundance in a desert or barrenness in a verdant forest. We are just beginning to understand that thoughts, although intangible, have tremendous power. They can be used to improve the quality of life. **Positive thoughts can change perspective, transform old behaviors, and attract good fortune.**

Outlines in coloring books remain obscure and lifeless until filled in with colors. The colors can be drab or cheery; they can clash or blend. In the same way, our emotions "color" the various situations we experience. **Until we react, the event is neutral. We give a situation meaning through our attitude and point of view.**

Anti-Prosperous Attitudes

To invite good fortune and success, learn to overcome anti-prosperous attitudes such as:

- It is his fault that I didn't get the promotion.
- If I share, there won't be enough for me.
- My expenses increase when I have more money, so why try to get ahead?
- I can't do this.
- I won't pay one dime more than my share!
- I earned my money the hard way. They can do the same.

Blame

Accepting Responsibility Puts You in Charge

It's easy to blame others for life's commonplace hurts and frustrations—the boss who overlooked a promotion, the child who ruined a new tool, or the slow cashier in a long grocery line. Blaming others for a pain or an inconvenience only adds to the problem and seldom makes the situation better.

Positive solutions exist for most problems, but they are far removed from blame. **Blame is a quick reaction that puts responsibility for your frustration "out there."** Most importantly, it never solves the problem. Cultivate your own garden, and let others do the same.

Scarcity

Scarcity is a belief that originates in fear and feeds on self-sacrifice. It says:

- There is not enough for everybody.
- Life is a continuous battle.

If you view life as a battle, you will need to keep "fighting." If you expect to be a victim, you will be dumped on with regularity. When this happens, working harder doesn't help you get ahead, and the work is not fulfilling. This reinforces the negative outlook that life is a continuous battle. To partake of the harvest, you must feel deserving. If you can change your beliefs to see an abundant world with ample resources and opportunities for everyone, you can **stop fighting and start giving thanks.**

More Is Better

Some people believe financial success means dining out more often, a bigger house, a newer car, or more clothes. We tend to equate financial success with more possessions, such as boats, luxury cars, and fine furniture. These things are only symbols of success.

Many work to achieve the symbol rather than what the symbol represents. They spend all the money they earn, then keep buying, not realizing possessions offer no real security and are a front for true wealth. Later, they realize owning more is not always better.

Sometimes a focus on getting **more** actually promotes a lesser life. This is especially true for those who buy beyond their means. They desire security, but burdensome monthly payments cause insecurity. **Security cannot be bought. It does not come from possessions; it comes from within. People care more about how you treat them than what you own.** So when you think "more stuff" enhances your life, step back and take an objective look. How do possessions complement your life and add to your self-worth?

Procrastination

We often think that tomorrow will bring more money, more time, stronger convictions, or greater happiness. The future always holds the promise of turning visions into reality. The thinking usually is: tomorrow I'll have increased abilities; tomorrow I'll have more time; tomorrow I'll have more money; tomorrow I'll be happier. The truth is desires only

We Usually Think: Tomorrow I'll Have More Time... Tomorrow I'll Have More Money... Tomorrow I'll Be Happier...

materialize by taking steps today to improve skills, to save money, and to make time for what is important to you.

Are You and Prosperity Compatible?

As a rule, when we expect good fortune, we find the right set of circumstances to create it. Remember, neither God nor the universe will send an instant promotion or put funds into your bank account. Just because you want more wealth doesn't mean you will find a bag of money on your doorstep. Wishing isn't enough. Life doesn't work that way. **Instead, life gives us opportunities and the free will to make choices. Often, misfortune is opportunity in disguise.** It can end a present direction that is not working and bring in a new one that will.

Opportunities are everywhere, but we must be positive and clear-thinking to recognize them. Muddled thoughts make decisive action difficult. **Clear thinking precedes determined action. Can you imagine yourself as successful, prosperous, and happy?** If you can't, you won't be. Your emotional acceptance is essential to its achievement.

The following stories tell about two people who received large sums of money and, in both cases, lost it. If used wisely, this money could have created lasting prosperity for them. As it turned out, their good fortune made only temporary changes in their life and no permanent improvements in their lifestyle.

The Westons

Mr. Weston inherited $250,000 from an uncle. At the time, he and his wife were living in a small trailer with their six children. Until the inheritance came, the Weston family was always broke. They never had enough money to make ends meet.

If the Westons had thought about their lifetime goals and dreams, they would have set aside money to buy their first home. Then, they would have purchased life insurance, put money in savings to cover emergencies, and opened a college fund for each of their children. As a bonus, they might have even planned a vacation. **They had an opportunity to stop struggling and start building their dreams.**

Unfortunately, they did not consider any long-range goals. Two years later, their circumstances had not changed. Instead of using a financial plan to direct their money, they went on a spending spree. This included dining often in expensive restaurants, buying new cars, new clothes, bikes, and televisions. They bought everything but a house! $250,000 disappears quickly without a plan.

As incredible as it seems, within twenty-four months, the Weston family still resided in their overcrowded trailer, with no money in the bank. After spending their inheritance, they were again struggling from paycheck to paycheck. The once shiny new cars became tarnished through neglect.

Obviously, Mr. and Mrs. Weston never learned how to take care of their possessions or how to use money to get ahead. Their habits were based on anti-prosperous attitudes. **Having more money made no improvement in their lifestyle because they did not use it wisely. Their self-worth did not match the money they received.**

Georgia

Georgia won $100,000 at a race track. Georgia went into shock when she talked to her tax advisor and discovered the taxes due would be more than her current salary. She could not concentrate on the positive—the $75,000 left after taxes.

Georgia was in her late forties and hated her job. The $75,000 left after taxes, used wisely, would be enough to fulfill her goal of early retirement and allow her to stop working at age fifty-five, ten years earlier than she had hoped. What an opportunity!

Unfortunately, Georgia never could get beyond giving up the $25,000 for taxes. She wanted the full $100,000. Her reward was still there, but she failed to see it. She had enough money left to reach her goal, although she lost one-fourth to taxes. Governments always tax income. Large gifts usually have strings attached and seldom come "free." Life is never 100% our way, but a continual compromise.

Yet, Georgia still wanted 100%. So, putting wise counsel aside, she invested in some high risk tax shelters. She tried not only to avoid taxes, but also to triple her winnings in a few short years. Had her plan worked, she would have been extremely lucky twice in a row. As it turned out, she lost most of her money. Will she retire early? Will she ever pursue the hobbies she loves? It's doubtful. She missed an opportunity to turn her life around because she wasn't willing to "pay her dues." Her expectations fell short of her winnings.

If you don't expect prosperity, it won't happen. Your expectations control the opportunities you recognize and therefore experience. Low expectations generate little opportunity. High expectations generate boundless opportunity. With low expectations, large sums of money can

With Low Expectations, Large Sums of Money Can Disappear Quickly, and Yet, with High Expectations, Small Sums of Money Can Increase Many Times Over

disappear quickly, and yet, with high expectations, small sums of money can increase many times over.

3
Basic Money Rules

To GET FROM where you are to where you want to be, you will need to use some basic money rules. Money at work is dynamic. Back in 1778, Ben Franklin wrote:

> "Money is of a prolific, generating nature. Money can beget money, and its offspring can beget more."

To build a fortune, you must put your money to work. Earning a high salary does little good unless some of that money also starts producing. When you save just a few dollars from each paycheck, eventually these dollars will earn more than you do—that is, if you give them enough time.

To Accumulate Wealth, You Must Put Your Money to Work

Shortcuts Do Not Work

Shortcuts to financial success seldom work. You gain wealth through joining MONEY, TIME, and GROWTH. All three must be present for lasting results, with no exceptions to this basic rule. Unless you are an heir to a sizable estate, you need to get some of your money working for you.

Money at work is the only reliable way to build a nest egg. All you need is an average wage and enough discipline to save consistently. **The discipline to continue putting money aside every month is more important than the dollar amount you save.** You can accrue an impressive balance with just a few dollars saved consistently over TIME.

The Importance of Money

To take advantage of Ben Franklin's idea and get money working for you, you need to first come up with the capital. Many people have built sizable fortunes through saving small sums consistently, then allowing TIME and the RATE OF RETURN to generate results. First you need the extra MONEY, even if it is a small amount. Without it, nothing can happen.

The Importance of Time

MONEY and TIME work together. More TIME permits fewer dollars to grow into sizable accounts. Money at work, however, doesn't double overnight. Just as apple trees need time to develop before they bear fruit, earnings need to mature before they start producing.

If you can't take advantage of TIME, it will be more difficult to accumulate wealth. **People waiting until their fifties to save and invest will need to put away over fourteen times more than those who start saving in their twenties.** By starting MONEY compounding early, you need fewer dollars to build an impressive account. Those in their twenties have an advantage; they have TIME on their side. This advantage, if used regularly, will guarantee financial success.

Table 3.1 illustrates "the time miracle." It shows how much money you need to save monthly at different ages to have $100,000 in today's dollars at age sixty-five if the money grows at 6%. Notice that you need to save over four times more at age forty-five than at age twenty-five to reach the same goal. By age fifty-five, with only ten years left, you need twelve times more! No wonder so many people in their fifties say, "Why didn't someone tell me to start saving when I was twenty?"

Table 3.1—The Time Miracle

AGE	MONTHLY AMOUNT NEEDED TO HAVE $100,000 AT AGE SIXTY-FIVE @ 6%
25	$ 49.26
30	$ 69.84
35	$ 99.06
40	$143.58
45	$215.35
50	$342.15
55	$607.17

More TIME creates wonders. For instance, $25 saved once a month, earning an annual yield of 6%, becomes $25,238 in thirty years. Yet, in just ten more years, this $25 per month almost doubles to $50,036! As you can see, small amounts grow significantly with enough TIME. If you only have a little MONEY to save, you can compensate by putting TIME to work, and TIME is free.

The Longer You Wait, the More You Have to Save to Achieve a Desired Amount

The Importance of Growth (Rate-of-Return)

MONEY and GROWTH also work together, because money invested doubles, then redoubles, at a pace set by the rate of return it receives. For most people, getting rich quick through an excessive return doesn't work, but neither does a low return that fails to keep pace with inflation and taxes. To get ahead, your money must earn more than average price increases.

Investments that take advantage of favorable market conditions will help you earn more on your money.

Generally, the reward of higher earnings offered on low to medium risk investments are worthwhile. You should avoid high and speculative risks offered through deals to "get rich quick" unless you are willing to gamble some or all of your principal. Few win, and many lose in these ventures. **On the other hand, a low, guaranteed rate of return may yield** a loss of purchasing power after inflation and taxes take their share. To get ahead, money needs to earn more than cost of living increases. (See Break-Even Rate of Return in chapter 20, Planning).

A higher rate of return generates higher profits. For instance, $10,000 earning 3% grows to only $18,180 in twenty years; but $10,000 earning 9% grows to $59,301 in twenty years. At 12%, this same $10,000 will grow to $106,409 in twenty years. Compounding at a higher rate of return produces nearly six times more money (from $18,180 to $106,409). This is the advantage of compounding. Examine Table 3.2 to see the results of saving only $25 per month ($300 a year) at four different compound returns: 3%, 6%, 9%, and 12% (the money is compounded monthly).

To Get Ahead, Your Money Must Earn More Than Average Price Increases

Table 3.2—Results of Saving $25 per Month

$25 SAVED PER MONTH				
	3%	6%	9%	12%
20 years	$ 8,228	$11,609	$ 16,822	$ 24,979
30 years	$14,605	$25,238	$ 46,112	$ 88,248
40 years	$23,209	$50,036	$117,911	$297,061

Notice that saving $25 per month at 6% produces $50,036 in forty years; but at 9%, the total grows to $117,911; at 12%, it reaches an incredible $297,061! Not bad for a $12,000 investment.

Compound Interest and the Rule of 72

Your money grows in a savings account by earning compound interest. The interest "compounds" when it is added to the principal, where it will earn interest for the next time period. The earnings are computed at the end of a compounding period, which can be daily, weekly, monthly, quarterly, or annually. The more frequent the compounding, the higher the yield, because each time the principal grows, it earns more interest.

Ben Franklin understood well how money grows and compounds over time. He left $5,000 to the city of Boston in 1791, with instructions that it should be left alone to compound for one hundred years. The $5,000 grew to $322,000 by 1891. The city built a school with some of the money, but they also followed Ben's wishes to set aside $92,000 for another hundred years. By 1960, this fund had grown to $1,400,000![1] Although you probably won't save your money for a hundred years, the dynamics of compounding can also work for you.

Rule of 72

> Divide 72 by Rate of Return
> Answer Equals Years Needed
> for Principal to Double

You will find the Rule of 72 valuable for predicting money growth on compound rates of return. **This rule shows how many years are needed for a sum to double at various rates.** Simply divide 72 by the rate of return, such as 6%. The answer tells the number of years needed for the principal to double.

For example:

$500 earning 6% doubles to $1,000 in twelve years (72 ÷ 6% = 12). $500 earning 12% doubles to $1,000 in six years (72 ÷ 12% = 6).

Table 3.3 shows $1,000 at work at annual compound rates, varying from 4% to 12%. The rate decides the number of years needed for the principal to double, then redouble, again and again.

Table 3.3—Rule of 72

$1000 will double in this many years	4% 18 years to double	6% 12 years to double	8% 9 years to double	12% 6 years to double
6 Years				$2,000
9 Years			$2,000	
12 Years		$2,000		
18 Years	$2,000		$4,000	$8,000
24 Years		$4,000		$16,000
27 Years			$8,000	
30 Years				$32,000
36 Years	$4,000	$8,000	$16,000	$64,000

Notice the wide spread in the thirty-sixth year—a $4,000 total from a 4% yield, compared to a $64,000 total from a 12% yield. Three times more interest (4% to 12%) does not net three times more money—it yields sixteen times more money ($4,000 to $64,000)! The higher rates that double in fewer years can create fortunes with only a few dollars.

Although 12% is higher than current market rates, it demonstrates the dynamics of compound growth. The last time we saw 12% interest rates paid by savings institutions was back in the late seventies. Several mutual funds today, however, advertise an annual compound rate of return close to 12%. The compounding from these funds comes from reinvested capital gains and dividends that are paid annually or quarterly. These funds have no guarantees, but over a five year period or longer, the potential increased profits might be well worth the minimal risk involved.

Simple and Compound Rates Compared

Simple interest rates use a different method to calculate rates of return. They are used with investments such as stocks, income producing limited partnerships, and mutual funds. If a mutual fund company converts their yield to a compound rate, their literature will clearly state so. Otherwise, assume the rate is "simple." With simple rates, the principal does not compound as illustrated in the RULE OF 72. If you invest $1,000, then six years later sell the investment for $2,000, you made a $1,000 profit, or 100% on your money. **With simple rates, the investor earns 100% each time the principal doubles.** Since it took six years in this illustration, the total profit divided by six (number of years) gives the annual yield of 16.7%. (100% ÷ 6 = 16.7%). Or, the profit per year, $167, can be divided by the principal, $1,000, to get the same, 16.7%.

The 16.7% simple yield used in this example is equivalent to a 12% compound yield. **That is, in six years, $1,000 earning 12% compound interest grows to $2,000; and, in six years, $1,000 earning a 16.7% simple rate of return also grows to $2,000.**

Assume a stock or mutual fund advertises a 20% annual yield. This means the earnings paid to investors would be $200 for each $1,000 invested ($200 ÷ $1,000 = 20%). **Most investments calculate yields using the simple method. Be realistic in making comparisons, and don't think the simple rate is always better because it is higher.** For example, if $1,000 earns a 14.4% compound return, the net result is the same as a 20% simple return. In both accounts, the money doubles in five years ($1,000 grows to $2,000).

Most Investments Calculate Yields Using the Simple Method

Since compound and simple rates are calculated differently, the best way to compare them is to look at how many years it takes for a given sum to double. This approach allows investors to make true comparisons between options using different payment methods.

Table 3.4 compares simple and compound yields by showing the years it will take for the amount invested to double. If you can receive a guaranteed 6% compound return, it makes no sense to take more risk to receive a higher simple rate of 8.3%, because the profits are the same.

To Compare Rates of Return, Look at the Years Needed for an Investment to Double

When the Profit Is the Same, Don't Take More Risk for Higher Yields

Table 3.4—Comparison of Simple and Compound Yields

YEARS TO DOUBLE	COMPOUND RATE	SIMPLE RATE
14.4 Years	5%	6.9%
12.2 Years	6%	8.2%
10.3 Years	7%	9.7%
9 Years	8%	11.1%
8 Years	9%	12.5%
7.2 Years	10%	13.9%
6.5 Years	11%	15.4%
6 Years	12%	16.7%
5 Years	14.4%	20.0%

When comparing growth opportunities, keep the anticipated end result in mind. Look at the earnings paid to investors over the years and how these profits have fluctuated. Also, realize that past performance is no guarantee for future performance, although it is the best indicator we have. Compare the investment's simple yield to the compound rate currently paid by banks and credit unions. What is the difference in earnings?

Look at the variations. Some mutual funds that pay consistent dividends convert their simple yield into a compound yield for ease of comparison. If this is the case, it will be clearly stated in the fund's literature, such as: this fund has averaged a 12.3% compound rate of return for XX years when all dividends and capital gains are reinvested.

On the other hand, some Certificates of Deposit (CDs) do not automatically compound the earnings. CDs pay a simple return for a certain time period. You can take the earnings in cash or reinvest them.

The difference between the two payment methods is **that a simple return does not automatically add the earnings to the principal to increase its value.** The following story illustrates the long-term results from simple and compound interest.

Sue's "Simple" Story

When Sue was born, her grandfather gave her a gift of $5,000. He placed the money in a savings account in her name at a local bank. The interest rate offered was 8% if it wasn't cashed in for fifty years. He left instructions that Sue was not to have the money until her fiftieth birthday. He thought he had invested prudently, but he failed to ask the bank how they paid interest. He never knew that it was a simple rate, paid annually.

Sue's grandmother also opened an account for Sue. The grandmother took $5,000 of her money and went to another bank. She also locked in an 8% interest rate for the next fifty years. Unlike her husband, she made sure Sue would receive compound interest on this account.

Time passed. On Sue's fiftieth birthday, she was still working and didn't need the money, so she renewed both certificates at the same 8% for another fifteen years. When she retired at age sixty-five, she went to the banks to collect her money.

First, Sue withdrew the account that her grandfather set up sixty-five years ago. The balance was $31,000. It had continued to pay 8% simple interest all this time, or $400 each year ($5,000 x 8% = $400). In sixty-five years, the earnings had grown to $26,000 ($400 x 65 = $26,000). Adding the $26,000 of earnings to the $5,000 principal equaled the current balance of $31,000.

Then, she drove across town to check on the account opened by her grandmother. Much to her surprise, she discovered that this account was worth $743,899. Receiving the 8% annual compound return since she was born meant that the bank added her interest to the principal annually. The first year she received 8% on $5,000; the second year, 8% on $5,400; then the third year, 8% on $5,832, etc. As the principal grew, her earnings increased. With compound interest, the principal keeps expanding to earn even more.

Just think, Sue had $774,899 when she retired from a $10,000 investment at work for her for sixty-five years. Of course, without a

Money, Time, and Growth Are All Necessary to Put Your Dollars to Their Wisest Use

compound return, she would only have had $62,000 ($31,000 x 2). On the other hand, if both accounts had earned compound interest, she would have retired with $1,487,798.

MONEY, TIME, and GROWTH are all necessary to put your dollars to their wisest use. Once you come up with the money, look at the time period you expect it to be invested. Growth makes an important difference in how quickly the money doubles. If you expect too much growth too quickly, you could lose it all. Chapter 8, Investments, tells about different opportunities to get higher rates of return.

Notes

1. Grace W. Weinstein, *Lifetime Book of Money Management* (New York: New American Library, 1987), 60.

Part 2
How Money Disappears

HOPEFULLY, some of the dollars you earn will multiply and grow to meet your future needs. Unfortunately, others will disappear before you get to use them. If you can identify where these dollars disappear to, you might be able to put more of them to work for you.

Consumer goods will take a portion of your money. Consumer debt, with its high interest charges, could be using more of your money than you realize. This is discussed in chapter 4. Chapter 5 covers rising prices or inflation, which sometimes works so subtly you may not be aware of how it erodes your dollars. Personal income taxes also take their portion. To give you a better understanding of what you must report as income, and what deductions you can take, chapter 6 gives the rules for figuring your personal income taxes.

With skill and persistence, you will be able to minimize you disappearing dollars and learn how to keep more of you income.

4
Consumer Debt

Consumables and Decreasing Assets

SPENDING your entire income on consumables like food and gasoline or items that decrease in value over time does not contribute to the goal of financial security. **Items that lose value over time cannot help you accumulate wealth.** Look at what you spend or have spent for:

- Automobiles and automobile accessories
- Furniture: beds, couches, tables, chairs, dressers, etc.
- Televisions, sound systems, speakers, VCR's, radios, and telephones
- Lawn mowers, snow blowers, and lawn and garden tools and equipment
- Saws, drills, and other power tools
- Computers, including all hardware, software, printers, and supplies
- Kitchen appliances: toasters, microwaves ovens, food processors, blenders, etc.
- Recreational vehicles and camping equipment
- Shoes, clothing, and other personal items

All these items serve an important purpose—they make daily living more convenient and more enjoyable. Goods like computers and power tools make it possible to earn more money in some jobs. Stylish clothing and recreational hobbies fulfill certain emotional needs and are important for happiness and self-esteem. **The fact remains, however, that these goods take a large percentage of income and will not add to net worth.** They are either consumed or decrease in value over time. The resale value is seldom worth the amount paid.

If overspending is a problem, **all of your money can disappear into consumable goods or depreciating assets. To change things around, you must make a conscious decision to put money aside. A growing net worth requires that you learn to PUT AWAY A PORTION OF EVERYTHING YOU EARN.**

Taking care of your long-term needs requires putting some money into assets that will increase in value as time passes. These include real estate, stocks, bonds, mutual funds, and savings accounts. Over time, they increase in value and are worth much more than their purchase price.

Appreciating Assets Help Your Net Worth to Grow

New clothes, appliances, or the latest software programs fulfill short-term needs. Often, your satisfaction with them wanes. Yet, you are left with monthly payments, a possession that is not worth what you paid for it, or both. **For your net worth to grow, you must have savings and investments appreciating in value.**

Every day you buy something you don't really need, you also decide not to save. **How you spend your money today decides your net worth tomorrow.** Only by saving and investing regularly do you give money the opportunity to work for you.

Some people feel they have little control over their present circumstances, so they do not give thought to how they can improve their position. **We constantly create our tomorrows through seemingly minor matters that take place every day.** These "minor matters," such as whether we spend or save, make a big difference over time.

Everyday You Buy Something You Don't Need, You Also Decide Not to Save

Saving and investing money takes deliberate action, based on caring about the future. **Don't let consumables and depreciating assets take away from your financial security. Make sure you also have assets working for you.**

Credit Abuse Robs Your Savings

The overuse of credit prevents many people from having extra money. This usually means any debt beyond long-term mortgages and auto loans. Credit cards make it easy to buy now without spending this week's cash. Because many companies encourage consumers to use credit, many people live beyond their means, never realizing that they continually spend more than they earn.

This month's paycheck may be completely spoken for by monthly bills, so any recreational pursuits or unexpected events must be financed with credit. Credit makes it possible to repair the car, buy gifts, and buy new clothes without directly spending your regular monthly income.

Instead of giving up one expenditure for another, credit makes it possible to have it all NOW.

Using credit cards has no ill consequences when you pay them off monthly. **The high interest charges on installment debt, however, turn potential savings dollars into healthy profits for the lending institution.** In contrast, this is money that could be growing in your savings account instead. Few people realize how long it takes to pay off installment debt once the bills start arriving. Charging is so easy.

Finance Charges Rob Your Savings

Tony and Lisa's Story

Tony and Lisa just purchased a new home. As new home owners, they didn't plan for the extra money needed for moving expenses and furnishing the house. They bought new furniture on credit because they couldn't afford to pay cash and also pay the required closing costs for their home. Interestingly, after closing escrow on their home, two banks mailed them new credit cards.

A vacuum, lawn mower, and garbage cans were all "necessities" not planned for. Neither were the lamps, light bulbs, and additional telephones. Their old towels and sheets looked out of place in the new home, so they purchased new ones. To buy all these items, they used their new Mastercard and Visa.

Although they intended to pay off their debt quickly, when the monthly bills came in, they could only afford the minimum payment. They then had difficulty coming up with cash to maintain their cars and to buy gas, so they applied for a gasoline company card. Although they tried not to charge, since cash was short, they couldn't avoid some new purchases. Around Christmas, they had no money to buy gifts, and their two credit cards were at maximum, so they mailed in an offer to get Visa #2. They charged over $2,000 in December on this new card. Over the next twelve months, they were able to make the minimum monthly payments on all their accounts but had little success in reducing their debt. The following tables show the details of their installment debt during the third year after they started charging.

Mastercard Credit Limit: $3,100 APR: 19.8%

	Monthly Payment	New Purchases	Finance Charge	New Balance
Jan.	85.00	158.00	47.89	2,924.84
Feb.	88.00	47.81	47.65	2,932.33
Mar.	88.00	0.00	47.44	2,891.77
April	87.00	127.74	47.99	2,980.50
May	90.00	0.00	48.26	2,938.76
June	89.00	18.00	47.65	2,915.41
July	88.00	0.00	47.96	3,103.70
Aug.	93.00	0.00	51.21	3,061.91
Sept.	92.00	0.00	50.52	3,020.43
Oct.	92.00	0.00	49.84	2,978.27
Nov.	88.00	0.00	49.14	2,939.41
Dec.	87.00	0.00	48.50	2,900.91
Totals	1,067.00	351.55	584.05	

Total Debt Reduction: $23.93

Visa #1 Credit Limit: $2,000 APR: 19.8%

	Monthly Payment	New Purchases	Finance Charge	New Balance
Jan.	57.00	0.00	30.75	1,872.82
Feb.	57.00	133.36	30.77	1,979.95
Mar.	60.00	0.00	32.03	1,951.98
April	59.00	0.00	31.58	1,924.56
May	58.00	0.00	31.17	1,897.73
June	57.00	18.00	30.78	1,889.51
July	57.00	0.00	30.34	1,862.85
Aug.	56.00	29.95	30.20	1,867.00
Sept.	57.00	0.00	36.06	1,903.06
Oct.	57.00	0.00	29.81	1,818.87
Nov.	54.56	0.00	30.01	1,794.32
Dec.	53.83	0.00	29.60	1,770.09
Totals	683.39	181.31	373.10	

Total Debt Reduction: $102.73

Visa #2 Credit Limit: $2500 APR: 16.9%

	Monthly Payment	New Purchases	Finance Charge	New Balance
Jan.	79.50	0.00	31.61	2,163.37
Feb.	64.00	204.00	30.88	2,334.25
Mar.	70.00	0.00	32.28	2,296.53
Apr.	68.00	135.80	33.25	2,397.58
May	71.00	0.00	33.14	2,359.72
June	70.00	0.00	32.69	2,322.41
July	93.50	100.00	36.30	2,299.71
Aug.	68.00	37.18	32.30	2,336.58
Sept.	68.00	0.00	35.39	2,336.58
Oct.	68.00	0.00	31.25	2,217.83
Nov.	66.54	0.00	31.27	2,182.56
Dec.	65.48	0.00	30.77	2,178.62
Totals	852.02	476.98	391.13	

Total Debt Reduction: $15.25

Furniture Credit Limit: $6,000 APR: 21.9%

	Monthly Payment	New Purchases	Finance Charge	New Balance
Jan.	123.61	0.00	101.83	5,558.02
Feb.	123.61	0.00	101.43	5,535.84
Mar.	123.61	0.00	101.03	5,513.26
April	123.61	0.00	100.62	5,490.27
May	123.61	0.00	100.20	5,466.86
June	123.61	0.00	99.77	5,443.02
July	123.61	0.00	99.34	5,418.74
Aug.	123.61	0.00	98.89	5,394.03
Sept.	123.61	0.00	98.44	5,368.86
Oct.	123.61	0.00	97.98	5,343.23
Nov.	123.61	0.00	97.51	5,317.13
Dec.	123.61	0.00	97.04	5,290.56
Totals	1,483.32	0.00	1,194.08	

Total Debt Reduction: $267.46

Gasoline Credit Card APR: 21.00%

	Monthly Payment	New Purchases	Finance Charge	New Balance
Jan.	45.21	91.89	4.10	300.04
Feb.	95.70	36.19	5.34	245.87
Mar.	95.70	36.04	4.32	190.53
April	45.72	68.10	3.33	216.24
May	51.89	12.00	3.78	180.13
June	43.23	82.00	3.15	222.05
July	30.01	0.00	3.88	195.92
Aug.	99.33	0.00	3.21	93.38
Sept.	23.21	79.97	1.51	151.65
Oct.	120.00	211.99	2.43	246.07
Nov.	95.00	61.33	4.26	216.66
Dec.	52.00	26.12	3.79	194.57
Totals	797.00	705.63	43.10	

Total Debt Reduction: $105.47

Tony and Lisa started the year with $12,819 of installment debt on their five accounts. During the year, they made $4,883 in payments, or an average monthly payment of $407. After making all these payments, their debt was still $12,335, only $484 less! Finance charges were $2,586. New purchases totaled $1,715, including $705 for gasoline. Sadly enough, their total debt reduction for the year was only slightly more than one month's payment.

If Tony and Lisa succeed in making no new purchases and continue making the minimum payment, it will take them approximately five years to pay off their Visas and Mastercard. The furniture, purchased through a finance company working with the furniture store, will take ten years to pay off.

Tony and Lisa's problem is that they don't have the extra money to make more than minimum payments on their installment debt. To correct their unfortunate situation, they must find ways to get the extra money to make higher payments and pay down the principal. **To make higher payments, they need to cut expenses and/or bring in new money.**

Getting out of Debt

If you can't see your way out of debt and can't work out a plan on your own, consumer credit counselors, affiliated with the National Foundation for Consumer Credit, are available in most cities. They will help work out a plan, often at no cost, for those who are overextended but have enough money coming in to make their payments. For those who are seriously overextended, they usually ask the creditors to accept smaller payments, then take the money from their client and pay it to the creditors. For this service, they charge a nominal fee. If you go in for credit counseling, be aware of credit clinics in business to make a profit. They could charge a large fee that increases your debt.

Before going in for credit counseling, do all within your power to correct the debt problem on your own. Try bringing in more income by working overtime or earning extra money from a second job. Cut down on expenses. Most importantly: **STOP CHARGING.**

High interest charges (often 16% to 24%) make it difficult to pay off the balance if you only make the minimum payment. If you have no extra money because of charge card payments, use one or more of the following suggestions to get out of debt.

- **Make no new credit card purchases.** Stop charging for perishable items such as clothing, gas, lawn furniture, and household equipment. If you don't have the cash, do without. It is too easy to make only the minimum payment, keep buying, and never get the balance paid off. **Thinking you will have more money tomorrow is seldom true unless you take realistic steps today to make it happen.**
- **Take out a bank loan.** See if you qualify for a lower interest bill consolidation loan through a bank or credit union. By reducing the interest charges and the monthly payment, you can pay off the debt faster. **If you do this, take the highest monthly payment and the shortest time period you can afford.**

For Tony and Lisa, such a consolidation loan through a bank or credit union would reduce their high interest charges from the 19% range to 9%. For example, a loan for $13,000 at 9% interest for three years would have payments of $413 per month. With this new loan, they could pay off all their debt in three years.

- **Take out a home equity loan.** Homeowners who have equity can turn around a difficult situation by borrowing against their

To Get Ahead, INTEREST Needs to Work for You, Not Add to Your Monthly Payments

equity. Interest rates for a home equity loan will be lower than those charged by credit card companies. The payments will be lower, and the interest will be tax deductible. Just remember, your home is the bank's collateral for the loan, and they will repossess it if you don't make the promised payments.

In Tony and Lisa's case, if they qualified for a home equity loan of $13,000 at 9% interest with payments for fifteen years, their monthly payment would be approximately $132. They could then make double or triple payments to pay off their loan in less time, or they could start saving $278 per month (the difference between their old and new payment).

- **Concentrate on paying off one bill at a time.** If you do not qualify for a home equity or bill consolidation loan, you must reduce the debt with your own systematic plan. To start, select your largest payment, or your most burdensome payment, or the one with the highest interest charges. If possible, double your payments on this bill so you can pay down the balance and, in doing so, reduce your finance charges.

Once You Pay Off Your Bills, Keep Making Payments—but Send the Money to Your Savings or Investment Funds

For example, Tony and Lisa feel their furniture bill, with an APR (annual percentage rate) of 21.9%, is their worst debt. If they decided to cut back in other areas and pay $250 each month toward this bill, the extra payment would reduce their balance owed at the end of the year from $5,290.56 to $3,611.09. This is a difference of $1,678.58. The additional $126.39 each month would be applied toward the principal, and a lower principal reduces the finance charges. If they had paid $250 per month from the beginning, they could pay off this loan in thirty-two months instead of ten years. Over the life of the loan, they would save $6,858 in finance charges. Compare the table on page 39 with the one shown on page 36 to see how the higher payment reduces the balance owed.

If you need to calculate finance charges, take the annual interest rate and divide it by 12. On Tony and Lisa's furniture loan, the APR was 21.9%. When divided by 12, the monthly charge is .01825 (.219 ÷ 12 = .01825). If the prior month's balance is $3,611.98, the next month's finance charge will be $65.92 ($3,611.98 x .01825 = $65.92).

Once you pay off your bills, keep making payments—but send the money to your savings or investment fund. To increase your net worth and get money working for you, you must spend less than you earn.

To take control of your finances, acquire the habit of paying cash for all consumable goods and depreciating assets. **It is smart to get into a**

Furniture Credit Limit: $6,000 APR: 21.9%

	Monthly Payment	New Purchases	Finance Charge	New Balance
Jan.	250.00	0.00	101.83	5,431.63
Feb.	250.00	0.00	99.12	5,280.75
Mar.	250.00	0.00	96.37	5,127.12
April	250.00	0.00	93.57	4,970.69
May	250.00	0.00	90.72	4,811.41
June	250.00	0.00	87.81	4,649.22
July	250.00	0.00	84.85	4,484.07
Aug.	250.00	0.00	81.83	4,315.90
Sept.	250.00	0.00	78.77	4,144.67
Oct.	250.00	0.00	75.64	3,970.31
Nov.	250.00	0.00	72.46	3,792.77
Dec.	250.00	0.00	69.22	3,611.98
Totals	3,000.00	0.00	1,032.19	

Total Debt Reduction: $1,819.65

"cash" habit. To help establish this habit, choose something you want to purchase but can't afford right now, perhaps a needed electronic appliance, an article of clothing, or a small trip or vacation. Work out on paper what you must put away during a six-month period to purchase what you want. Take the total needed and divide by 6 (months) or 24 (weeks) to know what you need to save each month or week. For example, if you save $10 a week, you'll have $240 plus a small amount of interest at the end of six months.

Acquire a Habit of Paying Cash

Why go through this hassle when you could more easily go to the store, use your charge card, and not have to wait? Because if you don't pay finance charges and if you earn some interest while saving to purchase, you will have more money working for you. Most importantly, you start a habit of saving. You also gain discipline in money management. When you pay cash, you often spend less because **your hard-earned dollars are spent today instead of a credit payment next month.**

5

Inflation,
the Subtle Saboteur

Rising Prices

INFLATION MEANS RISING PRICES. This chapter explains why prices keep going up. Inflation started after the Great Depression of the 1930s when the federal government implemented policies to create jobs and stimulate the economy, and it has been with us ever since.

Inflation is a subtle saboteur—at least this has been true since 1939. Each year, it steals some of your money. **The first year, you may not notice, but a few years down the road, your dollars have disappeared. Inflation cuts away at your purchasing power, so each year your dollar buys less. In 1962:**

- a first class postage stamp sold for $.04,
- a gallon of gasoline sold for $.31,
- the maximum social security tax had risen to $150, and
- the average price for a new home was $19,300.

People were just starting to complain about the high cost of living. Their concerns were well-founded, because prices had risen steadily by 2% to 3% each year since World War II.

During the next seventeen years, prices rose an average of 7.15% a year. **By 1979:**

- the first class postage stamp sold for $.15,

- a gallon of gasoline sold for $.79,
- the maximum social security tax had risen to $1,404, and
- new homes averaged $68,300.[1]

In 1979, 1980, and 1981, the United States experienced double-digit inflation, with annual price increases of 11.3%, 13.5%, and 13.9% respectively. Rising prices, or inflation, became a national concern. The Reagan administration tried to solve the inflation crisis with their "Program for Economic Recovery." This administration gave Americans some relief from inflation but initiated no meaningful solutions. **The inflation rate eventually dropped to under 4%, but the federal deficit continued to grow.[2] As you will learn, fighting inflation with more debt is like eating chocolate to lose weight. The two are not compatible.**

By 1997, Americans had experienced more than a decade of low inflation (under 4%). Nevertheless, **by 1997:**

- the postage stamp sold for $.32,
- a gallon of gasoline was $1.39,
- the maximum social security tax, which now separates FICA and Medicare, had risen to $4,055, with Medicare an additional 1.45% of wages with no ceiling, and
- new homes averaged $153,200.[3]

As you can see, even when the inflation rate is low, prices rise substantially over several years.

These subtle increases erode personal income. In fact, inflation will ruin the best thought out financial plan if its long-term influences are not considered.

Table 5.1—Thirty-Five Years of Inflation—1962–1997

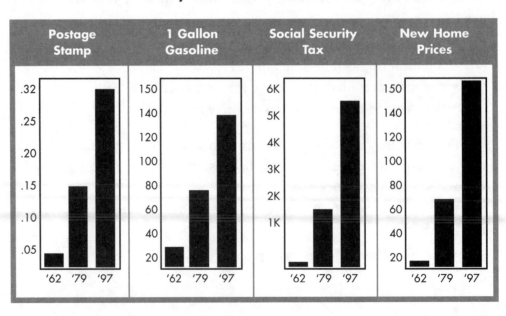

What Causes Inflation?

Inflation is rising prices due to increased spending. The value of all goods and services produced by a nation are referred to as the gross national product or GNP. Economists use the GNP to measure a nation's economic health. **When prices rise but our production of goods and services (GNP) does not, inflation results.**

Small price increases (such as 2.5%) are considered normal for a growing economy. Moreover, when prices go up 4% but you also receive a 4% salary increase, your purchasing power remains the same. **No noticeable change takes place as long as rising incomes balance with price increases.**

Usually, when spending and production are out of balance, inflation follows.

For example:

Assume all the people in a small, remote town must attend a weekly auction to buy their groceries. The town provides each of the one hundred households $50 to spend each week at the auction. The groceries are auctioned until gone. When one hundred people attend and everyone spends their allotted $50, they spend a total of $5,000. This $5,000 is exactly the value of the available groceries. As long as everyone shows up with their $50, the $5,000 of available money buys $5,000 of available goods, and everything stays in balance. If ten households do not come to the auction (a rarity), $500 less (or $4,500) will purchase the $5,000 of groceries. Those who do show up will get more for their money. On the other hand, if the town gives an extra $10 to each of the households, they now collectively have $6,000 to spend. If the available goods do not increase proportionately, the town's people pay more for the same groceries, their dollar loses value, and they experience inflation.

If the people attending the auction could increase their purchasing power through a line of credit at the bank, it would have the same effect. **Anytime more money buys the same supply, the price goes up. Consequently, the dollar loses purchasing power. The same loaf of bread that cost $.89 yesterday costs $.99 today.**

How the Federal Government Stabilizes the Economy

The 1930 Depression

Many seniors today remember the hard times of the early 1930s that started with the stock market crash in October, 1929. Following the crash, people feared losing their savings at the banks, so they showed up en masse to withdraw their money. **Because so many people showed up at the same time to make total withdrawals, the banks could not meet the demand.** The lucky ones managed to retrieve some of their savings, while the unlucky lost out completely.

Along with bank failures, production was down everywhere. Auto production declined 65%, residential construction declined 95%, and the steel industry was down over 80%.[4] **Many businesses failed because people just didn't have the money to buy goods.** Banks gave very few new loans because the job market was so unstable. **Especially in the cities, people suffered from massive unemployment and had no welfare or unemployment insurance to help them survive.** Nearly two million people were forced to live on the streets. The fortunate ones, those who had jobs, saw their wages reduced.

Unlike other depressions before it, this one did not correct itself. Thus, it lasted longer and was more severe. An economist by the name of John Maynard Keynes said **before conditions would improve, someone had to spend money to get the economy moving again. He said if the government created jobs, it would give people money.** With money, they would start buying; the renewed consumer spending would help businesses. **Finally, when other plans failed, the government did step in and start spending to create jobs. It worked just like Keynes predicted.**

The Role of Government Has Changed

Employment and Government Contracts

Since its major involvement bringing the country out of the Great Depression, the federal government's role changed. For instance, in 1929, the federal government employed less that 2% of the work force, but today, it employs, directly or indirectly, more than 25% of the total work force. Government workers receive steady wages that can help offset

• Production Was Down
• Businesses Failed
• Massive Unemployment Was Everywhere

The Government Started Spending to Create Jobs—This Put Money Back into the Economy

other depressed markets. **This large percentage of "guaranteed" employment helps keep some money circulating.**

Along with being a major employer, the federal government is also a primary purchaser of goods. The government buys airplanes, missiles, machinery, and office equipment. **Many businesses depend on government contracts to keep them going.** Government expenditures for goods and services totaled $9 billion in 1929, compared to an estimated $1,638 billion in 1997.

Payments to Individuals

The government also redistributes money to individuals. These payments include social security, education and social services, veterans' pensions, housing credits, welfare, Medicare, and subsidies to farmers. These payments have increased from $3.7 billion in 1929 to approximately $895 billion by 1997.

FDIC Insurance

Another major change since the Great Depression is the creation of the Federal Deposit Insurance Corporation (FDIC) to guarantee individual bank accounts. This guarantee prevents another panic like the one in 1929 when millions of people tried to withdraw their funds at the same time. **Accounts at FDIC insured banks give people security during bad times.** People know their savings are backed by the federal government, so they do not rush out to withdraw their funds even when bank reserves are low.

Money Supply

"Like an engine that runs on gasoline, the economy runs on money."[5] The Federal Reserve Board has the specific duty of monitoring the money supply. They accomplish this by deciding how much money will pass through the banking system. When they require commercial banks to keep a large percentage of their money in reserve, the banks must hold back more funds and therefore have less money available to loan to businesses, farmers, and individuals.

Fewer loans result in businesses cutting back and laying off their employees, less money circulating, and rising interest rates. On the other hand, when the Federal Reserve lowers the reserve requirements, the banks have more money to loan. **This increased lending leads to business expansion, more money in circulation, lower interest rates, and reduced unemployment.**

The Federal Reserve Controls the Money Supply

HIGH BANK RESERVES	LOW BANK RESERVES
• Tight Money	• Easy Money
• Less Money to Loan	• More Money to Loan
• Higher Interest Rates	• Lower Interest Rates
• Fewer Loans	• More Loans
• Little Business Expansion	• Business Expansion
• Fewer Jobs	• More Jobs

By controlling the money supply, the Federal Reserve Board indirectly influences business expansion. "Easy money" encourages business expansion and creates jobs to help solve high unemployment. "Tight money" reduces available credit and holds the reins on inflationary pressures.

The federal government stabilizes the economy through:

- Direct Employment
- Indirect Employment through Government Contracts
- Payments to Individuals
- Bank Account Guarantees
- Control of the Money Supply

Deficit Spending

Increased government control protects us from the ill effects of another great depression, but it also requires huge expenditures. These expenses exceed federal revenues. **Insufficient income to meet needed expenses has created a huge national debt.**

The term "deficit spending" comes from using credit (debt) as a source for additional funds. The difference between what the government takes in and what it spends is the federal deficit. Primarily, federal revenues come from taxes that individuals and businesses pay, such as: individual and corporate income taxes, employment, estate, gift, and excise taxes.

The money collected then goes out to support the military, the disaster relief fund, our judicial system, housing, social security, agricultural programs, government research, the space program, wages for government employees, services for the poor, services for the elderly, and other programs. **When the government's cost for these items is higher than the amount of money they collected, deficit spending results.**

The Difference between What the Government Takes in and What It Spends Is the Federal Deficit

Expanded government support of many public programs increases government spending. Such financing has created an enormous national debt that will be difficult to correct. As the debt increases so do the interest payments, adding to the tax burden of all citizens. If the debt were divided equally among all citizens, we would each owe $19,725. For fiscal 1996, the public debt was $5,182 billion; the interest charges alone were over $241 billion. Table 5.2 shows how the total national debt has increased since 1960.[6]

Government Support of Many Public Programs Increases Government Spending

Table 5.2—National Debt—1960-1990

NATIONAL DEBT	
1960	$ 284.1 Billion
1970	$ 370.1 Billion
1980	$ 907.7 Billion
1990	$3,233.3 Billion

Inflation

Dependence on government controls makes our economy vulnerable to inflation. **More money put into circulation with no offsetting increase in productivity dilutes the value of the dollar.** Inflation results.

My neighbor told me that when he cooked dinner, friends and relatives often stopped by just before the meal was ready. So, he started grating potatoes into the ground meat to stretch it to feed more people. Using this as an example, deficit spending affects the dollar in the same way the potatoes affect the meat. Both dilute the end product, reducing the quality by increasing the quantity.

Another way to look at inflation is through the dollar's loss of purchasing power. The same dollar buys less. Perhaps you've seen advertisements in old magazines selling a cup of coffee for a dime, a candy bar for a nickel, a steak dinner for $.99, or even a gallon of gasoline for $.21. No doubt, you know what these items cost today.

When Prices Go Up Each Year, the Dollar Buys Less

Ad from *Life* Magazine,
1955 Vol. 39, No. 21

Ad from *Life* Magazine,
1966 Vol. 60, No. 3

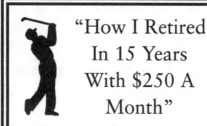

"How I Retired
In 15 Years
With $250 A
Month"

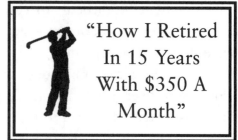

"How I Retired
In 15 Years
With $350 A
Month"

Consumer Price Index

The Consumer Price Index (CPI) measures the annual inflation rate. The U.S. Bureau of Labor Statistics publishes this index monthly. They track costs of household items used throughout our country, then compile the data to show price trends. The CPI is based on the average cost of over four hundred items categorized as: food, shelter, rent, fuel and utilities, apparel and upkeep, transportation, medical care, entertainment, and commodities.

In 1967, the CPI was arbitrarily set at 100 for ease in measuring future increases. **The monthly or annual CPI increase is the same as the inflation rate.** For example, the CPI rose from 100 in 1967 to 104.2 in 1968. Purchases, based on average costs, that were $100 in 1967 rose to $104.20 in 1968. The percentage increase of 4.2% was the inflation rate for that year.

Goods = $100 in 1967
Goods = $104 in 1968
This Is a 4% Increase
Inflation Rate = 4%

Keep in mind that cost-of-living increases are averages, and averages can be misleading. Prices for different items vary from one section of the country to another. For instance, housing is more expensive in California and Hawaii. Oranges are cheaper in Florida than Alaska, while a cord of wood is cheaper in Vermont than Nevada. Lobster is cheaper in Maine than Chicago. Along with these regional differences, families seldom make the same purchases or use the same services. Some may need to buy a new car, others a new washing machine, and still others require no major purchases. **Translated into real dollars, with the current CPI at 480.6, it now takes $480.60 to purchase what $100 bought in 1967.**

Table 5.3—Annual Increases in the Consumer Price Index[7]

Year	CPI Index	Increase	Year	CPI Index	Increase
(Base) 1967	100.0	———	1983	298.6	3.80%
1968	104.7	4.70%	1984	310.3	3.90%
1969	111.2	6.20%	1985	322.1	3.80%
1970	117.4	5.60%	1986	325.6	1.10%
1971	121.3	3.30%	1987	339.9	4.40%
1972	125.4	3.40%	1988	354.9	4.40%
1973	136.3	8.70%	1989	371.2	4.60%
1974	153.1	12.30%	1990	393.9	6.10%
1975	163.7	6.90%	1991	406.1	3.10%
1976	171.7	4.90%	1992	417.8	2.90%
1977	183.2	6.70%	1993	429.1	2.70%
1978	199.7	9.00%	1994	440.7	2.70%
1979	226.2	13.30%	1995	451.7	2.50%
1980	254.5	12.50%	1996	466.6	3.30%
			1997	480.6	3.00%
			Average = 5.42%		

If you look closely at Table 5.3, you will see why inflation was such a major concern from 1973 through 1981. Prices increased a total of 83.2% during those nine years, an average of 9.24% per year. Fortunately, between 1984 and 1994, the inflation rate remained low, averaging less than 4%. Will it always stay that low? Probably not, since its history has shown rising and falling rates.

The average inflation rate for the past thirty years, since 1967, has been 5.42%. With 5.42% inflation, prices double every 13.2 years (remember the Rule of 72). Sometimes price increases cause national concern, as they did during the late 1970s and early 1980s. Recently, increases have been so slight that we hardly notice them. **Regardless, the compounded, long-term effect erodes the buying power of your dollar.**

The Compounded Long-Term Effect of Inflation Erodes the Buying Power of Your Dollar

Why Inflation Won't End

Inflation is here to stay. We can't stop it; we can only slow it down. Inflation compounds just like interest, with each annual increase becoming the starting point for next year's escalation. If the inflation rate is a constant 4%, prices will double every 18 years.

Stopping inflation is almost impossible. It would require large cutbacks in government spending and would again leave us with a volatile economy, subject to dramatic ups and downs. The cures for inflation, at this point, seem worse than the consequences. The following factors make it a certainty that inflation will continue:

Indexing Adjusts Payments to the Consumer Price Index

People demand indexing when they notice inflation as a problem. Indexing occurs when a payment increases annually, the same percentage as the Consumer Price Index. Social security payments are one example of indexing. If the Consumer Price Index rises by 4%, social security payments will be 4% higher.

Once indexing starts, it becomes part of the economy and doesn't stop. A cycle then begins, with one end feeding on the other. Workers ask for higher salaries to keep up with the Consumer Price Index, but higher salaries help contribute to the Consumer Price Index rising. The companies they work for charge more for the goods they produce to fund the higher wages. We now have indexing for some wages, social security payments, personal income taxes, and many other items. Higher prices are commonplace; lower prices are rare.

Social Security Payments Continue to Rise

Many Misunderstand the Purpose of Social Security

Many Americans have misunderstood the purpose of social security. Although Congress designed the system to be a supplemental, not a primary source of income, many people retiring today depend on social security payments to meet their necessary living expenses. More people must learn not to depend on social security. When the eighty million baby boomers retire (those born between 1943 and 1964), the social security system will have more dependent retirees than contributing workers for the first time in our history.

People age sixty-five and older increased in number from 4% of the total population in 1900 to 12% of the total population by 1990. This number is expected to grow to 20% over the next thirty years.[8] These increasing numbers combined with decreasing mortality rates mean more payments to more people for longer time periods. More payments and more recipients translate into even higher employment taxes, a reduction of benefits, or both.

Taxpayers Pay for the Failed Thrift Institutions

Expenses for taxpayers increased with the government bailout of thousands of failed savings and loans. Between 1981 and 1991, 1,345 thrift institutions failed.[9] The funds were guaranteed by the federal government through FSLIC (Federal Savings and Loan Insurance Corporation) insurance. As it turns out, most of the assets that the S & L's were supposed to have to back up the savings accounts were in overappraised real estate. Therefore, the government had to return the "misused" funds to the savers. Since 1989, the government has paid out an average of $9,000 on the twenty-two million insured accounts. The total cost to taxpayers over the next thirty years will be over $150 billion.[10] **Taxpayers pay out more but get nothing in return.** This additional cost adds to inflation.

Cutbacks in Spending Make Politicians Unpopular

Politicians need public support to get reelected. Their backing often comes from campaign platforms that lead to even more government spending. Again, more spending translates into higher taxes and an increased federal deficit.

Can you imagine a politician getting elected into office by saying they would:

- Increase taxes
- Allow banks to fail and let people lose their money
- Allow corporations to go under without offering government assistance, leaving thousands of workers unemployed
- Provide no compensation for the needy
- Decrease social security payments
- Increase the employer and employee social security taxes AGAIN
- Raise interest rates to discourage borrowing
- Abolish Medicare and Medicaid
- Stop providing funds to improve interstate highways
- Freeze wages for all government workers and freeze pensions for all government retirees
- Freeze military spending

Politicians Need to Be Popular

In theory, we readily agree to cut back on government services—until it affects us personally. Because politicians need to be popular, no elected official would stay in office by supporting employment cutbacks and tax increases. That is the main reason why THE GOVERNMENT CAN'T AND WON'T DECREASE SPENDING TO FIGHT INFLATION.

Inflation Is Not All Bad

Continual rises in the cost of living are not necessarily bad if your income and/or assets also increase. By understanding inflation and planning to live with it, your wealth need not diminish. Inflation, however, does change many of the old money rules.

Inflation hurts those living on fixed incomes. People living on fixed pensions and other sources of fixed income will see their dollars diminish in purchasing power each year. If the inflation rate is 4%, a retiree who receives $800 a month this year will receive only $768 of buying power the following year, then $737 the next year on the same $800 a month check. At a steady 4% inflation rate, that $800 of monthly income erodes to $665 of purchasing power after ten years.

Table 5.4 shows how $1,000 decreases in purchasing power in just ten years with inflation rates of 3%, 4%, 5%, and 6%.

Table 5.4—Declining Value of $1,000

Year	3% Inflation	4% Inflation	5% Inflation	6% Inflation
0	$1,000	$1,000	$1,000	$1,000
1	$ 970	$ 960	$ 950	$ 940
2	$ 941	$ 922	$ 903	$ 884
3	$ 913	$ 885	$ 857	$ 831
4	$ 885	$ 849	$ 815	$ 781
5	$ 859	$ 815	$ 774	$ 734
6	$ 833	$ 783	$ 735	$ 690
7	$ 808	$ 751	$ 698	$ 649
8	$ 784	$ 721	$ 663	$ 610
9	$ 760	$ 693	$ 630	$ 573
10	$ 737	$ 665	$ 599	$ 539

Savers who earn fixed interest lose with inflation unless their fixed interest earnings exceed the inflation rate. The difference between the interest rate and the inflation rate represents the real earnings on an account. Interest at 4% with inflation at 3% gives 1% net earnings before taxes. After paying income taxes on the interest earnings, the account has lost buying power and, therefore, has decreased in value.

In times of high inflation, debtors win and creditors lose. Each year that a debtor pays back a fixed amount on a loan, he is repaying with dollars that have declined in value. In fact, banks now protect themselves from losing much of their profit to inflation through variable rates. Understandably, banks do not want to be left holding thirty-year mortgages that have lower than market yields, so when interest rates go up, their adjustable mortgages go up as well.

Interestingly enough, **sometimes inflation can help to create wealth.** People benefit when their investments increase in value faster than the inflation rate. Those who bought real estate in the right location prospered from the inflation cycle between 1973 and 1982. Along with all real estate, home values skyrocketed during this period, especially in California. Many homeowners were able to double or triple their equity within four to eight years.

An investment that goes up in value as prices rise will protect your dollars from losing buying power. **In the past, real estate and stocks have been excellent inflation hedges.** The pivotal questions are: Where will real estate values continue to go up? What stocks will increase in value? Will gold, oil, or silver values increase? As the population representing senior citizens grow, what services and products will expand? Will it be health care facilities, computer technology, or recreational facilities? **The "winners" will make money and become inflation hedges for those lucky or clever enough to invest in them.**

Your challenge is to be on guard against inflation. **Don't put yourself in the position of having only a fixed income in an economy where prices keep rising.** Instead, participate in that economy with investments that increase in value. If your income doesn't grow to match rising price levels, what may seem like a lot of money today can put you on the poverty level tomorrow.

An Investment That Goes up in Value as Prices Rise Will Protect Your Dollars from Losing Power

If Your Income Doesn't Grow to Match Rising Levels, What May Seem Like a Lot of Money Today Can Put You on the Poverty Level Tomorrow

Notes

1. "Compounding Inflation," *Forbes*, 11 June 1979, 108.

2. James K. Gailbraith, *Balancing Acts* (New York: Basic Books, Inc. 1989), 53–76.

3. Postage stamp and gasoline prices taken from personal knowledge. Social security tax taken from 1997 tax tables. Median priced homes, *The Wall Street Journal Almanac, 1998* (New York: Ballantine Books, 1997), 457.

4. John Case, *Understanding Inflation* (New York: William Morrow & Co., Inc., 1981), 135–45.

5. Case, 111.

6. *The Wall Street Journal Almanac, 1998*, 132.

7. *The Wall Street Journal Almanac, 1998*, 160.

8. Gerber, Wolff, Klores, & Brown, *Life-Trends* (New York: Avon, 1990), 3.

9. *The World Almanac and Book of Facts 1993* (New York: Pharos Books, 1992), 128.

10. TMI Tax Service, *Quickfinder Handbook 1993* (Minnetonka, Minn.), 18-3.

6
Personal Income Taxes

THIS IS A LONG CHAPTER with many details. You may want to refer to Mindmap II at the beginning of this section if you need to find specific information quickly.

If you do not know the basic rules for taxing personal income, you could lose "extra" dollars. This is especially true for the years where you have additional income from investment sales, bonuses, or a business boom. Our tax laws have become so detailed that many citizens just shake their heads and say, "taxes are too complicated." Then, to make matters worse, Congress changes the rules and forms every year. What is true this year is likely to change next year. In spite of the many details and ongoing changes, if you know the general concepts for taxing personal income, you will maintain an advantage that will help you keep more of your dollars. This chapter will show you:

- What you must report as income
- What you can take as deductions from your income
- The importance of tax planning
- How to use the tax forms so you can prepare your own taxes or verify the work done by someone else

Understandably, you stand to benefit the most by reducing your tax bill. If you know the basics—where to get reliable information, what income is taxed, and what deductions are allowed—you have a good

chance of saving some extra money. Knowing the rules for taxing personal income helps you plan tax saving strategies either on your own or with the help of a tax professional.

Free Information

It is easy today to be aware of changes in tax law. Many newspapers feature tax saving tips and provide information on current legislation. When you need more information on specific topics, the Internal Revenue Service provides an abundance of it free of charge.

A service called **Tele-Tax** offers taxpayers in every state the opportunity to hear prerecorded tax information over the telephone. Through this service, the IRS provides information on about 140 pre-recorded topics. You can also get automated refund information.

Also, tax forms are available on the Internet. The public can download free current tax forms, instructions, and IRS publications. The Web site for IRS products is located at: http://www.irs.ustreas.gov.

Tax forms via fax machines are available at any time by dialing (703) 487-4160.

Along with Tele-Tax, the IRS also provides **booklets** giving the current tax law on many subjects. A complete listing of the Tele-Tax topics, the free booklets, and other IRS resources are listed in Publication 910, *Guide to Free Tax Services*. To order it, call : **1-800-424-FORM (3676)**

General Rules

Who Is Required to File?

Age, gross income, and filing status determine if an individual needs to file a tax return. **All taxpayers are allowed two deductions:**

- the PERSONAL EXEMPTION(S) and DEPENDENT(S) deduction(s), and
- the STANDARD DEDUCTION, or ITEMIZED DEDUCTIONS.

When a person's taxable income exceeds the standard personal exemption and the standard deduction amounts, he/she must file. For example, for 1998 tax returns and a single person under age sixty-five, the personal exemption is $2,700 and the standard deduction is $4,250. When a single person has taxable income above $6,950 ($2,700 + $4,250), he/she

Take Advantage of Free Information

All Taxpayers Are Allowed Two Deductions

needs to send in a tax form. Married couples and senior citizens over age sixty-five have higher standard deductions, so they can have more taxable income before they must file.

The following people should file a tax return. **They are exceptions to the gross income filing requirement.**

- Self-employed persons with net earnings above $400
- People who received advanced earned income credit from their employer
- Those applying for a refund of income tax withheld

Interest and Penalties

When the IRS owes you money on a prior year return, they pay you interest of 2% above the short-term federal rate. But, they charge you interest of 3% above the short-term federal rate for all taxes not paid on time. In both cases, the interest compounds daily.

When you don't have the money to pay your taxes, still file your tax return. When you file but don't pay, the IRS assesses a penalty of 1/2% per month on the balance due (to a maximum of 25%) for not paying on time. In addition, the separate penalty for not filing is 5% per month of the unpaid tax (to a maximum of 25%). The minimum penalty for not filing is the lesser of $100 or 100% of the unpaid tax. Besides the late payment penalty and the failure to file penalty, the IRS will charge current interest on the balance due. Penalties plus interest can quickly amount to a substantial bill.

When you owe taxes and you can't pay, the worst thing to do is to ignore IRS bills and letters. They have the right to freeze your bank accounts, garnish your wages, and put liens on your property. You can save this hassle and embarrassment by communicating with them and working out a payment plan to retire your tax bill.

Withholding and Tax Estimates

For taxpayers who have income under $150,000, the tax law requires individuals to pay in, through withholding or estimated payments, either 90% of the tax due or 100% of the previous years' taxes. You will be charged another penalty, underpayment of estimated tax, if you don't pay in enough tax during the year. Form W-4 tells your employer how much tax to withhold (deposit on your behalf) from your paycheck. The number of exemptions you claim, along with your filing

Your Income Determines if You Need to File

Never Ignore IRS Bills and Letters

status (married or single), increases or decreases your withholding taxes. You can modify the amount withheld by amending Form W-4 with your employer.

Anytime you have a situation that reduces your tax liability, such as large financial losses, a new home with higher mortgage interest and property tax write-offs, a new dependent, large charitable contributions, or a reduction in income, you may be able to decrease your withholding to give yourself more monthly income.

Although it is wise to avoid penalties for under-withholding, it is also wise to avoid banking with the IRS. They don't pay interest on a current year's refund money. Additionally, you have no access to your money until your refund check arrives. So, when expecting a large refund, adjust your withholding on Form W-4, and put the extra money in savings. This way you have access to your money and its earnings.

Similarly, if a situation occurs during the year that increases your taxable income, do a tax estimate to see if you are having enough withheld (see Annual Tax Projection in chapter 20, Planning). Higher taxes result from salary increases and bonuses, making a profit on investments, selling real estate or business property at a profit, or losing an exemption or previous deduction.

When you expect to owe more tax than you have withheld, make sure you pay in enough to avoid the under-withholding penalties. Then, put the balance you expect to owe into a money market account or a bank account where it will earn interest until you file your tax return and need the money to pay. Do not make estimated payments beyond the amount required. Doing so gives the government an interest-free loan. Instead, put the interest earnings in your account.

Example:

Joel's prior year tax liability was $6,000. This year, Joel made a $20,000 profit on some investments and expects to owe an additional $5,600 in federal tax. As long as Joel pays in $6,000 (100% of the prior years tax) and pays the additional amount owed ($5,600) by April 15, the filing deadline, he will incur no penalties. Strategically, Joel should "save" the $5,600 in his own account and not pay the tax until it is due on April 15. The interest earnings on this money are now his to keep.

Extensions

Erroneously, many people who owe taxes think they can have three more months after the April 15 deadline to pay the tax due if they file an

Form W-4 Tells Your Employer How Much to Withhold from Your Pay

Don't Bank with the IRS

extension. **True, the IRS allows an automatic extension of three months (from April 15 to August 15) for all taxpayers who file Form 4868 by April 15.** If you wait until August 15 to pay, however, the IRS will charge you interest from April 15 on the amount due.

Another two month extension will give you until October 15 to file your taxes. This extension, Form 2688, requires IRS approval, so send it in several weeks prior to the August 15 extended deadline when you need more time. **Just remember, the IRS will charge interest from April 15 on all money you owe regardless of allowed extensions.**

An Extension Gives You More Time to File, Not to Pay

Amended Returns

If you neglect to take a deduction or to report additional income in one year, you cannot make it up by reporting these changes in a subsequent year. Instead, you must amend your return for the year of the error. **Report changes made to a previously filed tax return on Form 1040X.**

Form 1040

Form 1040 is the required tax form for individuals. Since it includes many backup schedules, it is referred to as "the long form." Forms 1040A and 1040EZ are shortened versions of Form 1040. Just remember, the shortened versions do not list all of the permitted deductions, so if you use 1040A or 1040EZ, check the long form periodically to make certain you haven't missed any applicable write-offs.

Since the two pages of Form 1040 summarize all of the other schedules, they contain a wealth of information. Being familiar with this form will help you:

- know what income you must report,
- know what you can subtract from your income,
- prepare or check your tax return for accuracy, and
- be aware of deductions that may apply on future returns.

Get Form 1040 to Look at while Reading This Section

For ease in going through the following information, get the most current year's Form 1040, the long form. Do not use 1040A or 1040EZ. All libraries have copies, or you could make a copy from a prior year's tax return.

The left margin divides Form 1040 into eight sections. Locate these sections on the tax form. The sections have not changed in years, although changing tax law adds or subtracts line items from these sections.

Get Pink, Yellow, Blue, and Green Highlighter Pens

The Major Sections of the Tax Forms Haven't Changed in Years

Marking Form 1040 with four highlighter pens: pink, yellow, blue, and green will give you a visual reference. If you highlight the title of each section in this text and/or highlight the actual tax form as you read about it, you will then associate the color with the section. This helps put the information into easy-to-remember categories. **Your right-brain needs a visual reference.** To begin, highlight what the colors represent:

> **Income is GREEN**
> > **Deductions are YELLOW**
> > > **Payments and credits are BLUE.**
> > > > **Taxes owed are PINK.**

Continue to highlight in this text and on Form 1040 all sections referred to as you read about them.

Form 1040 Has Eight Sections:

1. Filing Status YELLOW
2. Exemptions YELLOW
3. Income GREEN
4. Adjustments to Income YELLOW
5. Tax Computation YELLOW & PINK
6. Credits BLUE
7. Other Taxes PINK
8. Payments BLUE

Filing Status YELLOW

(Locate and highlight this section on Form 1040)
Each filing status has its own tax table or tax rate schedule. Also, each category qualifies for different standard deductions. The four filing categories are:

1. Married Filing Joint, and Surviving Spouses
2. Single
3. Head of Household
4. Married Filing Separately

Each filing status has different income levels for the different tax rates. In any year that you experience a major life change, such as the death of a spouse, marriage, divorce, separation, or the addition or deletion of a dependent, your taxes will change. For 1998 taxes, the 15% tax bracket ended at $25,350 for singles, at $33,950 for a head of household, and at $42,350 for married filing joint.

All taxpayers start at a 15% tax rate then, as taxable income increases, move up to the 28%, 31%, 36%, and 39.6% rates. **Each year, the IRS adjusts the tax tables for inflation.** They increase the base taxable income by the inflation rate. This adjustment is made according to the inflation rate from August 31 of the preceding year to August 31 of the current year. This annual inflation adjustment allows the percentage taken for taxes to stay relatively stable as wages increase to keep up with the cost of living.

Example:

In 1996, the 15% bracket for a single person ended at $24,000
In 1997, the 15% bracket for a single person ended at $24,650
In 1998, the 15% bracket for a single person will end at $25,350

Filing Choices

Singles and heads of households have no filing choice, but married couples can choose to file jointly or separately. The filing separate option is not advantageous, however, unless one or both spouses can take large expenses that would be disallowed on a joint return. For instance, higher joint income could disallow some deductions that must exceed certain percentages, such as employee business expenses, medical expenses, and casualty and theft losses. Sometimes by filing separately, the individual claiming the lower income may be able to write off deductions that would be lost on a joint return.

Married couples who choose to file separately will find that a higher tax rate applies, and once reaching a certain income level, they will lose deductions. Also, if one spouse itemizes instead of electing the standard deduction, the other spouse also must itemize. Furthermore, unless they file jointly, married couples cannot claim the earned income credit, the dependent care credit, the credit for the elderly, or take an IRA deduction for a non-working spouse.

If One Spouse Itemizes, the Other Spouse Also Must Itemize

Your Filing Status gives you a deduction. YELLOW

Exemptions, Personal and Dependent YELLOW

(Locate and highlight this section on Form 1040)

The second section of Form 1040 covers personal exemptions and the additional exemptions allowed for dependents. **Generally, taxpayers can deduct a set amount for themselves and each qualifying dependent.** This amount also changes each year to adjust for inflation.

- For example, the $2,550 personal exemption deduction allowed in 1996 rose to $2,650 in 1997, and to $2,700 in 1998.

Dependents two years of age or older must have social security numbers. You can claim a child born anytime during the tax year, even if born on December 31st. Also, if a qualifying person you support dies at the beginning of the year, you still claim him/her as a dependent for the entire year.

Five Tests Determine if You Can Claim a Person as a Dependent

1. Support. You must contribute over one half of their total support.

2. Member of Household or Relative. The dependent must be a relative or someone who lives with you full-time (cousins do not count as relatives).

3. Gross Income. The dependent's gross income must be less than the exemption amount ($2,450 in 1994). Two exceptions to this test are children under nineteen years of age and students under age twenty-four. You still must meet, however, the other dependency tests.

4. Joint Return. If you claim a married, dependent child, he/she cannot file a joint return with his/her spouse unless it is merely to claim a refund of withheld taxes.

5. Citizenship. Finally, your dependent must be a U.S. citizen or national, or a resident of the United States, Canada, or Mexico.

To claim parents or other relatives, your support must exceed their total support costs. Divorced or separated couples must decide who will claim the children from their marriage. When divorced couples disagree, tax law allows the parent who provides more than half of the child's support to claim the exemption. **Generally, tax rules consider the parent who has custody of the child for the greater part of the year as the one who provided more than one-half of the support.** The custodial parent can release the exemption to the noncustodial parent by signing a written declaration on IRS Form 8332.

Income GREEN

(Locate and highlight this section on Form 1040)

Report all income in this section. Report the entire amount of pensions along with the taxable portion, even though only the taxable portion will count. Although it is not taxed, you must also report tax exempt interest. It is used to determine taxable social security. The sale of investments, business assets, rental properties, partnerships, and businesses will produce additional income or a loss. **Total income is the result of adding all the positive and negative numbers. Lines showing negative numbers (losses) reduce other income dollar for dollar.**

In most instances, if tax law requires a taxpayer to report income, another person or business took a deduction for that sum. Employers deduct gross wages paid to employees from their profits; employees report these gross wages as income. Banks, corporations, credit unions, mutual fund companies, and others who pay interest and dividends deduct the payments made to shareholders; the recipient counts the payment as income. The spouse who pays alimony writes it off; the spouse who receives the payments counts it as income.

Generally, income is taxed only once. When contributions to IRA's, pension plans, or tax sheltered annuities are excluded from income and the earnings accumulate "tax free," all money coming out of the account is 100% taxable. When no deduction is allowed for the contribution, but the earnings accumulate "tax free," upon withdrawal, only the interest is taxed. This is the case with nondeductible IRA's and annuities purchased with regular money. The exception is the Roth IRA. You receive no deduction for the contribution, and qualified withdrawals are tax free.

Annuities are an investment that function under some special IRS rules. They can be purchased with regular after-tax money, through life insurance, or through some retirement plans. They can only be written through life insurance companies. The nature of the money withdrawn determines how it is taxed. For example, **if an annuity is purchased with regular after tax money, the interest accumulates tax free until the owner withdraws it.** Current law states that the interest must be withdrawn before the principal. That means the taxable portion comes out first, the tax free basis comes out last. **If the owner selects a life income option, or one of the other annuity options, the taxable earnings are prorated with the untaxed contributions making only a percentage of each payment taxable.**

If the annuity is purchased with "before tax" money, such as through a retirement plan, the earnings accumulate "tax free," and all distributions are 100% taxable. Annuities purchased as retirement plans, or 403(b) tax sheltered annuities (offered by schools and hospitals), the contribution is deducted from gross salary so the distributions are 100% taxable.

The following checklist gives an overview of many sources that should be reported as income on Form 1040. Remember, adding positive and negative numbers gives total income. Those items with a "☆" are usually added to gross wages with an explanation on the **W-2 (Wage and Tax Statement** issued to all employees by their employer in January for the preceding year).

Items to Include as Income:

___Alimony Received

___Awards & Prizes

___Back Pay ☆

___Bonuses ☆

___Business Income (loss)

___Capital Gains (losses)

___Commissions

___Dismissal Pay ☆

___Dividend Income

___Gambling Winnings

___Gross Wages

___Interest Income

___Partner's Share of Partnership Income or (loss)

___Pension and Annuity Income (taxable portion)

___Personal Use of Business Auto ☆

___Rental Income (loss)

___Royalties

___S-Corporation Income (loss)

___Sale (loss) of Business Property includes farming and fishing

___Severance Pay

___Sick Pay ☆

___Strike Benefits ☆

___Taxable Social Security Benefits If AGI exceeds certain limits

___Tips ☆

___Unemployment Compensation

___Vacation Pay ☆

Adjustments to Income YELLOW

(Locate and highlight this section on Form 1040)

From total income, subtract all adjustments. The most common adjustments to income are:

- deductible IRA, Keogh, and SEP IRA, and SIMPLE contributions,
- penalties for early withdrawal of savings,
- special deductions for self-employed individuals,
- alimony paid,
- non-reimbursed moving expenses for a job relocation, and
- student loan interest (starting in 1998).

These adjustments, subtracted from the total income, give your adjusted gross income, referred to as "AGI."

Moving Expenses

You can deduct unreimbursed moving expenses due to a job relocation if the distance between the new job and your former home is fifty miles or more. If you are an employee, you must remain in the new location for at least thirty-nine weeks during the twelve month period following the move. Self-employed persons must stay in the new location for seventy-eight weeks.

You can write off the full unreimbursed cost of moving your household goods and personal belongings. This includes fees paid to a moving company or money paid to rent a truck and to purchase packing materials. **You can also deduct the full transportation costs for moving yourself and members of your immediate family to the new location.**

Adjustments Give a Deduction YELLOW

Tax Computation

Personal Exemptions YELLOW

(Locate and highlight this section on Form 1040)

In the tax computation section, subtract from adjusted gross income (AGI) the personal exemption deductions for yourself, your spouse, and all your dependents. As mentioned earlier, this 1998 amount of $2,700 will increase each year according to the annual inflation rate.

Standard and Itemized Deductions YELLOW

(Locate and highlight this section on Form 1040)

The standard deduction is another write-off with a set amount for each filing status. It also increases each year according to the inflation rate. In 1998, it was $7,100 for couples filing jointly, $6,250 for heads of household, and $4,250 for singles. Blind persons and/or taxpayers over age sixty-five qualify for additional deduction amounts. These amounts increase each year, again with the inflation rate.

Taxpayers with deductions that exceed the standard deduction can claim a larger sum by filing Schedule A—Itemized Deductions. When taxpayers itemize, they deduct amounts paid for state and local taxes, home mortgage interest, charitable contributions, and other expenses. Some of the deductions that have limitations are medical expenses, casualty and theft losses, and employee business expenses. For most taxpayers, itemizing is not possible without the write-off from home mortgage interest and property taxes. An explanation of itemized deductions follows this information about Form 1040.

For Most Taxpayers, Itemizing Is Not Possible without the Write-Off from Home Mortgage Interest and Property Taxes

Taxable income is: AGI (Adjusted Gross Income) minus personal exemptions and either the standard or itemized deduction amounts. You use taxable income to figure your tax liability. The tax tables cover taxable incomes between $0 and $50,000; taxable incomes over $50,000 must use the tax rate schedules.

This Section Calculates	
Deductions for: YELLOW • Personal and Dependent Exemptions	
• Standard or Itemized Deductions	Tax Liability PINK

Tax Credits BLUE

(Locate and highlight this section on Form 1040)

Some credits reduce tax liability dollar for dollar, while the IRS gives others as a payment. Those credits given as a payment can be located on the tax form under the "PAYMENT" section. Lower income individuals qualify for an **Earned Income Credit.**

Childless workers between the ages of twenty-five and sixty-five with incomes of less than $9,000, who are not the dependent of another taxpayer, qualify for a reduced amount. The maximum credit for 1997 was $332. Couples and heads of households who work and have one or more children and an adjusted gross income below a certain amount ($29,290 for 1997) qualify for a larger credit. The maximum credit for two or more children was $3,656 in 1997.

The Earned Income Credit is given as a payment. It will be applied toward taxes owed or paid to the taxpayer who has no tax liability. Sometimes, employers will advance the earned income credit to qualifying employees to increase their current monthly income and help them meet their living expenses.

The Earned Income Credit Is Given as a Payment

Dependent and Child Care Credits reduce tax liability. Current tax law gives a 20% credit for those with incomes over $28,000. The credit increases from 21% to 30% for those with incomes under $28,000. A maximum of $2,400 in expenses can be used for one qualifying person, and a maximum of $4,800 for two or more qualifying persons. For those with adjusted gross incomes over $28,000, the top credit (20%) is $480 for one qualifying person and $960 for two or more qualifying persons. These limits apply regardless of how much is spent on child care.

To take dependent and child care credits, both spouses or the head of household must work. Also, the children must be under age thirteen or disabled. For married couples, the credit is figured on the lesser of the two incomes. If one spouse doesn't work, no credit is given. To receive the credit, in addition to the amount paid, the IRS requires the name, address, and tax identification number (social security number) of the person or facility performing the child care services.

Some employers offer a **flexible spending account for child care.** Up to $5,000 per year can be used from this account to pay for qualified child care expenses. Instead of taking the child care credit explained above, your wages are reduced by $5,000, allowing you to pay for child care with "pretax" money. These pretax contributions usually provide a larger tax savings than the dependent care credit for those with tax brackets over 15%.

Some Employers Offer a Flexible Spending Account for Child Care

Starting in 1998, a taxpayer may claim an annual **Child Tax Credit** of $400 per child. As of January 1999, the credit will be $500 per child. An eligible child must be under the age of seventeen by the end of the tax year in which the credit is taken. The child must be a dependent child, a dependent grandchild, a dependent stepchild, or a dependent foster child of the taxpayer. The credit is reduced by $50 for each $1,000 of modified adjusted gross income above $75,000 for singles and $110,000 for joint returns.

Starting in 1997, an **Adoption Credit** of up to $5,000 may be claimed for the qualifying costs of adopting a child under age eighteen or a person who is physically or mentally incapable of self-care. The credit is phased out for those with adjusted gross incomes between $75,000 and $115,000. After 2001, the adoption credit applies only to qualified expenses for adopting an eligible child with special needs. Adoption credits are taken on Form 8839.

Starting in 1998, the **Hope Scholarship Credit** can be taken for tuition and related expenses incurred in the first two years of post-secondary education. The maximum credit is $1,500 per student, per year. This credit can be taken for two years only, regardless of how long the student is in school.

The **Lifetime Learning Credit** covers tuition and related expenses paid after June 30, 1998. It applies to costs of improving job skills through a training program or to costs of undergraduate and graduate students. A 20% credit will be given for qualified expenses up to $5,000. The Hope Scholarship Credit and the Lifetime Learning Credit are phased out for modified adjusted gross incomes for single taxpayers between $40,000 and $50,000 and for joint filers between $80,000 and $100,000. **These credits cannot be claimed for any year that funds are withdrawn from an educational IRA.**

The **Credit for the Elderly and Disabled** is for persons age sixty-five and older who receive little or no social security or railroad retirement benefits. Persons under sixty-five receiving disability income, who are permanently and totally disabled, also qualify.

Those who receive foreign income or who temporarily live in a foreign country or a U.S. possession can take a **Foreign Tax Credit** for foreign taxes paid. Another credit is available for mutual fund shareholders for the tax paid by the mutual fund on its **undistributed capital gains**.

Finally, other credits include a **Fuel Tax Credit**, a credit for the tax on **diesel fuel**, a tax credit for interest paid on qualifying **mortgage certificates**, and numerous **general business credits**.

Credits Reduce Your Taxes

Credits Reduce Your Tax BLUE

Other Taxes PINK

(Locate and highlight this section on Form 1040)

In certain situations, you may have to add other taxes. One such tax is the **self-employment tax**. It is assessed against all persons who are in business for themselves. **This tax covers their contributions for FICA and Medicare. Since the self-employed have no employer paying into social security on their behalf, they must make a double contribution.** Although social security tax is subject to change, the self-employed will pay twice the amount paid by employees through withholding. They must pay for themselves and the "employer." Half of the self-employment tax qualifies for a deduction as an adjustment to income.

Individuals under age fifty-nine who take money out of qualified retirement plans such as IRA's, 401(k)'s, and Keogh's must pay an additional 10% tax penalty on the distribution; no offsetting deductions can reduce this tax penalty. After 1997, the 10% penalty will not apply to withdrawals for up to $10,000 for first-time home buyers and for higher education costs, such as tuition, books, room, and board.

Persons who receive tips and do not report all of them to their employer will pay social security tax on this tip income when they file their tax return. **These "allocated tips" are identified on Form W-2, the wage and tax statement given out by employers in January.** They write in the amount owed for the additional social security tax in this section.

Alternative Minimum Tax affects the higher income brackets and those with tax preference items. It can add as much as an additional 21% to the balance due.

Other Taxes Increase Your Tax Liability PINK

The Self-Employed Must Pay for Themselves and the "Employer"

Payments BLUE

(Locate and highlight this section on Form 1040)

Payments indicate the amount withheld by your employer for all taxes as well as other payments made during the year to meet your tax liability. These include estimated tax payments, payments made with extensions, and refunds applied from prior years.

Any tax credits given as payments also show in this section. They include: earned income credit, tax paid on gasoline and fuels (special situations only), and the mutual fund credit on undistributed dividends.

Other payments shown here are excess social security taxes and excess RRRA taxes withheld.

Applying the total payments against the total tax liability will show either a balance due or a refund.

Payments Are Applied toward Taxes Owed ^{BLUE}

Summary of Form 1040

Each of the sections on Form 1040 are important in determining the amount of personal income tax due. The simplified forms 1040A and 1040EZ go through a similar process but with fewer steps.

- Determine your **filing status** and the number of **exemptions** you can claim.
- Add all your income, including negative numbers or losses.
- Subtract adjustments from income to come up with **adjusted gross income (AGI)**.
- From **adjusted gross income,** subtract standard or itemized deductions and exemptions. This gives **taxable income.** The tax tables and tax rate schedules show the **tax liability** for different incomes and
  filing status' based on taxable income.
- **Additional taxes** and/or **credits,** when applicable, will lower or raise tax liability.
- Apply all **payments** to the total tax due for either a **balance due** or a **refund.**

Table 6.1 gives a summary of this process. Highlight each section with the appropriate color.

Table 6.1—Summary of the 1040 Sections

Color	SECTION	RESULT
GREEN	**INCOME** Add all income and losses	TOTAL INCOME
YELLOW	**ADJUSTMENTS** Subtract all adjustments from total income	ADJUSTED GROSS INCOME
YELLOW	**TAX COMPUTATION** Subtract the deduction for exemptions and standard or itemized deductions from adjusted gross income	TAXABLE INCOME
PINK	Take taxable income to: 1) the tax tables (under $50,000), or 2) the tax rate schedules (over $50,000)	TAX LIABILITY
BLUE	**CREDITS** All credits reduce tax liability. Some are entered as payments.	NEW TAX LIABILITY
PINK	**OTHER TAXES** Add other taxes owed to the new tax liability	TOTAL TAX LIABILITY
BLUE	**PAYMENTS** Add all payments, including credits given as payments	TOTAL PAYMENTS
REFUND OR BALANCE DUE **Apply payments to tax liability**		

Itemized Deductions (Schedule A)

Schedule A is also divided into sections. Locate one of these forms, and identify each section as you read about it. When certain write-offs exceed the standard deduction, taxpayers can take the higher amount by showing the details that reflect that higher amount on Schedule A, Itemized Deductions.

The expenses falling into these categories are:

- Medical Expenses
- Taxes
- Interest
- Contributions
- Casualty and Theft Losses
- Miscellaneous Deductions

Medical Expenses

To Deduct Medical Expenses, They Must Exceed 7.5% of Your Adjusted Gross Income

You can only deduct medical expenses for yourself, for your spouse, and for your dependents to the extent these expenses exceed 7.5% of your adjusted gross income. For example, if your adjusted gross income is $30,000, you must subtract $2,250 from your total medical expenses before you have a deduction ($30,000 x .075 = $2,250). This 7.5% limitation removes medical expenses as a write-off for most taxpayers. For many, the deduction only applies during years when income is low or when unreimbursed medical costs are high.

Allowed medical expenses include payments made for prescription medicines and drugs, and payments made to doctors, dentists, nurses, hospitals, and medical laboratories. Also deductible are amounts paid for insurance premiums, hearing aids, glasses, and dentures. When you put medical payments on a charge card, you can deduct the full amount in the year the charges occur.

In addition, the IRS permits deductions for meals, lodging, and transportation costs directly related to medical treatments. The IRS publishes a standard mileage rate when personal automobiles are used for medical travel, or they allow for the actual cost of other transportation. They also allow a per-day lodging expense up to a certain limit.

If you have a handicapped dependent, you can deduct qualifying school expenses. Also, if you must alter your home to accommodate a dependent's handicap, you can deduct all or part of the alteration expense.

If you are unable to claim a dependent relative only because their income is too high, but you pay for their health care, you may be able to take off the portion you pay. Generally speaking, all unreimbursed costs for treating an ailment or handicap suffered by yourself or someone you support are eligible expenses.

The IRS does not consider health or beauty maintenance a medical expense. So health club dues, vitamins, bottled water, cosmetics, toiletries, and weight loss programs are not deductible. If a doctor, however, prescribes a certain weight loss program because one's health is in danger or prescribes vitamins to treat a specific ailment, the expenses then qualify for a deduction.

Flexible Spending Accounts

Some employers offer a flexible spending account for medical expenses. You agree to an amount that is deducted from each paycheck and deposited into a separate account. As expenses incur, you are reimbursed from the account. These pretax contributions reduce your taxable income and allow you to avoid the 7.5% adjusted gross income floor.

F.S.A. funds can be used to pay for the annual deductible, copayments made to physicians, eye examinations, eyeglasses, or for orthodontic and dental expenses. The F.S.A. funds cannot be sued to pay for the regular health insurance premiums. Only expenses incurred during the year can be sued, and what you don't use by the cut off date (generally April 15), you lose.

Medical Savings Accounts

Medical Savings Accounts are available for self-employed individuals who have high deductibles on their health insurance. Medical costs can be paid for with pretax money. If you are self-employed, read about this great opportunity in Section IV, The Self-Employed.

Taxes

You deduct taxes in the year paid. This includes real estate taxes, state and local income taxes, and personal property taxes assessed by local or state governments. If you pay a prior year's property taxes in another year, you should deduct them in the year paid.

Prepaying state and local taxes may increase deductions enough to allow itemization in certain years. Be aware, however, if you consistently or deliberately overpay your state taxes just to secure this write-off, the IRS can disallow the deduction.

Interest Expense

You can deduct home mortgage interest on two homes as long as your total debt on both mortgages doesn't exceed one million dollars.

Also, you can deduct points paid to get a loan to purchase a new home if:
- the charging of points is an established business practice in your area,
- the points are not excessive, and
- the money you pay for total closing costs is equal to or greater than the points paid. Money for "deductible" points cannot come from loan proceeds.

If you refinance to use some of your home's equity for other expenses, up to $100,000 of the new loan will qualify as home mortgage interest. The points charged on a refinance must be amortized over the life of the loan. If you pay off this refinanced loan at a later date, the points not deducted can be taken in full the year the loan is paid off. When you refinance to remodel or do home improvements, the rules differ, and points allocated toward money used for improvements can be deducted in full in the year paid.

Personal interest, such as car loans, credit card interest, and bank loans are no longer deductible. **Investment interest (interest on loans used to purchase investments) can only be used to offset investment income.**

Charitable Contributions

You can deduct donations made to qualified, nonprofit, charitable organizations. You can donate either money or property. If you donate property, your deduction equals the item's fair market value—the price you could sell it for at a garage sale or through an advertisement. In order to claim a write-off for noncash contributions that exceed $250 in value, the items donated, their purchase price, and fair market value need to be listed on Form 8283.

All property items, other than publicly traded securities, exceeding $5,000 in value must be appraised. If your total for charitable contributions exceed a certain percentage of adjusted gross income, deduction limits apply, but you will have a carryover on the excess to be used the next year.

If you buy a ticket for a sporting event, a dinner, or a program offered through a charitable organization, you cannot write off the total amount. You can only deduct the contribution, not the amount that covers the dinner or the activity enjoyed. The organization should be able to tell you the amount of your charitable contribution for each ticket purchased.

You Can Deduct Donations of Money or Property Made to Nonprofit, Charitable Organizations

You can take a mileage deduction for travel when you donate your time to a charity. You can also deduct unreimbursed meal and lodging expenses incurred while volunteering your services in charitable projects. Under no circumstances can you write off the value of your donated time.

Casualty and Theft Losses

A casualty loss results from a sudden and unexpected event, such as an earthquake, a hurricane, a fire, a flood, or an automobile accident that destroys personal or business property. Theft losses must be verified by a police report.

If your loss is insured, you must file an insurance claim for the damages. The amount of loss is the lesser of the property's adjusted basis or the decrease in its fair market value after the casualty or theft. This amount must then be reduced again by the amount of the insurance reimbursement.

Each personal casualty and theft loss is first reduced by $100. Then, the total of all unreimbursed losses must exceed 10% of your adjusted gross income before you have a deduction. For example, if your adjusted gross income is $30,000 and you have a loss of $5,000 after insurance reimbursement, you can only deduct $1,900.

$5,000 Loss	$30,000 AGI	$4,900 Allowed Loss
- 100	X 10%	- 3,000 10% of AGI
$4,900	$ 3,000	$1,900 Casualty & Theft Loss Deduction

Unlike personal losses, you can deduct a business casualty and theft loss in full. Damaged or stolen property used partially for business generates a partial business deduction and a partial personal deduction. Only the personal portion is subject to the $100 and the 10% of adjusted gross income reduction.

Special Rules Apply to Designated National Disaster Areas

If you suffer a loss of property in an area designated as a national disaster area qualifying for federal assistance, special rules apply. You can take the loss either in the year it occurs or in the preceding year. If taking the loss in the previous year, you can file an amended return and claim an immediate refund for prior taxes paid.

Example:

Bob and Betty paid $8,460 in taxes in 1997. In 1998, they lost their home and most of their possessions in a fire. The area was later designated a national disaster area. After insurance reimbursements, their loss of $80,000 brought their taxable income to zero. They could immediately file an amended tax return (Form 1040X) for 1997 and use the 1998 loss to receive a refund for the $8,460 they paid in 1997. They can carry forward the amount of loss not used in 1997 to offset positive income.

Miscellaneous Deductions

Most miscellaneous deductions must exceed 2% of your adjusted gross income before any permitted deduction can be taken. The most common are employee business expenses, such as uniforms, unreimbursed travel, union dues, professional dues, job hunting expenses, and 50% of business meals and entertainment. Other deductions include tax preparation fees, appraisal fees for casualty losses and/or charitable contributions, IRA, Keogh, and other administrative fees, and management and investment expenses.

Capital Gains and Capital Losses

(Reported on the income section)

A capital gain or loss occurs when you sell real estate, limited partnerships, stocks, bonds, collectibles, hard assets, and many other investments. **Selling an investment or asset for MORE than its net cost, results in a CAPITAL GAIN. Selling an investment or asset for LESS than its net cost gives a CAPITAL LOSS.** The IRS has no limit on capital gains. **Currently, the maximum tax rate you will pay on capital gains is:**

- 20% for assets held eighteen months or longer—long-term rate
- 28% for assets held more than twelve months but less than eighteen months—mid-term rate
- Fully taxable—short-term rate

Collectibles, depreciable real estate, business property, and small business stock have different rules. **The IRS does limit capital losses to a total deduction of $3,000 each year.** This means if Kirk loses $5,000 in one year from selling an investment, he can only write off $3,000 and must carry forward the balance ($2,000) to the next tax year. You can carry a capital loss forward for as many years as necessary to absorb the entire loss, but you can deduct no more than $3,000 in any year.

Tax Deferred Exchanges (1031 Exchange)

Generally, a nontaxable exchange postpones a recognized (taxable) gain. No taxable event occurs when you exchange one piece of property for similar property. You can defer the gain until you sell the property received in the exchange. **Many types of business and investment property, such as real estate, stocks, and bonds, can be used in a tax free exchange.** You can postpone part or all of a possible taxable gain when you trade for "like" property that has an equal or greater value. **The properties exchanged can have NO personal use.**

Example:

Wilma and Kevin own a piece of land worth $125,000. They paid $30,000 for it. If they sell the land, they will have approximately $95,000 to pay in capital gains (minus sales expenses). They can trade this land for another piece of land and owe no tax until the new property sells, if they follow all the rules for a tax free exchange.

If Wilma and Kevin decide to do an exchange, all the proceeds from the sale must go into a trust fund held by a qualified third party, such as a title company. They have forty-five days from the sale of the old property to identify another property, then six months to purchase that property. Any cash received from the transaction is taxable. Also, if they have a mortgage on the property traded that the buyer assumes, the mortgage must be accounted for in the trade. In some cases, relief of mortgage debt becomes a taxable event.

Numerous rules, not mentioned here, apply to tax free exchanges. Because the rules are complicated, be sure to seek tax advice and know what you are doing before attempting one of these trades.

Record Keeping

Keeping tax records in order doesn't have to be complicated. A few labeled file folders or a labeled accordion file work well. **Saving time is an important consideration, so set up an easy system where you can simply drop receipts and statements into the designated pockets throughout the year.** This saves looking through drawers, desks, shoe boxes, and glove compartments at tax time to find the needed receipts. Select file labels that fit your situation. You might want to color-code your labels

Keeping Tax Records in Order Doesn't Have to Be Complicated

to correspond with the sections on Form 1040. **Whatever system you use, KEEP IT SIMPLE. Two to four file folders in your pocket system are adequate for most taxpayers. If you have business expenses, rental properties, or buy and sell numerous investments, you will need to expand your record keeping system.**

These Are the Records You Need

Check the ones that apply to your situation.

Income GREEN

___ W-2 wage statements from employers

___ All 1099's for commission income, interest, dividend, and miscellaneous income

___ Statements showing state tax refund

___ Pension/annuity statements or Form W-2P

___ Disability and/or unemployment statements

___ Year-end bank statements showing interest earned

___ Records showing alimony received

___ If you sell investments such as real estate, stocks, bonds, mutual funds, or limited partnerships, statements showing:

    Amount paid and date of purchase

    Date of sale and amount received

___ K-1's for all limited partnerships and trusts

Deductions YELLOW

___ IRA and Keogh deductions

___ Alimony paid

___ Out-of-pocket medical expenses exceeding 7.5% of AGI

___ Total medical insurance reimbursement

___ Home mortgage interest paid

___ Real estate taxes paid

___ Additional state/local taxes paid (other than withholding)

___ Personal property taxes paid

    Includes automobiles, recreational vehicles, etc.

___ Cash charitable contributions

    Name of organization if over $3,000

___ Non-cash charitable contributions

If over $250, itemized list showing purchase price, date of purchase, and fair market value of all items. Name of organization who received the property. Signature of recipient and appraisal is needed for all items over $5,000.

___ Total of each casualty or theft loss and insurance reimbursement

___ All employee business expenses and reimbursements
Include uniforms, union dues, meal expenses, and job hunting expenses.

___ Tax preparation fees

___ Investment expenses
Custodial fees, safe deposit box, brokerage fees, etc.

Payments and Credits BLUE

___ Child care expenses

___ Estimated tax payments made

___ Taxes paid with extensions

Tax Notices PINK

___ IRS notices and letters

Special Tax Situations

Buying or Selling a Home

___ Escrow closing statement for home sold

___ Escrow closing statement for home purchased.

___ Closing statements or tax return showing purchase price, costs, and amount of any previously deferred gains

___ Receipts for all home improvements

Claiming Dependents (other than children living with you)

___ Total amount paid for support

___ Total income received by person being claimed

___ Proof to show you provided over 50% of their care. Include expenses for lodging, food, child care, clothing, education, and health care.

Moving Expenses for Job Relocation

___ Cost of moving household goods

___ Mileage from former residence to new job site

___ Total reimbursement by employer

Part 3
How Money Grows

DOLLARS WILL MULTIPLY and grow only when you put them to work. Chapter 7 tells about safe options for savings accounts. Bank savings offer a federal guarantee, small minimums, and convenience. Banks have several types of accounts. Government securities or a contract with an insurance company are options that can increase your yield with little compromise in safety.

When you are serious about making your money grow, consider investments. Although investments have higher risks, they also have higher rewards. How investments are sold, why they rise and decline, and the numerous choices available to investors are covered in chapter 8. For many, home ownership has been a wise investment. The details are discussed in chapter 9. Chapter 10 is all about Retirement Plans and shows you the value of tax deferred growth. This entire section explores many available opportunities that you have to put your money to work.

7
Savings

Short-Term Savings

AN IMPORTANT STEP **for a secure financial future is having a liquid, cash account.** Its purpose is to cover emergencies and unplanned expenses. Consider this account your "ace-in-the-hole." When in need, you'll have backup funds to pay for living expenses if you are suddenly off work, for emergency car or home repairs, or for a trip to visit a loved one who is ill. Only use your short-term account for emergencies. **Then, if you spend some of the money, replace it as soon as possible so you always have funds available.**

A good rule of thumb is to keep liquid enough money to cover three to six month's of living expenses. Whether it be $4,500 or $20,000, you should feel comfortable with the amount, and it should fit your lifestyle. **After determining the right amount for your lifestyle, make this "emergency fund" your first financial goal.** When you have this "ace-in-the-hole" in place, it will add to your security and peace of mind. Having this account will give you strength in dealing with the unexpected.

If you don't have a savings account now, start a systematic plan to save the maximum you can afford. Take a minimum of 10% (more if possible) from every paycheck, and pretend you never earned it. Put it into savings, and leave it alone. Keep saving until you reach your goal.

Start a Systematic Savings Plan and Save the Maximum You Can Afford

Don't pursue other long-term investments until you have what you need in this short-term emergency account.

Table 7.1 will help you see how much money you can accumulate over a certain period when you save consistently. Interest earnings will help your dollars grow.

Table 7.1—How Weekly Savings Accumulate with Interest and Time

Save $15 a Week			
	1 Year	2 Years	3 Years
4%	$795.50	$1,623.45	$2,485.17
5%	$799.44	$1,639.84	$2,523.31
6%	$803.40	$1,656.45	$2,562.21

Save $25 a Week			
	1 Year	2 Years	3 Years
4%	$1,325.83	$2,705.75	$4,141.96
5%	$1,332.39	$2,733.06	$4,205.51
6%	$1,339.10	$2,760.74	$4,270.35

Save $50 a Week			
	1 Year	2 Years	3 Years
4%	$2,651.66	$5,411.49	$8,283.91
5%	$2,664.78	$5,466.13	$8,411.03
6%	$2,677.99	$5,521.48	$8,540.70

Save $100 a Week			
	1 Year	2 Years	3 Years
4%	$5,303.32	$10,822.99	$16,567.83
5%	$5,329.57	$10,932.25	$16,822.05
6%	$5,355.98	$11,042.97	$17,081.41

If the amount you can save seems inadequate, consider taking money from other sources. Can you contribute your next tax refund to this account? Do you have overtime or bonus pay that you could contribute?

Also, once funded, don't let too much money accumulate here. Investments (covered in the next chapter), although they have less liquidity, offer higher returns and/or tax advantages.

Passbook Savings Accounts

You can open a passbook savings account at a local bank or credit union for as little as $5. Interest compounds and is paid either monthly or quarterly. Each account is federally insured up to $100,000, and you can take your money out at any time without penalty. Passbook savings accounts offer small deposits, convenience, liquidity, and guarantees. The drawback to passbook accounts is that the interest earnings are minimal. Therefore, if you have enough to open a money market account, do so, because they pay higher interest rates.

Advantages of Passbook Accounts
Convenience, Small Minimum, Liquidity, Guarantees

Money Market Accounts

The money market offers higher yields than banks offer while maintaining short-term liquidity. It is called the money market because the investments are in money such as U.S. Government Securities and short-term corporate debt called commercial paper. For a minimum purchase of $100,000, corporations use the money market to "park" their extra cash for a few months.

Banks, credit unions, and mutual funds now offer affordable money market accounts to their investors. They take the funds from many investors and purchase a broad range of high yielding, liquid money investments, similar to those purchased by corporations. These money market accounts make it possible for individuals with smaller amounts of money to have liquidity while earning higher than passbook interest.

Money Market Accounts through Mutual Funds

Money market accounts with mutual funds are one fund within a family of funds, often referred to as their "cash" fund. The cash fund will invest only in money investments such as short-term commercial paper and U.S. Government Securities. This cash fund is designed to offer the

highest possible yield and remain 100% liquid. The fund has a professional manager who purchases new money investments when the older ones mature. For example, the manager may purchase a $1 million, 5% interest note for three months. When that note matures at the end of the three months, the manager will buy another money investment.

To participate in money market mutual funds, you need not purchase other funds within the family. Most money market accounts have initial deposits between $500 and $1,000 and accept additional contributions as small as $25. Once funds have been on deposit for thirty days, you are allowed unlimited check writing with no fees. The minimum check varies for different funds, but most range from $100 to $500. **Money market accounts have no sales charges, and the balance can be withdrawn at any time without penalty.** The interest rate changes daily and compounds daily. Most major newspapers list the prior day's annual yield. Generally speaking, money market mutual funds pay a higher interest rate and have fewer restrictions than similar accounts offered through savings institutions.

Money market mutual funds are not federally insured. They are considered "safe," however, since they only purchase short-term money investments. If a guarantee is important to you, you can purchase money market accounts through mutual funds that are federally insured. They will pay a lower yield, but they invest 100% in U.S. Government Securities that are backed by the full faith and credit of the United States government.

Money Market Accounts through Savings Institutions

Money market accounts offered by banks and credit unions have minimum deposits, usually $1,000, and are federally insured. Most have limited check writing privileges. They usually have higher yields than passbook accounts but may have maintenance fees. In mutual funds, interest is paid daily, and one rate is paid to everyone regardless of the size of their account. In contrast, savings institutions will pay higher interest on their larger accounts. Some pay interest daily, while others pay monthly. The rate can change either daily (like the mutual funds) or be locked in for a month. The only advantage money market savings accounts have over money market mutual funds is that the savings accounts are federally insured. **Be aware that if you buy a money market mutual fund through an investment advisor working at a bank, it does not come with the bank's guarantee.**

Bank and credit union savings accounts and money market funds can be redeemed at any time without penalty. This liquidity makes them the most suitable accounts for emergency money needed within the first three months. Money needed after that can go into other savings options that might pay higher yields but aren't immediately liquid without losing some of the interest earned.

Longer Term Savings

Certificates of Deposit

Nearly all savings institutions offer certificates of deposit, referred to as CD's. By giving up some liquidity and tying up your money for a fixed time, you might be able to earn higher interest in CD's. **The minimum deposit for CD's range from $500 to $10,000 and up. Interest is guaranteed for the life of the certificate, which can vary in length from three months to several years.** The only time earnings compound is when you "roll" the entire amount from one certificate into a new certificate at the end of the term.

The most common CD's have a term of six or twelve months. It is possible, however, to lock in an interest rate for several years. Be aware that if interest rates rise while you have your money tied up in a long-term certificate, you will lose the advantage of the higher rates unless you withdraw your funds, take a penalty for early withdrawal, and then reinvest the money at higher rates.

The Only Time Earnings Compound Is When You "Roll" the Entire Amount into a New Certificate

U.S. Government Securities

All U.S. Government Securities are debt obligations offered by the U.S. Treasury. The U.S. government pays a fixed interest rate guaranteed by the government through its ability to print money. You can buy government securities direct, through a broker or bank, or through a mutual fund that invests in government securities (mutual funds are covered in detail in chapter 8, Investments).

Investors purchase government securities for a certain time. Like certificates of deposit, the interest does not compound automatically at the end of the term. The owner must reinvest the principal plus earnings into another account to gain the benefits of compound growth. **U.S. Government Securities offer a tax advantage for those who have high**

state taxes since the interest earned is **not taxable by state or local governments.** Their drawback is a higher minimum deposit, often not affordable for the small saver. Accordingly, government securities are often purchased by banks, insurance companies, corporations, mutual funds, and foreign governments, as well as individual investors. Table 7.2 shows the tax advantages of investing in U.S. Government Securities for different state tax brackets.

Table 7.2—Equivalent Yields for U.S. Government Securities

Yield on U.S. Government Securities	3.5%	4.0%	4.5%	5.0%	5.5%	6.0%
	(Taxable Equivalent Yield in Shaded Box)					
State Tax Bracket: 5%	3.68%	4.21%	4.74%	5.26%	5.79%	6.32%
6%	3.72%	4.25%	4.79%	5.32%	5.85%	6.38%
7%	3.76%	4.30%	4.84%	5.38%	5.91%	6.45%
8%	3.80%	4.34%	4.89%	5.43%	5.98%	6.52%
9%	3.85%	4.40%	4.95%	5.49%	6.04%	6.59%
10%	3.89%	4.44%	5.00%	5.56%	6.11%	6.67%
11%	3.93%	4.49%	5.06%	5.62%	6.18%	6.74%

Treasury Bills

Treasury bills, referred to as "T-Bills" are offered and guaranteed by the U.S. government. **They are short-term debt instruments with maturity dates of three months, six months, or twelve months.** Their yields are usually higher than bank CD's. The minimum investment is $10,000, with additional purchases in $1,000 increments. For example, you could buy a $11,000 or $12,000 T-Bill.

T-Bills can be ideal for that portion of emergency savings you don't need for three to six months. Three and six-month T-bills are sold at weekly auctions. **The Treasury Department has a Treasury Direct system where you can buy T-bills without a charge.** (See Appendix A for a full listing by city of addresses and phone numbers where you can purchase T-bills and other U.S. Government Securities without a charge). You can also buy treasury bills from a bank or a broker for a fee. Typical fees are $50 to $75 and sometimes more. Be aware that if you buy a T-bill direct and need to cash out early, you must first transfer your account to a bank or broker and pay a fee before it can be sold.

Treasury bills are sold at a discount then held to maturity to collect the interest. For example, if you buy a $10,000 treasury bill at 8% interest for one year, you would pay $9,200 to purchase the bill and receive $10,000 one year later. The discount of $800 is the 8% interest earned on $10,000.

Treasury Notes

Treasury notes are longer term debt instruments of the U.S. Government. **They pay interest semi-annually, similar to many CD's.** They have a guaranteed yield with varying maturity dates. The minimum investment for treasury notes is $5,000 for maturity dates of less than four years, and $1,000 for maturity dates ranging from four to ten years. Notes are competitively auctioned through the Federal Reserve System.

Series EE Savings Bonds

Series EE savings bonds have low denominations. **The minimum purchase is $25 for a $50 bond, with increasing amounts up to the maximum of $5,000 for a $10,000 bond. Series EE bonds are bought at a discount then held to maturity to receive the interest.** When held at least five years, these bonds pay 85% of the average rate for treasury securities or 4% interest, whichever is greater. For bonds purchased after April 30, 1995, interest is added every six months. Rates are announced each May 1 and November 1. Like other U.S. government obligations, the interest is exempt from state and local taxes. **The owner can elect to pay interest annually or pay the interest when the bonds are redeemed.**

When people at least twenty-four years of age buy these bonds to fund college tuition and fees for themselves, their spouse, or their dependents, and use all of the proceeds for qualified educational expenses, all of the interest is exempt from tax. If this might fit your situation, check the rules, as income restrictions apply. (See chapter 20, Planning, for more information about using Series EE Bonds to fund a college education. Also see Educational IRA's in chapter 10, Retirement Plans)

The Owner of Series EE Bonds Can Pay Interest Annually, or when the Bonds Are Redeemed

Insurance Companies

Cash Value Life Insurance

Cash value in a universal life or whole life insurance policy can also serve as emergency savings if the money isn't needed immediately. You need a flexible policy that pays current rates and has a low interest loan. **The cash value within a life insurance policy offers the** advantages of compound, tax deferred growth, with a guarantee backed by **the assets of the insurance company.** A drawback to each policy is that it takes several years to build up the cash value in a policy before the owner has money available to borrow. Also, once you request a loan, it could take ten days or longer to receive a check from the insurance company. When using this option, be sure to ask the company or your agent how long you will typically wait before receiving a check after you make a loan request.

With savings in a life insurance policy, the policy owner must borrow from the cash value to take money out. Borrowing money and paying it back normally has no tax consequences. **If you do not pay back the loan, the amount payable to beneficiaries will be reduced accordingly.**

Fixed Annuities

For persons over age fifty-nine and a half, annuities have several **advantages.** The interest is often higher than that paid by banks, and it grows tax deferred. **With most contracts, after the first year, you have access to 10% or more of your policy face value without penalty.** Should you die, the accumulated value of the policy will pass to your named beneficiaries and avoid probate, an advantage in many situation.

Each annuity contract is written for a set period, normally ranging from five to ten years. When you take out ALL of the moneys prematurely, penalties apply. For example, if you purchase a five-year contract, the penalty for premature withdrawal during the first year might be 5% of the contract price. The second year, it declines to 4%, the third year to 3%, etc. With most companies, all of your principal and some interest are guaranteed.

Most contracts allow you to take out 10% of the face value of the policy each year penalty free. For example, if you purchase a $30,000 annuity, you could withdraw $3,000 (10% of $30,000) without penalty after the first year. With some companies, the 10% free withdrawal accumulates. If you didn't use it the first year, you could take 20% the second year. Then, if you didn't use it the second year, you could take 30% the third year and so on. After taking 50%, this feature often ends.

For people under age fifty-nine and a half, these contracts do not work for an emergency fund. Under age fifty-nine and a half, withdrawals that do not fit one of the exceptions are subject to the 10% tax penalty on retirement plans. For more information see, chapter 10,

Retirement Plans: Early Withdrawals, and chapter 6, Personal Income Taxes: Other Taxes.

Summary

Where you place your savings dollars is not as important as your decision to save. Start the habit of saving consistently so money will be available when you need it. First, fund a short-term emergency account with a minimum of three months' living expenses. Bank savings accounts or money market funds are best, because they are always available without penalty. Money you need in savings after the third month can go into certificates of deposit or treasury bills. Before tying money up for a longer time period, make sure the increased interest paid is worth the loss of liquidity.

Series EE savings bonds, treasury notes, cash value life insurance, and fixed annuities all require a longer holding period before they become liquid. For those who have saved for a longer time, these accounts can work well for emergency funds.

When choosing an account for your savings dollars, consider:

- **Safety.** Is the money guaranteed? By whom? If not, is the risk minimal?
- **Liquidity and access.** How quickly and easily can you get your money with no or minimal penalty for withdrawal?
- **Minimum investment.** The required deposit needs to be an amount you can realistically save.
- **Tax advantages.** Are the interest earnings fully taxable to both federal and state governments, or is a portion of them exempt?
- **Method of paying interest.** How frequently do the earnings compound? Daily, monthly, or quarterly? More frequent compounding will generate a larger return.

Table 7.3 gives a summary of the many options available for your savings dollars.

Where You Place Your Savings Dollars Is Not as Important as Your Decision to Save

Table 7.3—Safe Options for Savings

Account	Federally Insured	Minimum Investment	Instant Liquidity	State Tax	Compound Interest
Passbook	Yes	$5	Yes	Yes	Yes
Certificate of Deposit	Yes	$500	No	Yes	Not Automatic
Money Market w/ Sav. Inst.	Yes	$1,000	Yes	Yes	Yes
Money Market Mutual Funds	No	$100	Yes	Yes	Yes
Series EE Bonds	Yes	$25	No	No	No
Treasury Bills	Yes	$10,000	No	No	No
Treasury Notes	Yes	$1,000–$5,000	No	No	No
Cash Value Life Insurance	No	Varies	Borrow	No	Yes
Annuities	No	$1,000–$5,000	Partial	Tax Deferred	Yes

8
Investments

Introduction to Investments

INVESTING allows you to increase your rate of return and overcome the bite taken out by inflation and taxes. For the higher return, you will lose one or more of the advantages offered by savings or cash accounts. You may give up the guarantee, the liquidity, the compound interest, or all of these.

You will read about BONDS, STOCKS, MUTUAL FUNDS, and LIMITED PARTNERSHIPS. All come in many varieties. (This book does not cover the more sophisticated, higher risk choices, such as puts, calls, warrants, options, and commodities.) To successfully invest, you must match the objective of the investment with your investment purpose.

Your investment portfolio should reflect your investment goals and your risk comfort level. For example, you would not be happy investing in small company growth stocks if you want consistent earnings and would worry about temporary market declines. **All investments have some kind of risk, and you as an investor need to be comfortable assuming that risk for the trade-off of potentially higher returns.**

The length of time your money will be invested is equally important. **If you have twenty years before you'll need the money, you can be more aggressive than if you'll need the money in three years.**

To Successfully Invest, You Must Match the Objective of the Investment with Your Investment Purpose

Generally, a higher risk generates a higher return, but if the risk is too high, you can lose your principal. **Most importantly, your investment dollars need a purpose.** You must decide if you need growth, income, or a combination of growth and income. (Investment purpose is covered in chapter 20, Planning.)

Rarely are investments guaranteed—if they were, they wouldn't be investments. **People who invest become "owners" or "loaners" in some aspect of American or world industry. Securities cover the broad spectrum of investments, which includes "loaners" who want a fixed income and "owners" who want a share of the action. Securities** include stocks, bonds, mutual funds, real estate shares, oil wells, mortgage pools, movie rights, and equipment. The makeup of each security determines its risk level and profit potential. Investments that "own" are often referred to as **"equities."**

SEC, NASD, and SIPC

The Securities and Exchange Commission Regulates the Securities Industry

All investments sold to the public raising over $500,000 must be registered with the Securities and Exchange Commission (SEC). **Congress established the SEC to eliminate potential abuses within the securities industry, such as investors not receiving all pertinent facts about an investment.** The SEC has many rules to enforce full disclosure and to protect investors. **One of their subsidiaries, The National Association of Securities Dealers (NASD), supervises brokerage firms and the representatives working for those firms.** Before taking an order, the NASD requires all salespersons offering public investments to give potential investors a prospectus. **A prospectus is a legal document, approved by the SEC. It discloses all relevant facts about the investment.**

The Prospectus Discloses the Important Details of the Investment

Although the SEC has to approve every public offering, this approval does not endorse the investment's safety. The SEC does require, however, that the offering party reveal all pertinent facts regarding the investment in a prospectus. **The prospectus covers the investment's objective, the financial condition of the offering party, how the money contributed by investors will be spent, the risks of ownership, sales charges, expenses, and management fees.** The information in the prospectus helps securities brokers, registered representatives, and investors to evaluate a security and determine its suitability.

Only representatives who are registered and approved by the NASD can sell securities. To become licensed, they must complete an extensive training program and pass a difficult securities test. The NASD also screens its applicants to see if they have any prior history of not working in the public's best interest. **The NASD supervises all investment firms and their representatives to assure that they follow the industry's rules of fair practice, written to protect investors from foreseeable abuses.**

The responsibility of the NASD is to assure that investors have the necessary facts to make informed investment choices. In addition, representatives must complete a "suitability questionnaire" for each prospective investor before making specific investment recommendations. This questionnaire, kept on file by the brokerage firm, shows the NASD that the individual investor has sufficient net worth to participate in the suggested level of investment risk. **Securities regulators help investors by requiring full disclosure and by imposing suitability requirements. No one, however, can stop securities from fluctuating according to their inherent market risks.**

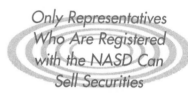

Only Representatives Who Are Registered with the NASD Can Sell Securities

To protect investors further, in 1970, Congress passed the **Securities Investor Protection Act, or SIPC**, to stop investor loss if a brokerage firm failed. SIPC is self-insured through each member firm paying an annual assessment to the SIPC fund. Then, should SIPC need more money, it has a line of credit with the United States Treasury. When a SIPC member cannot pay off its customers, SIPC takes over and appoints a trustee to liquidate the assets of the firm and make the promised payments.

SIPC insurance covers all stocks, bonds, notes, and certificates of deposit held by a covered member brokerage firm. The trustee can settle claims up to a maximum of $500,000 for each customer, but this settlement can contain no more than $100,000 in cash. **SIPC insurance does not protect a brokerage account from market ups and downs; it protects the assets of an account when a member of SIPC fails and cannot meet its obligations.**

Summary

The Securities and Exchange Commission and the National Association of Securities Dealers provide important protection for investors:

- The prospectus or offering circular discloses all important investment details.
- The NASD regulates and monitors member investment firms and their representatives.
- SIPC insurance guarantees brokerage accounts if a member firm fails.

Bonds

When you buy bonds, you LOAN your money to a corporation, a state, a city, or the federal government. Bonds sell in $1,000 increments, although some require a minimum investment of $5,000 or more. Because all bonds pay a fixed interest rate until they mature, they are referred to as **fixed income securities**. Fixed income securities include treasury notes, treasury bills, and treasury bonds. The maturity dates of bonds will be **short** (one year or less), **intermediate** (one to ten years), or **long** (ten to thirty years). A bond purchaser agrees to loan money to the issuer for a certain time period. **During this "loan" period, the issuer agrees to pay a fixed interest rate for the use of the money. At maturity, the full investment or principal is returned.**

Ratings

Bonds have varying degrees of risk based upon the financial strength of the issuer. The lower rated bonds pay higher interest. Two major independent agencies that rate the investment quality of bonds are STANDARD AND POORS and MOODY'S INVESTOR SERVICES. After looking at the assets and liabilities of the issuers, they base their rating on the issuers ability to make the payments as promised. The bond ratings range from prime for the highest grade to very speculative for the lowest grade. Table 8.1 shows bond ratings.

Table 8.1—Bond Ratings

Standard & Poors*	Moody's	
AAA	Aaa	Prime or highest grade
AA	Aa	Excellent or high grade
A	A	Good quality
BBB	Baa	Medium quality
BB	BA	"Junk bonds." Commercial banks do not invest at this level.
B	B	Risky
CCC	Caa	Riskier

* This rating may include a (+) or a (-) showing the bond in the upper or lower segment of a certain category.

All bonds are subject to an interest rate risk. **Discount bonds** have lower prices because interest rates went up after they were issued. They sell for under $1,000. An investor who buys bonds at a discount receives the full $1,000 at maturity and pays capital gains on the profit. **Bonds selling at a premium sell for more than $1,000. They are worth more because interest rates dropped after they were issued.**

Yield

If a previously issued bond has five years to maturity and pays 6% interest, but the current interest rate for similar bonds is 8%, the 6% bond could not be sold if it were not "price" discounted. So, to be competitive with the current higher interest rate, the $1,000 par value is reduced. The 6% bond with five years to maturity might sell on the current market for $905.65. For each year to maturity, the older bond is discounted in value to make up for the higher interest on the new bond. An investor who holds the older bond to maturity to claim the full $1,000 value will not make more money because he also lost out on the higher interest. Similarly, when interest rates drop, bonds with higher than market yields become more valuable and sell for a premium (more than their $1,000 par value).

The Face Value of Bonds Fluctuate to Balance Out Rising and Falling Interest Rates

Since bonds pay fixed interest and are guaranteed for a certain time period, an investor who sells before the maturity date can make money or lose money on the increase or decrease of the par value. Bonds are extremely vulnerable to the rise and decline in interest rates.

The face value of all bonds at maturity is quoted at $1,000. If interest rates have changed since the bond was issued, the market price will be different. Newspapers quote the market price as a percentage of face value. A bond quoted at 76.5, sells for 76.5% of $1,000 or $765. A bond quoted at 106¼ sells for 106.25% of $1,000 or $1,062.50. Newspapers also quote the fixed, payable interest rate, such as 9.75% or 7.12%. **The interest rate is based on the $1,000 maturity value (same as par value). The interest rate will differ from the current yield if you pay more or less than $1,000 for the bond.** To calculate the current yield, divide the interest rate by the bond price. For example, a bond purchased for $765 with an interest rate of 5% has a current yield of 6.5% (5%, interest, divided by $765, price = 6.5%). The 5% interest on $1,000 pays $50. This $50 divided by the price of $765 will also equal the current yield of 6.5%.

Bonds Decrease in Value when Interest Rates Rise

A Callable Bond Can
Be Redeemed by the
Issuer before Maturity
A Convertible Bond
Can Be Exchanged for
Common Stock

Bond issuers often protect themselves against falling interest rates by having a recall provision. Bonds with this provision are "callable." This allows the issuer to redeem their bonds at the stated price before they mature. Never pay more for a bond than its recall price. **Some bonds are "convertible."** This provision allows the investor to convert the bond to common stock under certain conditions.

Before purchasing bonds, always check the rating, the yield, the maturity date, and the recall provision. Also, consider if interest rates are expected to rise or decline. Fixed income securities offer steady, safe income, but the principal will decline in value if interest rates rise after the bond is issued. If this happens and you sell before the bond's maturity date, you will lose some of your principal.

Municipal Bonds

If you are taxed high, you can increase your net yield with municipal bonds. Municipal bonds have lower yields but offer interest free from federal income tax, and free from state income tax in the state where the bond originates. (Remember, federal treasury bonds are exempt from state and local income taxes but not from federal taxes.) You can buy bonds with tax free federal interest, tax free state interest, or both. A tax free bond could pay 3%, while a taxable bond pays 5%. Look at your tax bracket and the taxable vs. tax free yields to see if tax free income benefits you.

Table 8.2 shows taxable yields needed to match tax free yields for various tax brackets. For example, someone in a 43% tax bracket (36% federal + 7% state) would have to earn a taxable yield of 8.77% to equal the tax free yield of 5%. A choice of 5%, 6%, or 7% for state taxes are added to the 28%, 31%, 36%, and 36.9% federal rates. **For help in determining your tax bracket, see Federal Tax Rates and State Tax Rates in Appendix C: Tax Bracket.**

Find the line of the tax free yield. Then find the column showing your tax bracket. The intersecting taxable yield will show what you would need to earn to make up for the taxes saved on a tax free investment.

Table 8.2—Taxable vs. Tax Free Yields

TAX BRACKET	28% Federal Only	33% 28% Fed. + 5% State	34% 28% Fed.+ 6% State	35% 28% Fed. + 7% State
Tax Free Yield	Taxable Yield Needed to Equal Tax-Free Yield			
3.0%	4.17%	4.48%	4.55%	4.62%
3.5%	4.86%	5.22%	5.30%	5.39%
4.0%	5.56%	5.97%	6.06%	6.15%
4.5%	6.25%	6.72%	6.82%	6.92%
5.0%	6.94%	7.46%	7.58%	7.69%
5.5%	7.64%	8.21%	8.33%	8.46%
6.0%	8.33%	8.96%	9.09%	9.23%
6.5%	9.03%	9.70%	9.85%	10.00%
7.0%	9.72%	10.45%	10.61%	10.77%

TAX BRACKET	31% Federal Only	36% 31% Fed. + 5% State	37% 31% Fed.+ 6% State	38% 31% Fed. + 7% State
Tax Free Yield	Taxable Yield Needed to Equal Tax-Free Yield			
3.0%	4.35%	4.69%	4.76%	4.84%
3.5%	5.07%	5.47%	5.56%	5.65%
4.0%	5.80%	6.25%	6.35%	6.45%
4.5%	6.52%	7.03%	7.14%	7.26%
5.0%	7.25%	7.81%	7.94%	8.07%
5.5%	7.97%	8.59%	8.73%	8.87%
6.0%	8.70%	9.38%	9.52%	9.68%
6.5%	9.42%	10.16%	10.32%	10.48%
7.0%	10.14%	10.94%	11.11%	11.29%

You can purchase **individual bonds** through a broker or a large **portfolio of bonds** through a mutual fund. Most mutual fund families have several **bond funds**. Some specialize in the higher income from lower rated bonds, some have only investment grade issues, some only include government securities, and some offer tax exempt income.

Remember that income is the primary purpose for a bond investment. With this criteria, investments under $10,000 make little sense since smaller amounts generate little income.

Stocks

When you buy bonds, you loan your money, but when you purchase stocks, you become a part owner in that company. Most companies raise the initial capital needed to start their business by selling stock. After the original funding, the stock of profitable companies increases in demand. The price goes up, and shares become more valuable when investors are willing to pay more for the stock. If a company experiences losses, the stock declines in value. Should the company go out of business, the stock can even become worthless.

As a rule, a company's earnings and its growth potential control the demand for its stock. When a company has a bright future, more people want to buy in, so the shares increase in value. In contrast, when demand is low and buyers are few, the price falls.

You make money owning stock when you receive dividends and when the price per share goes up. **Because individual stocks have the potential of increasing in value as well as paying dividends, stocks attract many investors.**

Stock Pays Investors through Dividends and Increases in the Price Per Share

Consider both dividends and increases in the stock's value to calculate your total yield. For example, assume you purchased one hundred shares of XYZ's stock at $80 a share ($8,000). It yields 5%, so it pays an annual dividend of $4.00 a share, or $400 total. The dividend per share divided by the price per share gives the stock's yield ($4 divided by 80 = 5%).

Consider Both Dividends and Increases in the Stocks Value to Calculate Total Profits

After five years of holding this stock, you sell it for $105 a share, or $10,500 total. You've made $2,500 (the $10,500 sales price minus the $8,000 purchase price equals the capital gain of $2,500). Your total return, however, needs to consider the dividends as well as the capital gain. Assuming this stock paid a steady 5% dividend for five years, you would have received $2,000 in dividends ($400 x 5 years = $2,000). The total dividends received, $2,000, added to the $2,500 capital gain shows a profit of $4,500 on this $8,000 investment during the five-year holding period. Therefore, your total yield is 56% or 11.25% per year ($4,500 divided by $8,000 = 56%, 56% divided by 5 years = 11.25% per year). The brokerage commissions, not considered here, reduce the yield slightly.

Each type of stock has a different objective. Some pay high dividends, while others emphasize growth. If the stock doesn't match your needs, you won't be happy with your investment.

Companies issue both preferred and common stock. **Common stock has many categories of growth and income, such as high income and low growth, medium income and medium growth, or low income and aggressive growth. Preferred stock pays steady dividends like bonds.** Preferred stock makes payments regardless of the companies profitability but usually has a lower yield and less security than bonds. Unlike common stock, it does not participate in the company's growth. Preferred stock, however, can offer provisions permitting it to be converted to common stock. If it cannot be converted, a bond or common stock probably will serve your needs better.

Each Type of Stock Has a Different Objective

Blue chip stock is from the large, stable corporations like Coca-Cola, McDonald's, and Wal-Mart. For the most part, their consistent earnings allow them to pay steady dividends to their stockholders. Normally, blue chip stock is a good investment for income. Sometimes, unexpected market situations or new inventions will affect profits and dividends paid, but as a rule, most blue chip companies are dependable performers.

Blue Chip Stock Is a Good Investment for Income

At the other end of the spectrum are the smaller, less known companies. Their stock costs less than the higher priced blue chip. **These companies expand by reinvesting most of their profit back into the company, so their stock is called growth stock. Growth stock has more risk because the company's future is unknown.** Many people, however, have made a lot of money from buying in on a new company with potential while the price was still low.

The blue chip companies all started small and became successful through solid management and a popular product line. The same can happen to other small, well-managed companies with increasing demands for their product or service. If a person succeeds in buying stock in the right company when the price is low and holds the shares until the company's earnings grow, he/she can double the original investment many times over.

Selecting the Right Stock Takes Expertise, Research, and a Sense for Future Needs

To illustrate the potential profits of growth stocks, look at the three examples on the next page showing what $10,000 invested on December 31, 1933, grew to in sixty-three years. These examples assume that all dividends were taken in cash and not reinvested to buy more shares.[1]

	Value December 31, 1933	Value December 31, 1996
Philip Morris	$10,000	$3,620,711
Proctor & Gamble	$10,000	$2,649,228
General Electric	$10,000	$2,433,848

Thousands of analysts work for various investment firms studying emerging new companies, hoping to pick a "sleeping giant" or, at second best, a successful performer. Selecting the right company takes expertise, research, and a sense for what business will be like in the future. Investments in growth stocks are exciting when you win but equally devastating when the company fails and your investment shrinks. But, if you pick just one big winner, it can make up for losses on other purchases. For many, playing the stock market and selecting the right company is a numbers game. They know if they succeed just 55% of the time, they will make money.

Stocks can only be bought or sold by securities brokers. The American Stock Exchange and the New York Stock Exchange are referred to as the "big boards." They trade the stock from large companies. The **NASDAQ** or National Association of Securities Dealers of Automated Quotations have an automated information network where they trade the smaller, lesser companies. The NASDAQ is also known as the **OVER-THE-COUNTER MARKET**. The closing price per share for the previous day's trades from these three exchanges are listed daily in most newspapers.

Mutual Funds

*Mutual Funds Make Sense for Investors Who Don't Have the **Time, Money, or Expertise** to Select Variety in Their Portfolio*

Unless you have enough money to buy a variety of stocks and bonds, along with the time and expertise to select and manage them, consider mutual funds. **Mutual funds are managed by investment companies that combine money from many investors to buy a wide selection of securities to meet specific objectives.**

Mutual fund investors are called shareholders since they purchase shares of a fund. Each share represents ownership in hundreds of companies. The price of mutual fund shares change as the securities within the portfolio rise and fall with the current market. If the price per share were $10, a $1,000 investment would buy one hundred shares.

Most companies have a family of funds, that is separate funds with different objectives under the same roof. Each fund has a professional manager or group of managers who take charge of that fund's portfolio. Fund managers purchase stocks, bonds, or money market investments. They watch the market and buy or sell as needed to get the highest possible return for shareholders while adhering to the overall objective of the fund. Through mutual funds, investors benefit from the expertise of professional management for a nominal fee.

Through Mutual Funds, Investors Benefit from the Expertise of Professional Managers for a Nominal Fee

Fees and Charges

All funds have expenses and fees, and some have sales charges. These fees and charges must be fully disclosed in the prospectus. Sales charges go to the securities brokers and their representatives for selling the fund. Sometimes their advice and continued service is valuable, making the fee worthwhile. **Good investment advice can save you far more than what you pay for a sales charge.**

Funds with sales charges are called "load" funds. If it is a front-end load, you buy in at the offering price, which will be higher than the fund's net asset value (NAV) per share. For example, if the newspaper lists the offering price of the fund as 10.00 and the NAV as 9.55, the sales charge is 4.5%. An investor must buy in at the higher price and sell at the lower price.

All Fees and Charges Must Be Disclosed in the Prospectus

The maximum sales charge allowed is 8.5%. Most funds today, however, have reduced their sales charges to the 3% to 6% range. You only pay a sales charge once. Thereafter, you can move your money from one fund to another within the same family with no additional charge. **Mutual funds with front-end sales charges are also referred to as "A" shares.**

Some funds have no initial sales charge but have a redemption fee that lasts for a specified time period. **These back-end loads are called "B" shares by fund companies.**

Load Funds Have an Offering Price Higher Than Their Net Asset Value or Redemption Price

A redemption fee discourages investors from buying into a fund then selling after a short hold. **An "R" next to a fund listed in the paper, or a reference to "B" shares, indicates a back-end load. It is possible to buy either "A" or "B" shares of the same fund.** To make this decision, consider your projected holding period and the fund's expenses for both class "A" and class "B" shares.

Some Funds Have a Redemption Fee Charged upon Selling

The paper lists **no load funds** with a quote for the NAV and an "NL" for the offering price. Given equal performance and equal fee schedules, you will come out ahead with no load funds. With a no load fund, however, you are your own advisor and must do your own research to keep tabs on the fund's performance.

The so-called load funds, which include both class "A" and class "B" shares, pay the sales charge to brokers and representatives for selling the fund. The no load funds usually spend an equal amount of their fund's profits but choose to put their money into advertising instead of paying salespersons. So, no load funds spend money on advertising in popular magazines and newsletters, while load funds depend on representatives to distribute their shares. One way or another, funds pay for the distribution of their shares out of the fund's profits. **The fund's performance and the net return to investors should be a more important consideration than how the fund chooses to do its advertising.**

All Funds Charge Annual Management and Expense Fees Ranging from .2% to 1%

All funds charge annual management and expense fees. These generally range from .2% to 1% of the net assets of the fund. Funds subtract these expenses before calculating the profits for investors. **The prospectus discloses all fees and expenses under Annual Fund Operating Expenses.**

Study a fund's past performance before you invest. Look at the preceding year, the preceding five years, and the preceding ten years. Mutual fund information can be found in publications such as *Money, Business Week, Changing Times, Forbes, Barons,* and *The Wall Street Journal.* Keep in mind that most of these magazines are biased and therefore print biased studies and articles because they receive huge advertising revenues from many fund companies.

An Unbiased Ranking of Funds by Performance Is Done by Morningstar and Weisenberger

To look up detailed, unbiased information with articles and surveys that are not influenced by promoters, two excellent reference books are available: *Weisenberger Investment Services* **and** *Morningstar.* **Most libraries have copies.** Both of these reference books rate ALL funds according to performance in their category. They also analyze the fund's portfolio, its management, and its risk level. They provide a valuable service, especially when considering the 3,500 plus mutual funds available today.

Fund Objectives

Most mutual fund families have MONEY MARKET FUNDS, INCOME FUNDS, GROWTH & INCOME FUNDS, and GROWTH FUNDS.

Many also have **GLOBAL** funds that invest worldwide and/or **SPECIALTY** funds. The prospectus outlines a fund's objective, its current portfolio (its investment holdings), and other important information. Portfolio managers select securities to meet the objective of the fund. To be happy with a fund, you must match its purpose to your own. **Let's look at the common investments selected by fund managers to meet different objectives.** All funds can keep a certain percentage of their assets in cash.

Your Investment Objective and the Funds Objective Should Be the Same

- Objective: LIQUIDITY WITH HIGHEST POSSIBLE YIELD. **MONEY MARKET FUNDS** buy short-term money investments, such as treasury bills, certificates of deposit, or commercial paper issued by corporations. These funds have check writing privileges, and their interest rate changes daily. Money market funds do not have sales charges, even those under the umbrella of "load" funds.

Money Market Funds Buy Treasury Bills, CD's, and Commercial Paper

- Objective: HIGH YIELD AND PRESERVATION OF CAPITAL. Generally, **INCOME FUNDS** hold various grades of bonds that pay interest. The higher yielding income funds often have lower grade bonds in their portfolio. **EQUITY INCOME FUNDS** buy blue chip stocks that pay consistent dividends.

Income Funds Buy Blue Chip Stocks, Bonds, and Money Market Investments

- Objective: GROWTH AND MAXIMUM CAPITAL GAINS. **GROWTH FUNDS** primarily select common growth stocks. The more aggressive funds naturally select more aggressive stocks from young, growing companies. In growth funds, the dividends are small, but as the stock held by the portfolio grows in value, the share prices of the fund also increase. Some managers sell often to take the profits or capital gains from these stocks and reinvest them. How often the manager sells shows the turnover of the portfolio. Some managers believe in buying quality and holding; others believe in taking profits often and reinvesting.

Growth Funds Buy Common Growth Stocks

- Objective: GROWTH AND INCOME. Funds seeking **GROWTH AND INCOME** might invest in both blue chip and growth stocks. **BALANCED FUNDS** promote long-term growth plus income, so they hold bonds, preferred stock, and common stock. Although growth and income funds and balanced funds usually have less growth than straight growth funds and less income than straight income funds, they deliver the important combination of steady growth combined with regular income.

Balanced Funds Buy Common Stock, Preferred Stocks, and Bonds

Many have excellent long-term track records. Many of these funds tend to hold their value during down markets.

Some funds get more SPECIALIZED than just growth and income. For example, they can produce income only from utility stocks, or tax free income from municipal bonds. **Many families have FEDERALLY INSURED FUNDS that purchase only government securities.** Other choices include **GOLD FUNDS** or funds in other precious metals. Some growth funds can buy **only AMERICAN STOCKS,** while others participate in the **WORLD ECONOMY.** Many global funds that invest worldwide have been added to typical U.S. fund families during the past five years. **Sometimes a fund can specialize in a particular industry, such as communications or health care.** Some funds are **environmentally aware** and will only buy stock of companies that do not harm the environment. By purchasing these funds, you can also make a political statement. Chances are, any investment offered to the public can also be purchased through a mutual fund.

REITS Buy Real Estate in a Mutual Fund

Another feature of mutual funds are Real Estate Investment Trusts or **REITS.** REITS operate like mutual funds but own various real estate investments instead of stocks and bonds. REITS are traded on the stock exchanges. **Although real estate investments are not liquid, well-selected real estate has kept up with inflation. REITS offer liquidity combined with well-selected real estate as their primary benefit. Before purchasing, look carefully at the fees and charges, because they are usually higher than other investments.**

For complete information, always check a fund's portfolio in the prospectus, and look at how the money is invested. Also, look at the fund objective, its risk level, its ratings in both up and down markets, and its past performance in *Morningstar* or *Weisenberger.* This gives you a good idea of what to expect for future performance. **Although past performance does not indicate future success, it is the best single indicator available.**

Dollar Cost Averaging

Dollar cost averaging is a method of investing that takes advantage of market swings. It is often difficult for investors to determine the best time to invest a large sum of money, especially when the market is high. If the market dips soon after your purchase, the value of your investment will drop. If you buy at a lower price, you can buy more shares.

Example:

$10,000 invested in a mutual fund at $19 per share purchases 526.32 shares. Should the price per share drop to $16 over the next year, those 526.32 shares are now worth $8,421 (526.32 x 16 = $8,421). If you invested $10,000 at $16 per share, you would purchase 625 shares. Then, when the price rises, you have more shares increasing in value. If these 625 shares increase in value to $19, your fund would be worth $11,875 (625 x 19 = $11,875).

Dollar cost averaging takes advantage of investing at various market prices and eliminates the guesswork. With dollar cost averaging, instead of investing one lump sum, you would invest the same amount over time, such as $400 per month for twenty-five months (400 x 25 = $10,000).

The following graph shows the price fluctuations of a hypothetical mutual fund over a twenty-five month period where the market declines then rises. It starts at $19 per share, drops to $16, then recovers and rises to $23 per share by the twenty-fifth month.

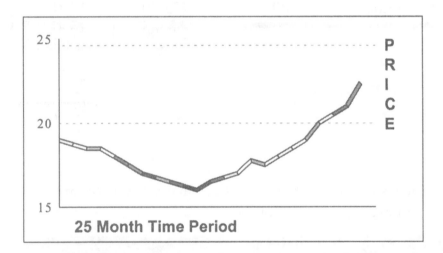

The best time to invest would be when the share price is at the low of $16, approximately the twelfth month. Accurately guessing a "low" is difficult, although some try by studying the fund's price fluctuations during different market conditions. The best alternative to reduce the risk of buying "high" is dollar cost averaging. Investing $400 per month over twenty-five months has the following results:

Table 8.3—Dollar Cost Averaging

Price Per Share	Shares Purchased	Price Per Share	Shares Purchased
$19.00	21.05	$16.40	24.39
$18.70	21.39	$16.80	23.81
$18.60	21.51	$17.00	23.53
$18.50	21.62	$17.50	22.85
$18.00	22.22	$17.70	22.60
$17.50	22.86	$18.00	22.22
$17.30	23.12	$18.50	21.62
$17.00	23.53	$19.00	21.05
$16.80	23.81	$20.00	20.00
$16.50	24.24	$20.50	19.51
$16.20	24.69	$21.00	19.05
$16.00	25.00	$22.00	18.18
		$23.00	17.39

Shares Purchased = 551.24

Amount Invested = $10,000 over twenty-five months

Value at end of twenty-five months @ $23 per share is $12,679

The results of investing at $19 per share, $16 per share, and using dollar cost averaging are as follows:

Amount Invested	Method Used	Price Per Share at Purchase	Shares Bought	Value of Shares at $23
$10,000	LUMP SUM	$19.00	526.32	$12,105
$10,000	LUMP SUM	$16.00	625.00	$14,375
$10,000	AVERAGING	VARIOUS	551.24	$12,678

Note: In this example, the price dropped steadily before it increased. Dollar cost averaging is not advantageous if the price per share steadily increases without a decline.

Dollar cost averaging eliminates the guesswork and reduces your risk by buying shares at various market prices. Usually, longer time periods show better results than shorter periods.

Special Features

If you plan to invest large amounts of money into a load fund, you can qualify for a breakpoint, or reduced sales charge. The first reduction for most funds is at $50,000 and will be explained fully in the prospectus. Funds also offer a letter of intent. This means if you, or members of your immediate family, intend to purchase additional shares during the coming year, you can sign this letter and qualify for the reduced sales charge. All purchases made within one family count toward the breakpoint.

Breakpoints Allow for Reduced Sales Charges on Large Purchases

You can redeem mutual fund shares at any time. Most newspapers list the value of mutual fund shares daily. The number of shares times the net asset value tells how much money you will receive if you liquidate. If you own four hundred shares with an NAV of $8 a share, you would receive $3,200 (400 x $8 = $3,200). When a fund receives a "redemption request," they mail a check within five business days.

Shares Are Redeemed at Their Net Asset Value within Five Business Days

To redeem shares, most funds offer a telephone redemption if you request this on the original application. Otherwise, a written request is needed, and it will need your signature guarantee. This can only be done by a commercial bank or stock brokerage firm. A word of caution here: credit unions and savings and loans cannot guarantee signatures unless they work with a commercial bank. If you invest in mutual funds, make sure you can easily get a signature guarantee, or request telephone exchange privileges.

Two basic types of funds exist: **OPEN-END FUNDS and CLOSED-END FUNDS.** Most of the funds on the market are the open-end type. They have no limit on the number of shares the fund can own, they are open to new investments, and shares can be redeemed at any time.

Unlike the open-end funds, the closed-end funds have a limit on the amount of money they can take in. **Once an offering for a closed-end fund closes, new investors cannot participate in that fund.** Shares of closed-end funds are traded like shares of stock; buyers decide the price they are willing to pay to purchase a seller's shares. Commissioned brokers complete these trades.

Advantages of Mutual Funds for Small Investors

Diversification Reduces Risk by Spreading Your Investment Dollars among Numerous Corporations

- Without a doubt, mutual funds have numerous advantages for small investors. **Many mutual fund families have SMALL INITIAL INVESTMENTS, ranging from $100 to $1,000, and accept ongoing deposits of $25 or more.** Some have no minimum.

- **Another major advantage is DIVERSIFICATION, which normally isn't possible without large amounts of money to invest.** The fund concept allows an individual to invest in a broad range of securities for a small amount of money. As already mentioned, diversification reduces risk by spreading the investment dollars among numerous companies and/or industries. This allows an investor to have variety in a small portfolio without paying excessive commissions and sales charges. Diversification, an important key for successful investing, is automatic with mutual funds.

- **PROFESSIONAL MANAGEMENT is another important feature of mutual funds.** Shareholders benefit from the expertise of the fund manager or group of managers who continually watch the market for advantageous times to trade the securities in the portfolio. The shareholders' money participates in all this activity for a small annual management fee assessed by the fund.

- **LIQUIDITY is an important feature of mutual funds. Funds offer several convenient ways to liquidate their shares.** They will send you a check monthly or quarterly: 1) for the dividends, 2) for the dividends and capital gains, or 3) for a specified amount. When this option is requested and the dividends and capital gains aren't enough, they sell enough shares to cover the amount.

- **With a mutual fund, you don't have to guess at your INVESTMENT'S PROGRESS; newspapers give the preceding day's closing price.** In addition, fund families keep shareholders well-informed. They send updates to the prospectus and annual reports to all shareholders for each fund owned. They also mail statements each time an account has a transaction, such as shares purchased, shares redeemed, and dividends or capital gains paid. These regular statements make additional investments in a fund easy because they include a payment voucher to mail in with a check.

- **EXCHANGE PRIVILEGES allow an investor to move money from one fund to another within the same family with no additional sales charge.** This feature provides great flexibility. If an investor's financial objective changes due to retirement, an increase in assets, an unexpected illness, or other reasons, he or she can easily move money to another fund or divide it among several funds at no cost. Switching funds within a family is easy, especially since most companies allow exchanges by telephone.

Fund Families Offer Exchange Privileges

> ### ADVANTAGES OF MUTUAL FUND INVESTMENTS
> - Small Initial Investment
> - Diversification
> - Professional Management
> - Liquidity
> - Convenience and Current Information
> - Exchange Privileges

Limited Partnerships

Limited partnerships, like mutual funds, work with the combined money of many investors. Here, the general partner forms the partnership, purchases the investment, and takes responsibility for the daily management. Real estate is a common limited partnership investment. **The pooled money often buys apartment units, mini-warehouses, shopping centers, and commercial buildings. General partners, however, put together many investments other than real estate holdings and sell them as limited partnerships.** Some common ones are: movie rights, oil and gas wells (either exploratory or income producing), equipment purchases and leases, and mortgage pools.

The General Partner Forms the Partnership, Raises the Money, Purchases the Investment, and Takes Responsibility for the Management

Limited partnerships are not traded like stocks and mutual funds on the open market, so they are not liquid unless the general partner agrees to purchase units back from investors. The original investment plus profits (minus fees and charges) are returned when the general partner sells the investment. Some limited partnerships purchase income producing investments to create an ongoing annual cash flow to the partnership.

Most Partnerships Are Not Liquid

The Benefits of
Ownership Pass
through to the
Limited Partners

Partnership Income and
Losses Are Passive

The benefits of ownership pass through to the limited partners. When the investment sells or earns income, the general partner and the limited partners divide the profits; limited partners usually receive 75% to 85% of the proceeds, the general partner receives the rest.

The 1986 Tax Reform Act drastically changed limited partnerships. Formerly, the depreciation from equipment and commercial buildings generated tax write-offs for the investor. Now, a subscriber cannot write off more than their initial investment. Furthermore, partners who do not participate in the management of the partnership cannot deduct depreciation and other expenses. These write-offs are now "passive" and can only offset passive income from the partnership.

Partnerships take one of two forms: PRIVATE PLACEMENTS or REGISTERED PUBLIC OFFERINGS. A private placement can have no more than thirty-five investors. They are limited to raising smaller amounts of money. **Typically, private placements are for experienced investors who often invest $25,000 or more.** Although these partnerships are not registered with the SEC, the offering circular must make full disclosure of all facts regarding the investment.

A registered offering is much larger, often raising millions of dollars from thousands of investors. It is registered with the SEC and sold as a security. Only qualified registered representatives can sell the shares. The cover of the prospectus states the maximum amount of money the general partner can raise. Once the general partner collects sufficient funds to purchase the assets, they form the partnership and close the offering.

All investors must meet certain suitability standards to invest. Minimum investments are usually $2,000 to $5,000 per unit for registered offerings. **At tax time, the general partner distributes a Form K-1 to all subscribers, showing their proportional share of partnership income and expenses. Again, the prospectus states the objective of the partnership. In growth partnerships, as in growth stocks, the future of the investment is unknown, so they assume more risk than income partnerships. Before investing in a limited partnership, be sure to consider the following:**

- The projected length of the partnership.
- After raising the required funds, how long does the general partner have to invest the money?
- If the general partner does not invest all the money, what happens to the remainder? Does it stay in the partnership as reserve cash, or is it returned to the partners?

- How often does the general partner communicate with the limited partners to inform them about the progress of their investment?
- Do distributions come from actual earnings, from earnings plus a return of capital, or from a return of capital only? Sometimes annual distributions include a portion of the money that limited partners originally invested.
- Are the limited partners liable for further assessments should the partnership be sued or something go wrong?
- How much do the limited partners give up for management fees, sales charges, and profits to the general partner?

Winning with Investments

When you own equities, you become an owner of an asset that you expect to increase in value. Investments can help your money stay ahead of inflation and make up for the amount given up for taxes. A minimum investment goal should be to earn at least a net 2% each year. See chapter 20, Planning: Break-Even Rate of Return. Your net yield depends on investment performance after subtracting sales charges, management fees, expenses, and other costs. **You also need to consider the portion of your profit given to taxes and the loss of buying power due to inflation.** If the inflation rate is 4% and you earn only 4% on your taxable savings account, you have only kept even; you have not moved ahead. Once you give up another 30% to taxes, you are behind.

Your Net Profit Depends on Investment Performance after Subtracting:

- Sales Charges
- Management Fees
- Inflation
- Taxes

With investments, you can expect higher yields than with fixed, guaranteed accounts. But remember, no investment program is foolproof. **It is the nature of investments to fluctuate. "Losers" are necessary to have "winners." Most importantly, what has proven true in the past, might**

not work in the future. The unpredictable often happens, and when it does, indicators are off. Market conditions always change, and as they do, they will influence the value of your investment.

Any time you take a chance with higher yields, you will also experience greater risks. You don't need to be overly concerned over market dips if your long-term profits keep going up. Many stocks and growth mutual funds show substantial gains during any five-year period, yet often show losses during shorter time periods.

If you buy stock or mutual funds when the price is low and sell when the price is high, you will always make money. Novice investors often do just the opposite; they jump into the market when everyone else talks about gains and high profits, and then they sell when prices are low.

Following the crowd is undependable and ill-advised. The best buying opportunity comes when everyone else is selling. If you watch general trends, develop a long-term investment strategy, take only comfortable risk, and trust your instincts, you can win with investments. Investments, although unpredictable, are not overly complicated. Many experts make investing seem complicated by trying to predict the future. Some have good results, others do not. It is impossible to predict the unpredictable consistently with 100% accuracy. **To be a successful investor, you must be willing to live with market ups and downs. Look at your long-term goals and your long-term growth opportunities.**

Wouldn't it be ideal if we could build sizable estates using only disciplined savings in fixed, guaranteed accounts? Inflation and taxes makes that ideal impossible. Since the cost of goods and services keep rising, and the tax on profits keeps going up, advancing financially requires earning higher than average rates of return. **When your earnings don't exceed the ongoing rise in the cost of such items as food, shelter, education, and transportation, at best you can only keep abreast, but cannot get ahead. Making headway in finances today requires ownership, in one way or another, in investments that will beat inflation.**

Advancing financially in the 1990s is similar to a predicament faced by Alice in Lewis Carroll's *Through the Looking Glass*.

Alice found herself in a strange country that she wanted to leave but couldn't. She tried running away, but it didn't work because she couldn't move forward. Even when she ran as fast as she could, she went nowhere. The queen yelled at her to run faster and faster, but she was already running as fast as possible. Alice didn't understand the problem until the queen explained that the world was moving at the same pace. She said, "…here you see, it takes all the running you can do to keep in

Investments Are Not Foolproof; Losers Are Needed to Have Winners

To Make Money, Buy Low and Sell High

The Cost of Goods and Services Keep Rising, So Advancing Financially Requires Earning Higher Than Average Yields

the same place. If you want to get somewhere else, you must run at least twice as fast..."[2]

In our world, prices, wages, earnings, and taxes all are accelerating. We can deplete our resources just trying to stay even. **To get ahead, we must beat the average increases.** We also have to take the queen's advice and "run twice as fast" to make any progress.

Our free enterprise system created rising prices and the inflation problem, but it also created a workable solution. That solution lies in the many investments available today that didn't exist fifty years ago. **This wide range of investment choices, offering more flexibility and diversity, can help us offset those rising prices and tax increases with increased profits.**

Notes

1. The American Funds Group, *ICA 1997 Investors Guide* (Los Angeles: Capital Research & Management Co., 1997), 8.

2. Lewis Carroll, *Through the Looking Glass* (Kingsport: Kingsport Press, Inc., 1979), 173.

9
Home Ownership

PURCHASING A HOME can be a wise investment that also helps you save on personal income taxes. If real estate appreciates at a healthy rate in the area where you buy, owning a home can also make money for you. Generally, you need to live in the home at least four years to recover the extra money paid for closing costs, loan fees, insurance, taxes, and other costs absent when renting. For shorter periods, you may get stung if forced to move when housing prices in the area have dropped due to lack of jobs or overbuilding.

A Wise Investment for Many Has Been Home Ownership

Real Estate Risks

All real estate investments, including private residences, are subject to risks in three major areas: **1) Market, 2) Political, and 3) Interest Rates.** An explanation of each follows.

MARKET. The market risk, based on demand, causes prices to go up or down. New construction in the area is a good sign because it reflects growth, high demand, and accompanying rising home prices. A constant danger in a growing area, however, is overbuilding. With too many available homes and not enough buyers, prices drop.

If the area has experienced above average price increases several years prior to your arrival, be cautious. It is difficult to know when prices have reached their peak or if the appreciation will continue. This is a guess, even for the experts. If possible, you want to avoid paying top dollar for a home if future appreciation is tenuous. The shorter your intended stay in the home, the more careful you need to be in your decision to buy and the more careful you need to be in your home selection.

POLITICAL. Political decisions create jobs as well as layoffs. One political risk in home buying hinges on available jobs in the area. If a major local employer has massive layoffs from losing a large contract, or for other reasons, people will need to move to seek new employment. The large number of vacant homes without buyers creates an oversupply so, accordingly, home prices drop. Another political risk is deductibility of home mortgage interest, because it can be changed by a political decision.

INTEREST RATES. Interest rates also affect housing prices. Lower interest rates reduce mortgage payments, making mortgages affordable for more people (see Table 9.2). Due to the lower rates, more buyers can qualify for a home. High interest rates have the reverse effect.

What Can You Afford?

Most lenders use a 28/36 ratio to test for mortgage qualifications with a 20% down payment. **Your mortgage payment, homeowner's insurance, and property taxes should not exceed 28% of your gross income. The total of all your loan payments, including the mortgage, should not exceed 36% of your gross income.**

Table 9.1—Formula for Mortgage Affordability

Mortgage Affordability		
1.	Gross Monthly Income =	$
2.	Affordable Monthly Payment = *Line 1 x .28*	$
3.	Total of All Monthly Debt = *Line 1 x .36*	$

Example:

You and your spouse have a combined gross monthly income of $4,167. You would qualify for a total monthly mortgage payment of $1,167 per month ($4,167 x .28 = $1,167). The total payment includes mortgage payment, property taxes, and homeowner's insurance.

You could spend up to 36%, or $1,500 per month ($4,167 x .36 = $1,500), for mortgage payment, property taxes, homeowner's insurance, and other loan obligations having payments beyond one year.

The 28/36 ratio is not written in stone. If you are willing to take an adjustable rate mortgage (ARM), if you have excellent credit, or if you can make a larger down payment, most lenders will raise the ratios slightly. Likewise, if you pay less than 20%, the mortgage lender will lower the ratios.

Before Purchasing a Home

Before purchasing a home, consider these factors:

- Are home prices in the general area rising, falling, or are they relatively stable?
- Are interest rates high or low?
- Do you expect to live in the home at least four years? For shorter periods, you may not recover your costs unless prices increase significantly during your ownership.
- If your purchase is for less than four years, what would you pay for a comparable rental? Compare the total costs of home ownership, including mortgage payment, closing costs, taxes, insurance, and upkeep for your intended stay to the amount you would pay in rent for this same period.
- If renting is less costly, what could you earn by investing the "extra" money you will save by renting?
- What are the tax benefits of home ownership for your situation? Do you have gains to defer from a prior home sale? Do you need a mortgage interest tax deduction? (Remember, mortgage interest is tax deductible, and no similar deduction exists for rental payments.)
- Do you have a growing family and need more living space? Can you rent a suitable home for a good price? A yard might be a necessary housing amenity. Homes often have yards, most apartments do not.

Moving Forward with the Decision to Buy

Once you make the decision to buy, move forward following these guidelines:

- Prioritize the features you want in your new home. You may have to compromise, so know what is most important to you.

    BEDROOMS—How many? How large?

    YARD—How large? Maintenance is expensive and time consuming but also rewarding for those who like it.

    KITCHEN AREA—Check for adequate cupboard space, and consider how much time you will spend in the kitchen.

    LIVING and **DINING ROOM** areas.

    LAUNDRY facilities.

    GARAGE and **STORAGE** space.

    How close are the **NEIGHBORS?**

    Is the area tranquil or bustling with traffic? Is there distracting street or freeway **NOISE?**

- **Find a good real estate agent to show you around the area.** You will not pay extra for this service—the seller pays. Agents know what is on the market in your price range. Have an agent give you a tour of an area that interests you. Look at the location of schools, recreational facilities, shopping, and public transportation.
- **Look at homes in the neighborhoods where you would like to live.** Real estate agents work on Saturdays and Sundays, so use this time to review what is on the market.
- **Know what you can afford for a mortgage** (See Table 9.2). Take your most recent pay stub and tax return to a prequalifying interview with a loan officer from a reputable mortgage lender in the area.
- **Learn the traffic patterns and commute time from the possible home sites.** Visit the neighborhood during a weekday to get a realistic idea of peak driving times and traffic noise. Visit the

neighborhood again on the weekend to get a feel for the activity level of the area.

- **Make an offer based on similar properties with recent sales** (past three months).
- **Before you sign the final papers, insist on a thorough home inspection.** It is a good idea to hire an independent inspector to look at the structure and appliances for you. The inspection may cost you several hundred dollars, but it will reveal potential flaws in the property, e.g., termites, unusable soil, poor drainage, needed roof repairs, and potential electrical or plumbing problems. The inspection could uncover problems you never considered. Furthermore, if you do find problems that are expensive to fix, you can renegotiate a better deal with the seller.

Surviving an Escrow Closing

If you can find a knowledgeable loan officer who will lead you through the loan process, this person is worth their weight in gold. An inexperienced or incompetent loan officer will test your patience, if not drive you crazy, and could cost you needless extra money.

The loan officer takes your application and prequalifies you for the loan. The loan officer obtains the required information for the loan package, then usually gets approval from a second source: an office manager, supervisor, or another department.

Generally, the completed loan package consists of:

A Knowledgeable Loan Officer Is Worth Their Weight in Gold

- Your completed, signed application
- A recent credit report
- A recent appraisal on the property you wish to purchase
- Verification of your employment
- Your most recent tax return, or if you are self-employed, a profit and loss statement and your three most recent tax returns
- Verification of your savings and checking account balances
- Verification of the balances owed on your monthly debts

You will be asked to make a "good faith" deposit up front between $400 and $500. Normally, it is non-refundable. It covers the up front costs of securing a credit report and an appraisal.

In completing the required information for the loan package, don't be overly surprised if skeletons you have forgotten about come out of the closet. You may be asked to explain why you were late making a $25 credit card payment several years ago, or you may discover that one of the institutions you borrowed from gave incorrect information, so you now have to prove that you really did pay off their loan. You may have to explain a late car payment when you were on vacation or out of the country. Written explanations to most of the questions raised through a credit check are usually sufficient to satisfy most lenders.

As you approach the closing deadline, your loan officer may ask you if you want to lock in the current interest rate. Once you lock in a rate, that is the rate you will receive on the loan even if general rates go up or down. If the officer doesn't provide you with interest rate information, ask for the interest rate guidelines. This is especially important if current rates are low and expected to rise.

Interest Rate on Your Loan Is Important

Your loan officer will work for a lending institution like a **bank, credit union**, or a **mortgage company**. A bank or credit union loans you the money directly. Many mortgage companies find an investor interested in buying your mortgage and sell it to them.

Buying a home is a legal procedure involving numerous details. Typically, an ESCROW COMPANY will draw up the FINAL SETTLE-MENT STATEMENT. It gives a break down of all your closing costs, payments made toward them, and the balance due. It also shows the contract price for the property. **The escrow company takes care of legalities such as:**

- **Title Search.** Making certain the property you are about to buy is legally registered to the seller and has no unusual liens or judgments against it other than the mortgage(s) revealed by the seller.
- Preparing the **Trust Deed** in your name and recording it with the County Recorder in the county where the property is located.
- **Prorating** taxes, insurance, interest, and other assessments **between you and the seller** on the final settlement statement. For example, if you are scheduled to take title on October 1, you will be charged with three months of property taxes and insurance. The seller will be responsible for paying these same charges for the first nine months of the year. If you do not close on the first of the month, you will be charged with a portion of the month's interest.

- **Pay taxes, interest, and other assessments** due to the appropriate parties.
- **Collect moneys** due from both parties, pay the seller, and pay off all existing mortgages or liens on the property.

Closing Costs and Final Settlement Statement

You will receive a settlement statement that shows all amounts paid by you and by the seller. If you will own the home as of October 1, you will pay for the annual city and county taxes for your three months of ownership. These may be collected as part of the closing costs. Mortgage interest (if you do not close on the first day of the month) and homeowner's insurance will also be prorated and paid in advance on this settlement statement.

Other closing costs normally paid by the borrower include a LOAN ORIGINATION FEE or LOAN DISCOUNT FEE, often referred to as "POINTS." The loan origination fee is a commission paid to the mortgage company or lending institution for preparing the loan package. A loan discount is an amount you pay up front to get a lower interest rate. It is the same as prepaid interest. **You can deduct these points on your income taxes in the year paid if the total amount you pay out of pocket for closing costs equals or exceeds the points paid.** You can also deduct property taxes paid in escrow.

You will pay for **title insurance.** It is required by lenders to protect their investment in the property. Through this insurance, lenders have a guaranteed dollar amount in the property if ownership is somehow contested through the courts and they should lose title. While title insurance and other costs, plus recording and transfer fees, are not tax deductible, you can add them to the price paid for the home to reduce your gain upon selling. All of these costs are called closing costs.

Private Mortgage Insurance (PMI)

Private Mortgage Insurance is available through most lenders. By taking out a policy to protect the lender, you can make a smaller down payment, such as 5% or 10%. The insurance protects the lender from declining prices when they have invested more than 80% of the market value in the property. Lenders have a guaranteed dollar amount in the property through the insurance even if real estate prices drop. **Private Mortgage Insurance is nearly always required when equity in the property is less than 20%.**

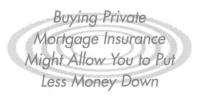

Buying Private Mortgage Insurance Might Allow You to Put Less Money Down

If you must obtain PMI, you can cancel it after two years if equity in the home grows beyond 20%. Your equity increases through general rising home prices, through improvements to the property, and/or a reduction of the principal balance on the loan. You (the borrower) need to petition the lender to cancel the PMI insurance. **Lenders are not required to notify borrowers when they no longer require this insurance.**

Your Mortgage

Several types of mortgages are available. **You can get a mortgage for FIFTEEN YEARS or for THIRTY YEARS. You can get a FIXED INTEREST MORTGAGE or an ADJUSTABLE RATE MORTGAGE, commonly referred to as an ARM. To determine the best type of mortgage for your situation, look at your taxable income, how much you can afford, and how long you expect to live in the house.**

Rising and falling interest rates change the size of a mortgage payment, thus influencing the amount you can afford. The following table gives the monthly payment due on principal and interest for various mortgages with differing interest rates.

The monthly mortgage payments for various interest rates are in the boxes to the right of the mortgage amount. $5,000 and $10,000 amounts are given in the table so you can easily add or multiply to get a wide variety of possible sums.

Example:

If you are looking at a $130,000 mortgage, take the $10,000 amount, multiply it by three ($10,000 x 3 = $30,000), and add it to the $100,000 amount.

Table 9.2—Monthly Mortgage Payments for Differing Interest Rates

Mortgage Amount	Interest Rate													
	7%		7.5%		8%		8.5%		9%		9.5%		10%	
	15 Yr.	30 Yr.	15 Yr.	30 Yr.	15 Yr.	30 Yr.	15 Yr.	30 Yr.	15 Yr.	30 Yr.	15 Yr.	30 Yr.	15 Yr.	30 Yr.
$ 5,000	45	33	46	35	48	37	49	38	51	40	52	42	54	44
$ 10,000	90	67	93	70	96	73	98	77	101	80	104	84	107	88
$ 50,000	449	333	464	350	478	367	492	384	508	403	522	420	538	439
$ 75,000	674	499	695	524	717	550	739	577	761	603	783	631	806	658
$100,000	899	665	927	699	956	734	985	769	1,015	805	1,044	841	1,075	878

Adjustable Rate Mortgages

ADJUSTABLE RATE MORTGAGES have changing interest rates. Most cannot increase more than 2% in any year or more than 6% over the lifetime of the mortgage, but do not assume these ceilings are part of your mortgage. Find out the parameters of the mortgage from the lender. **Law requires lenders to give full disclosure on all features of the ARM. Most ARM's move with:**

- the three month or six month TREASURY BILL RATE,
- the Federal Home Loan Bank Board's "COST OF FUNDS" RATE,
- the yield on TREASURY SECURITIES maturing in one, three, or five years, or
- the "NATIONAL AVERAGE MORTGAGE RATE." This is an average of loan rates during a specified period.

Each lender will markup the cost of the loan to include their profit. These markups vary, so ARM's based on the same index will also vary according to the lender's profit margin. **This makes loan shopping important.**

ARM'S are a good loan choice for those buyers who expect to have the mortgage for only a few years. But, before signing any documents, make sure you know:

- Which index the ARM is tied to, such as the Cost of Funds Index or the Treasury Securities Index. Have the lender show you a history of how these rates have changed over the past several years.

- The profit margin for the lender that is added to the index to set the actual rate of the mortgage.
- How often the rate changes and the limits on these changes in any given year and over the life of the loan. Don't assume your cap will be 2% each year and 6% over the life of the mortgage.
- If the ARM is convertible to a fixed rate mortgage? If it is convertible, how often, and at what cost?

Fixed Interest Rate Mortgages

Fifteen- and Thirty-Year

Looking at the mortgage interest payments in Table 9.2 shows that the thirty-year mortgage has lower payments than does the fifteen-year mortgage. **The thirty-year mortgage has lower payments because you have double the time to retire the principal.** Some people like the idea of a fifteen-year mortgage because they will pay considerably less interest over the life of the loan and have their house paid off in fifteen years instead of thirty.

To take advantage of the benefits of a fifteen-year mortgage and maintain more flexibility, take the thirty-year loan, then make double principal payments to reduce the balance. This plan will pay off the loan in fifteen years, but it doesn't tie you in to the higher monthly payments required under the fifteen-year schedule. Should you experience unexpected cash flow problems, you can miss several of the "double principal" payments and make them up later when you have the money (see section below on Prepaying Mortgages).

Take the Thirty-Year Loan and Make Double Principal Payments to Reduce Your Balance

Prepaying Mortgages

By prepaying next month's principal with your current mortgage payment, you save that entire month's interest expense. An amortization schedule for your loan is necessary to determine the breakdown between principal and interest so you can add next month's principal to this month's payment. Table 9.3 shows an amortization schedule for one year for a $95,000, thirty-year mortgage at 8% interest. The monthly payment is $697.08. Over the life of this thirty-year loan, $155,949 would be paid in interest. By prepaying next month's principal with this month's payment, you can pay off the loan in fifteen years. The additional principal payments over this fifteen-year period total $22,058, an average of $1,471 per year. But, making these additional payments will

Prepaying Next Month's Principal with This Month's Payment Saves an Entire Month's Interest Expense

save a whopping $103,417 in interest! The total interest paid over the fifteen years by making double principal payments is $52,532, compared to $155,949 under the thirty-year loan. Also, as you pay more principal, you increase your equity in the home.

Look at the amortization schedule below. Add the principal from payment #2 to payment #1. Add the principal from payment #3 to payment #2, etc. Each time you make an additional principal payment, cross it off your list. Continue adding next month's principal to this month's regular monthly payment.

As You Pay More Principal, You Increase Your Equity

Example:

Payment 1   Add $64.17 to scheduled payment of $697.08
Payment 2   Add $64.60 to scheduled payment of $697.08
Payment 3   Add $65.03 to scheduled payment of $697.08

Table 9.3—Loan Amortization

$95,000 Loan @ 8% for 30 Years Payment: $697.08 Per Month			
Payment #	Principal	Interest	Balance
			95,000.00
1	63.75	633.33	94,936.26
2	64.17	632.91	94,872.09
3	64.60	632.48	94,807.49
4	65.03	632.05	94,742.47
5	65.46	631.62	94,677.01
6	65.90	631.18	94,611.11
7	66.34	630.74	94,544.78
8	66.78	630.30	94,478.01
9	67.22	629.85	94,410.77
10	67.67	629.41	94,343.00
11	68.12	628.95	94,274.98
12	68.58	628.50	94,206.40

Additional Principle Paid			
Year 1	793.61	Year 9	1,501.85
Year 2	859.46	Year 10	1,626.49
Year 3	930.79	Year 11	1,761.52
Year 4	1,008.05	Year 12	1,907.71
Year 5	1,091.71	Year 13	2,066.04
Year 6	1,182.35	Year 14	2,237.52
Year 7	1,280.48	Year 15	2,423.23
Year 8	1,386.77		
Total Paid $22,057.58			

People use various methods for prepaying mortgages. Some send the lender an additional 10%. Some lenders even have a plan of paying mortgages using biweekly instead of monthly payments. Paying biweekly can pay off the mortgage nearly ten years sooner. Before starting a prepayment plan, it is a good idea to notify your lender of your intentions. Then make a notation on each payment voucher of the extra money you have sent in. You can also pay the additional amount with a second check to make record keeping clear if discrepancies arise.

Second Homes

Currently, Congress allows taxpayers to deduct home mortgage interest on two homes as long as the total owed on both homes does not exceed one million dollars. (Is this because most politicians have two homes?) These second homes can be:

- **VACATION HOMES** are those the owner rents and also uses personally. The rental income is tax free if rented for fourteen days or less.
- **TIMESHARES** if they are deeded timeshares where the taxpayer owns the property, and if the owner uses it less than fifteen days per year.
- **BOATS** and **MOBILE HOMES** that have basic living facilities.

Any second home that you rent is also referred to as a vacation home. **If you own a second home, a boat, mobile home, or timeshare that qualifies as a second home, you can take advantage of a tax law that permits you to rent it up to fourteen days without claiming the income from the rental.** If you rent beyond the fourteen days, the rules change, and you must claim the income. However, you can also take offsetting expenses.

Refinancing and Home Equity Loans

REFINANCING occurs when you replace your current loan with a new loan. Consider refinancing when current mortgage rates are 2% or more below your existing mortgage rate. **Before redoing your loan, find out how much you will pay for closing costs, points, and other fees, and how much you will save with your new mortgage payment over the old.** Then, look at how many months it will take you to recover the costs of refinancing. If you plan to stay in the house beyond this "recovery" period, refinancing is worthwhile.

Points paid for refinancing are NOT tax deductible, even if fully paid out of pocket. They must be amortized over the life of the loan. This means if you pay \$2,000 in points for a new thirty-year loan, you can only deduct \$67 each year (\$2,000 ÷ 30 = \$67). If you pay off this refinanced loan, you can deduct the points not taken in the year the loan is paid off.

Home equity loans are available for those who have more than 20% equity in their home. The lending institution will carry a second trust deed on the property for the amount of the home equity loan they give you. For example, if the market value of your home is \$150,000 and you have a first mortgage of \$90,000, and you have a good credit rating, you would qualify for a home equity loan of approximately \$30,000 (150,000 x 80% = \$120,000). Some lenders give loans up to 10% of equity but charge higher interest and/or fees. **Most lenders will loan up to 80% of the market value of the home.**

A Home Equity Loan Is Secured by a Second Deed of Trust on the Property

A HOME EQUITY LINE OF CREDIT gives you a line of credit up to your qualifying amount, also secured by a second trust deed. The lending institution will give you checks that you can use against the credit balance. It works like revolving credit. You can "charge" up to your limit, then when you pay off or pay down the balance, you can reuse the available credit line for another purpose.

The advantage of a home equity loan or home equity line of credit is that the interest rate is much lower than credit card rates. The money can be used for any purpose, and within limits, the interest is fully deductible as "mortgage interest" on your personal income tax. **Current tax law limits deductible home equity debt secured by second trust deeds to $100,000 for couples and $50,000 for singles. These amounts are totals allowed on ALL home equity debt for first and second homes.**

Tax Benefits of Home Ownership

MORTGAGE INTEREST and PROPERTY TAXES paid on a home are normally the deductions that allow a taxpayer to take itemized deductions. Tax law allows a taxpayer to take either a standard deduction or itemized deductions, whichever is greater. With itemized deductions, in addition to writing off mortgage interest and property taxes, a taxpayer can also deduct state and local taxes paid, charitable contributions, and varying percentages of employee business expenses, investment expenses, casualty and theft losses, and medical expenses. Without the mortgage interest deduction, most taxpayers do not have enough applicable expenses to itemize, so they lose the write-offs.

Because mortgage interest is tax deductible, it saves money that would otherwise be paid in taxes. Use your tax bracket (see Appendix C: Tax Bracket) to determine your net costs for a mortgage.

For example:

If your mortgage interest is $900 a month, or $10,800 a year, and your tax bracket is 35% (28% federal + 7% state), you will have a $3,780 tax reduction due to the mortgage interest you paid ($10,800 x 35% = $3,780). Considering you save $3,780 in taxes, your net cost of the mortgage is $7,020. Table 9.4 shows the net after tax cost of a home mortgage for various tax brackets and interest rates.

Table 9.4—Net Cost of a Mortgage

| | Interest Rate on Mortgage | | | |
	7%	8%	9%	10%
Tax Bracket	Net or Real Cost of Mortgage:			
22% (15% + 7%)	5.46%	6.24%	7.02%	7.8%
35% (28% + 7%)	4.55%	5.20%	5.85%	6.5%
38% (31% + 7%)	4.34%	4.96%	5.58%	6.2%
43% (36% + 7%)	3.99%	4.56%	5.13%	5.7%
46.6% (39.6%+7%)	3.74%	4.27%	4.8%	5.34%

Most Gains Now Excluded on Sale of Principal Residence

New tax law now makes it possible to avoid tax on the sale of a principal residence. **Single persons can avoid up to $250,000 of gain and married couples who file jointly can avoid up to $500,000 of gain** for sales after May 6, 1997.

To qualify for the exclusion of capital gain on a primary residence sale, **you must have owned and occupied the home as your primary residence for an aggregate of two years out of five before the sale.** Periods of use do not have to be consecutive. Furthermore, this is not a one time benefit. **As often as you meet the ownership and use test, you may claim the exclusion.**

Less Than Two Years

If you are forced to sell your home before the two-year period due to change of employment, health reasons, or unforeseen circumstances, the excludable gain is prorated. The IRS will define unforeseen circumstances in upcoming regulations. For example, if after owning a home for one year, you develop serious life-threatening asthma and the doctor recommends you move to a warmer, drier climate, you would be able to exclude 50% of the gain. The same rule applies if you must move because of job relocation.

Home Owners Incapable of Self-Care

A home owner who becomes physically or mentally incapable of self-care and needs to be admitted to a licensed care facility can still qualify for the exclusion as long as the homeowner has owned and used the residence for at least one year out of the five preceding years. **Time spent in the care facility counts as time spent in their own home.**

Real Estate, Leverage, and OPM

Leverage is using borrowed money to make money. It is also referred to as OPM, "Other People's Money." The rate of return on the amount of money you make is based on the amount of money invested. With leverage, you can take advantage of the appreciation on the total value of a property, although you put down only 5% to 20% of its market value.

If you select real estate in the right location, leverage can make money for you. Historically, real estate has been a good inflation hedge. The value increases each year to keep up with, or ahead of, overall rising prices. To make money in real estate, location is everything. The higher the demand, the greater the increase in value. If the property isn't in demand, the price won't go up.

When you purchase real estate with a down payment and a mortgage, you use leverage or OPM to make your profits. As the property owner, you receive ALL of the benefits of ownership, whether they be tax benefits or an increase in equity through appreciation on the property. The bank or lender does not share in these benefits with you. With leverage and a good loan, you stand to earn more than if you owned the property outright.

Assume you purchase several acres in an area where you expect to see future growth. You pay $50,000 for the land. Over the next two years, the property increases in value to $75,000. The property taxes are $500 per year. To see the power of using leverage and OPM, let's compare the difference in profits if you had paid $50,000 cash for the land as opposed to the down payment and the mortgage approach. **To calculate your rate of return, look at the money you make with the money you spend.**
Example:

In the **leverage** example, you purchase the land with a 20% down payment of $10,000 and a mortgage for $40,000 at 8% for fifteen years.

The payment on the mortgage is $384 per month, and the property tax is $500 a year. At the end of the two-year period, you have made $9,216 in payments.

In the **cash or outright purchase** example, you pay $50,000 cash for the same piece of land. Taxes remain the same at $500 per year.

Money Spent				
Leverage			**Cash**	
Down Payment	$10,000		Purchase Price	$50,000
Money invested in monthly payments $384 x 24	$ 9,216			
Property Taxes (2 Yrs.)	$ 1,000		Property Taxes (2 Yrs.)	$ 1,000
Total Money Spent	$20,216		Total Money Spent	$51,000

Yield and Profit				
Leverage			**Cash**	
Sales Price	$75,000		Sales Price	$75,000
Balance on Mortgage	$37,002		Balance on Mortgage	0
Profit to Owner based on total money spent	$37,998		Profit to Owner based on total money spent	$24,000
Profit per year	$18,999		Profit per year	$12,000
Annual rate of return on money spent	94%		Annual rate of return on money spent	23.5%

This simplified example does not include commissions, fees, and other expenses. The profits would be lowered by the cost of these additional expenses but would be the same in both cases, so it would not change the difference that leverage makes in the rate of return. **Many people have made money by taking advantage of real estate appreciation with a minimum purchase in the property. You can even use the equity buildup to get a loan to purchase additional properties.**

Like all investments, real estate also has its risks. **If no buyer exists for the property, you are stuck with it.** Some real estate is not easy to buy

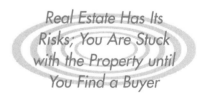

Real Estate Has Its Risks; You Are Stuck with the Property until You Find a Buyer

into, while other real estate is not easy to get out of. To make money, the property must be in demand. Demand will make it appreciate in value. A change in zoning laws, a surge in interest rates, or a downturn in the market can all affect what you hope to earn.

10
Retirement Plans

WORKING FOR THIRTY YEARS for the same company and then retiring with an adequate pension plan from that company is rare. Corporations today have discovered that they can't afford to pay for employee benefits and also totally fund retirement for their employees. Therefore, the retirement funding has shifted away from the employer and the former defined benefit plans to the employee who must now fund his/her own retirement through a company sponsored plan. Many companies contribute a percentage or a matching contribution but leave the majority of the funding up to the individual employee.

The most common company sponsored plan is the 401(k), named after Section 401(k) of the Internal Revenue Code, where you can find the rules governing the plan. Tax sheltered annuities, or 403(b) plans, referring to Section 403(b) of the Internal Revenue Code, are used in non-profit organizations such as hospitals and schools. Deferred Compensation Plans, governed by Section 457 of the Internal Revenue Code, are offered by some companies, while small employers may offer the new SIMPLE plan. The self-employed individual can set up their own plan through a SEP IRA or a Keogh plan. In conjunction with all of these plans, individuals can also contribute to Individual Retirement Accounts, better known as IRA's. The contributions may or may not be tax deductible. New in 1998 are the Roth IRA and the Education IRA, which really isn't an IRA at all.

Although the rules are many and cumbersome, **the benefits under most of these plans are similar.** Unless you qualify for financial need, distributions before age fifty-nine and one-half will have a 10% tax penalty (see Early Withdrawals later in this chapter). Typically, contributions come out of your pocket and go into an account that is held in trust for you. **For the 401(k), 403(b), Deferred Compensation, SIMPLE IRA, SEP IRA, Keogh, and deductible IRA, you get a tax deduction or dollar for dollar write-off for the contributions.** When you take the money out of the plan, it is then taxed at your current tax bracket. **For the new ROTH IRA, there is no deduction, but contribution and earnings will be tax free when withdrawn.** With nondeductible IRA's only, the earnings will be taxed when the money is taken out.

Since the multitude of rules and variety of plans can be overwhelming, try to **focus on the benefits and features of the plans that apply to you.** There is no better way to make your money grow than through a tax deferred retirement plan. This tax deferral, combined with an employer's matching contributions (offered by many employer sponsored plans), can't be beat for building a future nest egg. If you do not qualify to participate in a company sponsored plan, you can still take advantage of tax deferred growth by setting up a SEP IRA, a Keogh, a TSA (403[b]), or an IRA.

The Power of Tax Deferred Growth

Tax deferred retirement plans through employers are funded primarily by salary reduction. You give up a portion of your salary, before tax, and it goes into your retirement account. So when you contribute to your company's 401(k), a SIMPLE IRA, or a TSA (403[b]), Uncle Sam also pitches in indirectly with the money you save in taxes. For example, if you contribute $600 a month, or $7,200 per year, to a 401(k) and are in a 35% tax bracket (28% federal and 7% state), your out-of-pocket cost would be $4,680. Uncle Sam would put in $2,520. Uncle Sam's $2,520 contribution is the amount you save in taxes. Your contribution of $7,200 is not included in your gross pay.

Taxable Income	Retirement Plan Contribution	Tax @ 35% Fed. 28% + State 7%
$35,000	0	$12,150
$27,800	$7,200	$ 9,730

$7,200 Contribution Costs You:	$4,680
Uncle Sam Contributes:	$2,520
	$7,200

Since the $600 comes "off the top" and is not included in gross pay, you do not pay federal or state taxes on it. You will, however, pay the employees share of FICA and Medicare taxes. The result is that your take home pay is not reduced by the full $600 contribution, since the federal and state taxes are reduced. Your out-of-pocket cost for saving this $600 could be as low as $390. Table 10.1 shows a pay stub BEFORE and AFTER a tax deferred retirement plan contribution.

Table 10.1—Net Take Home Pay before and after Tax Deferred Retirement Plan Contribution

Before		After
$2,917	Gross Pay	$2,917
0	Retirement Plan	600
2,917	New Gross	2,317
817	Federal Tax	648
204	State Tax	162
223	FICA and Medicare Tax	223
$1,673	Net Pay	$1,284

The above example shows that it only costs you $389 to save $600! When you contribute to your retirement plan, **dollars that you would normally lose to taxes can earn interest for you instead.** This advantage allows you to earn 40% to 65% more. You control the timing of your tax liability and can choose to withdraw funds when your tax rate is lower, such as after retirement when your income is significantly reduced.

Retirement plans are also attractive because the earnings accumulate tax deferred. (With the new Roth IRA, earnings are tax free. This is covered later.) The following example illustrates the power of tax deferred growth.

Example:

Account A is fully taxed (35% tax bracket), and Account B is tax deferred. Assume that both accounts earn 10% per year and each account receives a $2,000 contribution at the same time each year. After twenty years, Account A is worth $74,464 after paying the annual taxes due out of its earnings. Account B has had to pay no taxes and is worth $114,560. Taxes will be paid on Account B as the money is withdrawn, but the balance will continue to grow tax deferred.

Another way to look at the power of tax deferred growth is to look at the amount you can save. When taxed at 35%, you must earn $1.54 to bring home $1.00. If your tax bracket is 40%, then you have to earn $1.67 to bring home $1.00. **However, with pretax savings, a dollar earned can be a dollar saved.**

401(k) Plans

When Taxed at 35%, You Must Earn $1.54 to Bring Home $1.00

A 401(k) is a qualified retirement plan that defers compensation to a future year. The employee (and sometimes employer) contributes to the plan for the employee. The contributions are held by a trustee until distributed to the employee.

If the employer makes contributions, the plan must have a vesting schedule. The vesting schedule tells when the employer contributions irrevocably become the employee's. **In other words, you give up money you would have been entitled to when you leave a job before you are fully vested.** Vesting schedules are based on length of service. Most contributions become 100% vested after six years. **Your own contributions are always immediately 100% vested.**

Employee contributions to 401(k) plans are done through salary reduction. This allows the employee to defer salary to a future year and have a tax free buildup of earnings within the plan until he/she makes withdrawals. Generally, the maximum contribution is 15% of salary, up to a maximum of $9,500.

Another advantage of the 401(k) is that **many employers offer low interest loans so their employees can have access to their retirement money without the tax consequences of adding it to income.** The maximum loan allowed by tax code is 50% of your vested account balance up to a maximum of $50,000. Loans must be repaid within five years unless they are used to purchase a primary residence.

Employers who have one hundred or fewer employees may elect to set up a SIMPLE 401(k). Employees can contribute only $6,000 annually to the SIMPLE 401(k). The employer must either put in a matching contribution, or 3% of the employee's salary, or 2% of salary for all employees whether or not the employees make contributions on their own.

403(b) Annuities for Nonprofit Organizations

The largest participators in 403(b) annuities are schools and hospitals. These plans are also called TSA's (short for "tax sheltered annuities"). The plan can invest in mutual funds or fixed interest contracts offered through insurance companies. Like the 401(k) plans, TSA's are also funded through salary reduction agreements. Generally, a participant can contribute 25% of one's salary, up to a maximum contribution of $9,500 for 1997.

Certain employees who have fifteen years of service but have not put in the maximum amount allowed each year may qualify for a special catch-up provision, which allows them to put higher contributions into their TSA contract. Agents working with and servicing these plans are familiar with the catch-up provision and can tell their clients the maximum amount they can contribute.

Government Employees

Federal government employees can defer 10% of their pay up to a maximum deferral of $9,500 in 1997 into a Deferred Compensation Plan, technically referred to as a 457 Plan. They pay into the Federal Thrift Savings Fund.

State and local government employees qualify for a similar deferred compensation plan, but their deferral limit for 1997 is $7,500. Catch-up provisions may apply to certain qualified employees.

Early Withdrawals

Before age fifty-nine and one-half, you will pay a 10% tax penalty on all withdrawals unless you no longer have your job, are disabled, or qualify for a financial need that cannot be met by other sources. Financial need includes the following when there is no other source of funds:

- down payment for the purchase of a "first-time" principal residence,
- tuition, fees, or room and board for the next year for "higher" education for yourself, your spouse, children, or other dependents,
- medical expenses for yourself, your spouse, or your dependents,
- to prevent eviction or mortgage foreclosure, or
- to pay funeral expenses for a family member.

Leaving an Employer

If you leave your job for any reason before paying off a loan, the loan balance is treated as a withdrawal subject to penalties and taxes.

Your retirement plan moneys can be transferred to a new company plan or to a rollover IRA if it cannot be left with the former employer. If you do transfer the funds, be sure to do a "trustee to trustee" transfer. Decide where you want to place the money, then have the new trustee send a letter to your former trustee and ask that the funds be transferred directly to them. You will never receive a check, as it will be made out to the new trustee for your benefit to be deposited into your new account.

If you do not follow the trustee to trustee transfer procedure, you will receive a 1099R at tax time, showing that you had a distribution from your retirement account. If you rolled the money into a new IRA within the sixty day limit, be sure to keep records of this transaction so the money is not taxable. **The biggest disadvantage in doing a roll over where you receive the funds is that the former trustee is required to withhold 20% when you do not have the money transferred directly to the new trustee.** Unless you have funds from other sources where you can deposit that same 20% into your new IRA rollover account, the 20% becomes taxable and must be added to your income in the year it is withheld. This is a little-discussed "revenue maker" for the government, so when changing companies, be aware of this pitfall.

When you leave your job, consider all the consequences before you rollover your 401(k) plan into an IRA. In most cases, it is better to keep these two plans separate. If you rollover your 401(k) into an existing IRA, you can no longer roll that 401(k) money into a future employer's plan. Remember, 401(k) money qualifies for five- or ten-year averaging when you take a lump-sum payout at retirement. This can significantly reduce your tax burden because you can spread the taxes due over five or ten years. IRA's have no provisions for this tax averaging. Remember also that loan provisions available with 401(k)'s are not available with IRA's.

In Most Cases, It Is Best to Keep 401(k) Money and IRA Money Separate

E.S.O.P.'s

E.S.O.P.'s, or Employer Stock Option Plans are another company sponsored retirement plan. Instead of cash, the employer places company stock into accounts set up for their employees. Sometimes E.S.O.P.'s are referred to as profit sharing plans because the employer contributes from company profits.

The company must allow an employee who is fifty-five or older and who has been in the E.S.O.P. for ten years to sell up to 25% of the stock. It is a good idea to take advantage of the "selling" rule just so you can diversify your account.

When you retire, if there is no available market for the stock and you need to withdraw your shares, the company must buy your shares at a price set by an independent appraiser.

SEP IRA's

SEP's are retirement plans for the self-employed. Most mutual fund and life insurance companies offer SEP Plans. The owner/employee can contribute an annual amount of 13.04% of net earnings from self-employment. The deadline for the contribution is the tax return filing date, so it could be as late as October 15 for a person who has approval for two extensions. All contributions are tax deductible, and earnings grow tax deferred. As with other plans, withdrawal restrictions apply before age fifty-nine and one-half.

Keogh Plans

Keogh plans are either **Defined Benefit Plans or Defined Contribution Plans.** Only sole proprietors or partnerships can set up Keogh plans for themselves and their employees. Employees who are at least age twenty-one and have at least one year of service must be allowed to participate. Employer contributions are tax deductible, and employees may be permitted to make nondeductible voluntary contributions to the plan. Keogh's must be set up before December 31 of the applicable tax year, but the plan can be funded as late as April 15, or the due date of the tax return approved with an extension.

A Defined Benefit Keogh allows the lesser of $120,000 or 100% of average net income during the three highest earning years. This can be a tremendous tax saver for individuals who need to boost their retirement and have high profits in their later years. When considering a defined benefit plan, make sure you follow the rules and use a qualified trustee for your plan administrator.

A Defined Contribution Keogh has three plans, 1) a MONEY PURCHASE PLAN, 2) a PROFIT SHARING PLAN, and 3) a COMBINATION of these two. With a money purchase plan, the contribution limit is 20% of net earnings, up to a maximum of $30,000. Once a money purchase plan is established, you must put in the same amount each year. The profit sharing plan allows a contribution of 13.04% of net earnings, up to a maximum of $22,500. The combination plan allows a contribution of 20% of net income, up to a maximum amount of $30,000.

Traditional IRA's

Annual contributions to the IRA remains at $2,000 for singles and now $4,000 for couples, regardless of whether the spouse works. The main features are the tax deferred accumulation of investment earnings and deductible contributions for those in lower tax brackets.

The income ceiling where contributions are not deductible increases in 1998. There is no deduction for singles who have adjusted gross income over $40,000 or for married couples who have an adjusted gross income over $60,000. If a married couple has no qualified retirement plan, their adjusted gross income can be as high as $160,000 before they lose the entire deduction. $10,000 below these income ceilings, the deduction starts to "phase out." No contribution is allowed to a traditional IRA after age seventy and one-half.

Under the taxpayer relief act of 1997, penalty free distributions are allowed up to $10,000 for first-time home buyer expenses and for qualified education expenses of the individual, spouse, child, or grandchild. All money withdrawn is still fully taxable.

The Roth IRA

This much talked about IRA features tax free accumulation of investment earnings like most other retirement plans. The Roth IRA differs from the traditional IRA because the annual contributions are not deductible, regardless of income level. All qualified distributions, however, are 100% tax free. **To be a qualified distribution, the money must have been in the plan for five years and the participant must be at least age fifty-nine and one-half.** Like the traditional IRA, all non-qualified or early distributions are subject to the 10% tax penalty if no hardship rule or exception applies.

All Qualified Distributions Are Tax Free from a Roth IRA

The Roth IRA is subject to income limitations. Phaseouts of contribution amounts occur for adjusted gross incomes between $95,000 and $110,000 for singles, and $150,000 to $160,000 for married couples. **Unlike the traditional IRA, contributions can be made to a Roth IRA after an individual reaches the age of seventy and one-half.**

Individuals who qualify for a Roth IRA may roll over contributions from existing IRA's into Roth IRA's before January 1, 1999, without penalty. All taxable distributions must be included in income, but the taxpayer has four years over which they can average the taxable distribution. Qualified distributions will then come out tax free.

Singles can contribute no more than $2,000 annually to any IRA, whether it be a traditional IRA or a Roth IRA. The same rule applies for married couples, except they can contribute $4,000, $2,000 for each individual.

If your tax bracket is higher now than it will be when you retire, then the traditional IRA is best for you. If your tax bracket will be the same now as when you retire, the results are the same with the Roth IRA and the traditional IRA. If you tax bracket will be higher in retirement than it is now, you will definitely benefit from the Roth IRA. Also, if you are making nondeductible contributions to a traditional IRA and qualify for the Roth IRA, you would be better off with the Roth IRA, because all qualified distributions come out tax free.

The IRA That Isn't an IRA: The Education IRA

This new IRA is for education expenses. Like the Roth IRA and other retirement accounts, all earnings accumulate free of tax. All contributions are nondeductible and limited to $500 per year, per individual. This contribution does not count in the $2,000 limit allowed in traditional or Roth IRA's for each individual. (The Education IRA really isn't an IRA.) No contribution can be made after the beneficiary reaches age eighteen, and all amounts in an Education IRA must be distributed to the beneficiary before age thirty. **Distributions will be tax free and penalty free only if used for educational purposes or transferred to another Education IRA for the benefit of another family member.**

To be eligible to make the $500 contribution, your income must be below a certain level. Singles must have adjusted gross income of $95,000 or below, and couples must have an adjusted gross income below $150,000. A phaseout of contributions occurs between $95,000 and $110,000 for singles and between $150,000 and $160,000 for couples.

When Retirement Benefits Must Begin

The longer you defer taking retirement distributions from your company plan or self-employed plan, the greater the tax free buildup of your fund. To stop this tax deferral, the law required minimum distributions to begin by a certain date. **Employees who continue to work after the year in which they reach age seventy and one-half can delay their first required minimum distribution until April 1 of the year following their year of retirement.** For example, if you reach age seventy and one-half in 1998 but do not retire until the year 2000, your first required distribution does not have to be made until April 1, 2001, the year after you retire. This new rule does not apply to those persons who are more than 5% owners of a business.

The Required Minimum Distribution Is Calculated by Using Annuity Tables That Show Life Expectancies

The required minimum distribution is calculated by using annuity tables that show life expectancies. You can use your own life expectancy or average the expectancy of you and your spouse. If you have a younger spouse, using the joint life expectancy will give you a smaller amount that you MUST take out. Ten years is the maximum amount that is used to calculate a younger spouse, even if the spouse is fifteen or twenty years younger.

Whether you are an employee, self-employed, or not working for a salary, a retirement plan is available for you. It is an excellent way to make your money grow over time. Contributing annually to a plan is one way to assure that you will have a comfortable retirement.

Part 4
Protection

YOU MAY THINK you have a better use for your money than spending it for insurance. The truth is, you cannot safely build your net worth without protecting your assets. Property is vulnerable to unexpected weather conditions. People are vulnerable to accidents and illness. Although insurance costs money, it is a good friend. If you suffer a large loss, owning the right kind of insurance can save you from financial disaster.

The money you spend to preserve assets such as: your earning power, your health, your home, and your possessions is money well spent. Without adequate protection, you stand to lose what you have worked so hard to get. No man or woman can avoid exposure to the hazards of life as long as he/she works, plays, and breathes. With exposure, potential tragedies do occur. **Be wise, and protect yourself against unexpected losses.**

11
Insurance Principles

Why Insurance?

WHEN YOU OWN INSURANCE, you have an agreement with the insurance company that the company will compensate you for covered losses. Typical losses include death, disability, illness, and destruction or theft of property. You buy a dollar amount of protection with the premium dollars you spend. Even if you have made only one premium payment, law requires insurance companies to pay the policy amount.

LIFE INSURANCE gives financial protection from the loss of a person's life so dependents do not suffer when the wage earner who supports them dies. Likewise, with "key man" life insurance, businesses do not suffer when a contributor to the business dies. HEALTH INSURANCE covers the medical bills for short-term and extended illness of all the persons covered under the plan. DISABILITY INSURANCE works to replace a percentage of the insured person's salary for the period he/she is unable to work. PROPERTY AND CASUALTY INSURANCE includes HOMEOWNER'S, RENTER'S, and AUTOMOBILE POLICIES. Homeowner's and renter's insurance covers dwellings and/or personal possessions from such losses as fires, floods, and thefts. These policies also offer liability protection. They protect the insured from lawsuits when a person is injured on the property. Automobile insurance

When You Own Insurance, the Insurance Company Compensates You for Covered Losses

*A Policyholder Files
a Claim with an
Insurance Company
to Collect Money for
the Damages*

pays for damages to persons and property when automobiles, trucks, boats, trailers, and recreational vehicles are involved in accidents, fires, thefts, and other hazards. Each type of insurance will be discussed separately after some ideas about how insurance started, how it is regulated, and how it is sold.

Background

The idea behind insurance is to collect a small sum of money from many people to raise sufficient funds to compensate those who suffer losses from accidents, illness, or death. When you own an insurance policy, you become a policyholder. Insurance companies "pool" policyholders' money through premiums paid to them. When a policyholder suffers a covered loss, he/she can file a claim with the insurance company to collect money for the damages.

Example:

One thousand men, living in a small town, want to provide a continuing income for their families should they suffer a premature death. The town's current statistics, based on what has happened in the past, show that five men out of the one thousand will die each year.

The men decide to each contribute $50 per month, or $600 a year, to a general fund that will be given to the families of those who die. In one year, their "pooled" money equals $600,000. That sum is enough to pay $120,000 each to the five families who lose their family member.

The men had a great idea but ran into numerous problems doing the supervision among themselves. It was a big job to collect $50 monthly from each of them and keep accurate records of when they made their payments. Also, someone had to put the money where it was safe and take charge of paying the claims. They had to keep having meetings to answer questions that came up, such as:

- How should they handle late payments?
- If fewer men died in one year than expected, did they refund the extra money or save it for a year when their death claims increased?
- If more men died than the expected number, should they pay a lesser amount or assess all the members more money to pay the agreed amount?
- Should the money be placed in a safe until needed, or should they invest it?

- What responsibility did the manager have for investing their money? How much investment risk could he take?

Collecting premiums, paying claims, and setting fair standards took full-time administrators. These administrators eventually formed the insurance companies that solved many questions and set standards for the insurance industry as we know them today. As more people bought insurance, the "pooled" money grew, and the earnings of the insurance companies also grew. This raised new questions. After paying all the claims and their administrative expenses, were insurance companies obligated to share these profits with their policyholders?

Many people soon saw the advantages of pooling their funds to insure property, health, and disability as well as the loss of life. As more people participated, insurance became big business. Politicians got involved and made laws to regulate the industry and to protect the policyholders. These laws became the insurance codes of each state. Each state's insurance code now regulates the insurance industry within that state. The state insurance code sets requirements for financial responsibility and establishes the guidelines that govern insurance companies in what they can and cannot do.

Although each state regulates the insurance companies doing business within their boundaries, the companies must adhere to certain national and industrial standards, e.g.:

- Life insurance policies allow a thirty-day grace period for late payments before they let a policy lapse.
- If a policyholder has been truthful and paid all premiums when due, the company must pay the claim.
- Upon the death of the insured, life insurance companies must pay the face amount of the policy, regardless of how many death claims are filed that year.
- Life insurance companies cannot assess more than the agreed premium, even when they have more death claims to pay than they anticipated.

Insurance Companies Must Adhere to National and Industrial Standards

Health and disability insurers and property and casualty companies will cancel a policy if they do not receive the premium by the due date. If policyholders let their policies lapse due to late payments, the company does not have to reinstate them upon receipt of the late payment. **At each renewal period, insurance companies can raise their rates on**

homeowner's, health, disability, and automobile policies. They often do when they have more claims to pay.

If insurance companies pay fewer claims than expected, they do not refund the extra money to their policyholders. They save the money to cover future claims or consider it "profit." Premiums paid are protection against uncertainty, not an investment that will give you a return.

Premiums Are Protection against Uncertainty; They Are Not an Investment

Insurance Commissioner

Each state has an elected insurance commissioner who oversees the insurance industry, making certain companies and licensed agents comply with the state insurance code. The commissioner has a major responsibility to check out a company's financial responsibility. Every company that does business in the state, and all products offered by that company, must have the commissioner's approval. Regulations do vary from state to state. A product approved in one state may not be approved in another state. The commissioner also oversees licensing procedures for insurance agents. He/she issues the licenses and sets the ongoing educational requirements for license renewal.

In addition, the commissioner handles complaints and sets penalties for agents and companies who violate the insurance code. These violations usually occur when agents or literature misrepresent a product. The improper handling of premiums or not paying claims as agreed are other serious violations. The commissioner can impose heavy penalties or fines and/or revoke the licenses of companies and agents who repeatedly commit violations.

> **State Insurance Commissioner**
> • Approves Insurance Companies and Their Products
> • Licenses Agents
> • Handles Complaints
> • Sets Penalties for Violators

Insurance Agents

You can buy an insurance policy only from licensed insurance agents. These agents must pass a test to get their license, and once licensed, they can sell life and disability products or property and casualty products. Some agents are licensed to sell both. They receive commissions for the policies they sell and service. Their ongoing educational requirements update them on changes in the insurance codes and keep them abreast of changes in their product line.

A good agent will keep you informed of industry changes and will work to save you premium dollars. When you have questions about coverage, claims, or premiums, call your agent for information and advice.

Agents often compete for your business. If a new agent offers you a new policy for considerably less money, make sure you have all the facts before switching policies. Many policyholders go with a new company that offers better rates, only to later find out they bought inferior coverage. It is a good idea to call the writing agent on your original policy before switching. This agent might know details about the new policy that you never considered.

Self-Insurance

"Self-insurance" refers to the amount you personally can afford to pay to cover a loss of life, a loss of property, an illness, or an accident. You can reduce your premium dollars if you take it upon yourself to provide a certain amount of self-insurance.

Example:

If your medical insurance has a $500 or $1,000 deductible instead of a $100 deductible, your premium will be much lower. The higher deductible is your self-insurance amount. It represents the sum you are willing to pay each year to have lower premiums. The same concept applies to homeowner's and automobile policies, because higher deductibles, the amount you pay, reduce your annual premium.

If you have money in savings or investments that your family can liquidate should you die, that extra money can be your "self-insurance." It will reduce the amount of life insurance you need to replace your income. Likewise, having less insurance requires a lesser premium.

Premiums

The fortunate ones, those who never have to file a claim, never collect on the premiums they have paid for pure insurance. Insurance companies use premium money to pay current claims. **Premiums buy peace of mind; they protect you, your family, and your business against financial loss should unfortunate accidents, illness, or death occur.**

A Good Agent Will Work to Save You Premium Dollars

The Fortunate Ones Never Collect on the Premiums They Have Paid for Pure Insurance

Insurance Is a Financial Guardian for Unknown Future Tragedies That Could Happen

You never know when you may die, become disabled, or get sick. If you own a home, it is subject to destruction by violent weather or fire. This could mean losing all of your personal possessions. Automobiles can be completely demolished in an accident. Along with the accident, if another person is hurt or killed by your automobile, you could be sued for the damages. The payment of insurance premiums give you protection against all of these perils. Insurance is a financial guardian for unknown future tragedies that could happen.

LIFE INSURANCE pays a sum of money for the loss of a life. The types of policies and the amount of protection you might need, if any, is covered in chapter 12. Chapter 13 then goes into **HEALTH and DISABILITY INSURANCE.** Many workers have health coverage as a fringe benefit paid through their employers. They may or may not have a choice of plans. This chapter will help you better understand your health insurance policy if you have one, or guide you to the best type of policy to purchase if you employer does not pay for it. Most workers do not have adequate disability protection.

HOMEOWNER'S and RENTER'S INSURANCE as well as **AUTOMOBILE INSURANCE** come under Property and Casualty Insurance, the topic for chapter 14. You will read about the importance of protection and available options for your policies.

12
Life Insurance

LIFE INSURANCE protects dependents from loss of income when their provider dies. It also can protect a business when a valued employee dies. The proceeds from life insurance "replaces" the insured person's future earnings or business skills.

Life insurance sold to businesses covers the life of an important person in the organization. The insurance proceeds make it possible for the business to buy the deceased's outstanding stock and/or replace his/her professional skills by hiring another professional.

The Proceeds from Life Insurance "Replaces" the Insured Person's Future Earnings or Business Skills

Policy Terms and Conditions

Life insurance policies are contracts between the **INSURER** (the insurance company) and the **POLICYHOLDER** (the one who pays the premiums), for the benefit of the **BENEFICIARY** (the one designated to receive the money). The **INSURED** (the person covered) may or may not be the policyholder. **The insurance company promises to pay the FACE AMOUNT of the policy when the insured dies or when the policy matures, as long as the policyholder keeps the policy in force by making the required premium payments.**

Exclusions and additions to the basic policy must be in writing and made a part of the policy. **All additions and exclusions to a company's basic policy must be brought to the attention of the insured for approval.**

An **INCONTESTABLE CLAUSE,** found in all policies, states that after the policy has been in force for a certain time, usually one to two years, the insurance company cannot void the policy except for nonpayment of premiums. If the insurance company discovers fraud because the applicant lied on a material point, they can cancel during the contestable period. Once the period ends, however, the company cannot void the policy even if the applicant committed fraud.

Most state laws require that an insurance company have a **GRACE PERIOD. They must give the policyholder a stated time (usually thirty days) to make a past-due premium payment before they cancel the policy.**

A life insurance company only issues a policy if the beneficiary has an insurable interest in the life of the insured. To have an **insurable interest,** the beneficiary must suffer an economic or emotional loss upon the insured's death. Usually, an insurable interest does not exist between friends, cousins, aunts, or uncles. **Relationships that have an obvious insurable interest include: husband and wife, parent and child, creditor and debtor, and business partners. You always have an insurable interest in your own life.**

If the policyholder is not the insured, it is up to the insurance company, based on information provided by the insurance agent, to make certain that an insurable interest exists between them before issuing a policy. **Once the policy is issued, and kept in force with paid-up premiums, the insurance company must keep their end of the bargain and pay the face amount at the death of the insured.** They can only cancel if they discover fraud during the contestable period.

Law requires life insurance companies to always pay **the face amount** of the policy. It doesn't matter how many death claims have been filed during the year or how long the policyholder has paid premiums—three months or fifty years. **A most attractive feature of life insurance is that the beneficiary receives the death benefit completely free of income tax. No other alternative will provide an immediate, tax free cash settlement for the loss of a life.**

Underwriting

The procedure of approving a person's health condition in order to issue a life insurance policy is called **UNDERWRITING.** When applying for life insurance, you may or may not need a complete medical exam before the company issues the policy. **Often, a paramedic, who comes to** your home, completes the required exam. **The extent of the exam varies according to age, type of policy requested, and the amount of coverage applied for.** Insurance underwriters normally require urine specimens and detailed answers to their health questionnaire before they approve an application for insurance.

The company considers a person with a preexisting health problem a higher risk. **Standard risks pay the normal premium. The higher risks or substandard risks pay higher premiums according to their substandard rating.** Insurance companies automatically consider smokers substandard risks and charge them higher premiums than nonsmokers. **Sometimes, in order to verify a person's health condition, the underwriters at insurance companies order medical records from various doctors and hospitals.**

People Who Are Higher Risks Pay Higher Premiums

Mortality Tables

Mortality tables show how long people are expected to live. The information comes from statistics gathered over past years showing the ages of the people who died. For example, the insurance commissioner's current mortality table might state that out of every 1,000 persons, 1.90 died at age twenty and 16.08 died at age sixty.

Mortality tables show the number of people who died within each age group. These tables decide the cost of insurance. **Since fewer people die in their early years, the cost of insurance is cheaper for younger people. Statistics show that the death rate increases as people age, so each succeeding year, the cost of life insurance increases.**

Mortality Tables Show How Long People at Various Ages Are Expected to Live

Group Insurance

Private businesses and federal, state, and local governments usually offer group life insurance to their employees. **In this case, one policy covers the group of people. The insurance company determines the premiums by the group's occupation and its average age.** The insurance company will admit all members of the group without a medical exam during a specified enrollment period. Most group plans only allow members to make changes or allow new members to enroll during a designated time of the year. **Group insurance uses decreasing term policies, discussed later in this chapter.**

During the Enrollment Period, Group Plans Insure All Members without a Medical Exam

How Much Life Insurance Do You Need?

Considerations

Do you have loved ones who are dependent upon your income? If they would suffer financial hardship if you should die prematurely, you need life insurance. **The amount of life insurance you need depends upon how much income your family will require if your earnings suddenly stop.** You need to consider:

- **The money your spouse or family counts on from you each year to meet LIVING EXPENSES.** Many insurance representatives use 75% of the family's current income as a benchmark when advising their clients how much insurance they need to purchase. If you have children, look at how much money your surviving spouse will need to raise and educate them.

- **Consider your SPOUSE'S SALARY. If your spouse is not currently working, look at his/her employability.** Would it be "easy" for your surviving spouse to find a job, and if so, what is the potential salary? If you have small children and your spouse is not working full-time now, your spouse will need additional funds for child care.

- **Then, look at the MONTHLY BILLS your surviving spouse would have to pay.** If you have many bills, such as car loans and other credit payments that could be a burden, consider sufficient insurance to pay them off in a lump sum upon your death.

- **Next, look at your LIQUID ASSETS. They can be used as "self-insurance" to reduce the amount of insurance you need to purchase from a company.** For instance, if you decide you need $200,000 of life insurance, but you have over $50,000 of liquid assets, reduce the amount of insurance you need to purchase by $50,000.

- **FINAL EXPENSES include funeral, burial fees, and hospital and doctor bills not covered by insurance.** Add an estimate for these charges to the total money needed by the surviving spouse.

- **Subtract from this "needed" income the amount your surviving spouse would receive from your employer's GROUP LIFE INSURANCE plan (if any) and from SOCIAL SECURITY (if any).**

Social Security Benefits

Social Security benefits for surviving family members vary according to the wages and contributions the deceased member made during his/her lifetime. For the family to qualify for benefits, the covered member must be "fully" or "currently" insured. "Fully" insured generally means at least forty quarters of contributions (ten years worth), and "currently" insured means at least six quarters of contributions during the most recent thirteen quarters.

Your spouse or divorced spouse, under age sixty, can receive benefits only if he/she cares for a child under age sixteen or cares for a child who was disabled before age twenty-two. Children under age eighteen (nineteen if still in high school) or those disabled before age twenty-two qualify for additional benefits. All family benefits are subject to certain income limitations.

All Family Benefits Are Subject to Certain Income Limitations

Example Cases: Need for Life Insurance

To help you evaluate your need for life insurance, compare your situation with the following three cases. Recommendations may differ based on personal preferences.

Case A:

Jean and Dennis have no children. Both work, and each earns approximately $35,000 a year. They have no debt except their $800 monthly house payment. Their total monthly living expenses are $1,500. They own stocks and mutual funds worth $40,000 and have $15,000 in a bank CD.

Recommendation:

Neither of them need life insurance, because the survivor would suffer no financial hardship. The salary for either, combined with their assets, would more than cover current expenses. Owning life insurance on each other, however, would increase their options while dealing with the trauma of losing a spouse. It is difficult to work when emotionally distraught, and the proceeds from the life insurance could fund a sufficient recovery period.

Case B:

Mike and Louise have two teenagers. Louise's annual salary is $40,000; Mike's is $25,000. Louise has a $75,000 group policy with her employer; Mike has no coverage. Their monthly house payment is $1,100, and their outstanding debt, including car loans and credit cards, equals $1,150 monthly. Each month, they spend between $3,000 and $3,200 for their house payment, upkeep, utilities, car payments, bills, food, clothing, and recreation.

Recommendation:

Should either Mike or Louise die, the other would have a difficult time keeping up with their monthly payments with the increasing costs of raising their children. They both need insurance policies to protect each other, at least until they accumulate some savings or investments and reduce their debts.

If Mike should die, Louise wants to keep working. She feels it would be difficult to raise the children, send them to college, and continue their present lifestyle without Mike's income. A $125,000 policy on Mike would give Louise an annual $12,500 income that would last for fourteen years if the $125,000 earned a consistent 5% (see How Long Will Your Money Last?, Appendix B).

If Louise had a $150,000 life insurance policy, in addition to her $75,000 group life, this $225,000 would give Mike and the children an additional $24,750 a year for twelve years if the $225,000 principal earned a consistent 5%. This amount, combined with Mike's salary would be sufficient to pay final expenses, continue payments on their ongoing bills, and provide extra money for the children to go to college.

Case C:

Jay and Maxine have four children. Jay's current salary is $30,000. Their only monthly debts are their house payment of $600 and their car payment of $150. They spend approximately $1,700 monthly for living expenses, including their house and car payments. Maxine is a home-maker and has never been employed.

If something happened to Jay, Maxine would not have enough money to provide for herself and the children. Since she has never worked, getting a job and working in addition to raising their four children would be most difficult.

Jay is fully covered by social security, so according to current social security tables and the amount Jay has contributed to the system, in the beginning, Maxine and the children could receive up to $1,200 a month in family benefits. Then, as each child reaches sixteen years of age, Maxine's payment would be reduced, with the child's benefit ceasing at age eighteen. Once the last child reaches age sixteen, Maxine would not be eligible for further benefits until age sixty.

Recommendation:

Social security alone would not be enough for Maxine to keep up with current living expenses. She would need at least $500 more each month, along with $5,000 for expected final expenses. An $85,000 insurance policy on Jay would give Maxine $567 monthly, if the money earned 8%. With a policy this size and with earnings of 8%, Maxine would not need to dip into the principal of $85,000 in order to meet her family's ongoing living expenses. But, if the money earned only 5%, she would need a $120,000 policy to receive $500 each month and also preserve the principal ($120,000 at 5% earns $6,000 annually, or $500 monthly). Alternatively, the $85,000 policy earning 5%, with Maxine withdrawing from the principal at 8% (see How Long Will Your Money Last?, Appendix B), would give her $6,800 annually, or $567 monthly, for twenty years. After the children get older, unless Maxine could go back to school and learn a marketable skill so she could work and support herself, a larger sum of insurance would be needed to fund Maxine's living expenses after the family support from Jay's social security benefits stops.

In this case, insurance on Maxine is also important. If anything would happen to her, Jay would have to pay an additional $300 each month for child care in order for him to keep working. Maxine needs $45,000 of coverage with Jay named as the primary beneficiary to cover child care expenses should she die. To save premium dollars, she can be added as a rider to Jay's policy. (Adding riders are discussed later in this chapter.)

For your own situation, first decide if you need life insurance. Then, look at the minimum coverage required by your survivors to avoid financial hardship. Next, get several quotes from different insurance agents for the same basic coverage. Be sure to compare "like" policies: term with term, universal life with universal life, etc.

The amount of life insurance you need will be based upon:
- what you can **afford for premiums,**
- **assets** that your surviving spouse can liquidate,
- the amount needed for ongoing family **living expenses,**
- the continuing payments on your **monthly bills** and **other obligations,**
- expected **final expenses** (funeral/burial) not covered by insurance,
- how much your surviving spouse will earn if he/she works (will money be needed for child care?), and
- expected benefits receivable under **group plans** and **social security.**

Types of Policies

Some insurance contracts require higher premiums but include a built-in savings plan. Others have lower premiums and are for "pure" insurance without the savings plan. In both types of policies, you can add to their coverage by purchasing riders.

The cost of life insurance for young people is inexpensive because so few die; but, the cost of insurance premiums for older people is very expensive because far greater numbers die each year. All insurance policies have one similarity; each year that a person gets older, the cost of insurance goes up. This fact is true in every contract. If the premiums do not get higher, it is because you have "prepaid" the increases through higher premiums in the earlier years or because the coverage decreases. Most differences between policies are created by the way the insurance contract treats the excess premium a policyholder pays to the company. Pure insurance among different carriers is similar.

The Cost of Insurance Increases with Age

Term Policies

Term insurance premiums are for "pure" insurance. These policies do not have attached savings account provisions. Term insurance is offered for a specified time, after which it is subject to renewal or termination. Term premiums are lower because the insured pays only for insurance coverage, nothing more. Each year that the insured grows older, the premiums increase. Most people who buy term insurance plan to keep the policy only until their children leave home or until they accumulate sufficient assets to self-insure.

Term Policies Include:
- **Annual Renewable Term**
- **Decreasing Term**
- **Level Term**
- **Deposit Term**

A definition of these policies, plus the advantages and disadvantages of each policy follows.

Annual Renewable Term

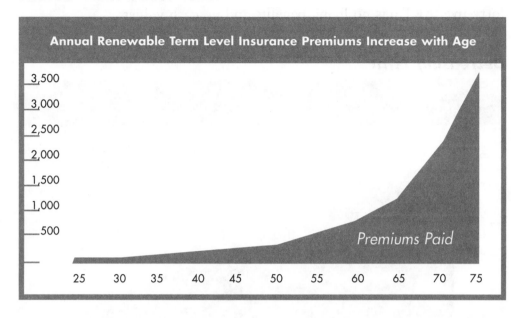

An Annual Renewable Term (ART) policy has a level face amount with increasing annual premiums. The policy must be renewed each year, and the company may require new proof of insurability before it does renew. Since we never know when or if we will become ill, and through the illness may then become a higher risk or even uninsurable, new proof of insurability in the future is an important consideration.

Most ART policyholders cancel when they get older and their premiums start to skyrocket. For example, a male age thirty who is a nonsmoker and in excellent health would pay $145 for $100,000 of term coverage. At age fifty, the premium would be $418 annually, and by age sixty-five, it would have risen to $1,350. Those who succeed in saving and investing can "self-insure" in other investment and savings accounts so they can drop the policy by the time the premiums become "unaffordable." Having no insurance later in life is not detrimental for these "savers," because they have adequate liquid assets in other accounts to provide equal protection.

Advantages of Annual Renewable Term. ART gives the highest coverage for the lowest premium. Due to low mortality rates, the premiums are affordable for young to middle-aged persons.

Disadvantages of Annual Renewable Term. Later in life, if the insured develops a chronic illness such as diabetes or heart disease, he/she may become uninsurable or have such high premiums that coverage is prohibitive. Some ART contracts allow renewal without evidence of insurability, but with most companies, this option expires around age forty-five. ART has no living benefits and no cash values.

Decreasing Term

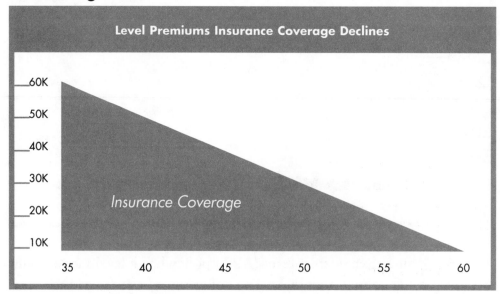

Decreasing Term has level premiums, but the amount of coverage declines each year. Group plans usually offer this policy type because the group can pay the same premium amount for all members of the group. The premium is the same because the coverage varies. When the group contract states coverage of $50,000, older members do not have $50,000 of coverage; their coverage may be only $20,000 or less.

Decreasing term is often sold as mortgage insurance or credit insurance. The coverage declines with the loan balance. Should the borrower die, the insurance pays off the loan. As the borrower retires the outstanding loan balance, the insurance coverage on the loan appropriately declines.

Advantages of Decreasing Term. Level premiums fit some needs. They are fair for group plans because employers can make equal contributions for all employees under the same policy.

Disadvantages of Decreasing Term. The amount of coverage decreases every year. Older members of group plans have less insurance than the face amount of the policy. Younger members of the group can often get more coverage elsewhere for the same premium, since the premiums are based on the group's average age. As with other term contracts, no cash buildup exists.

Level Term

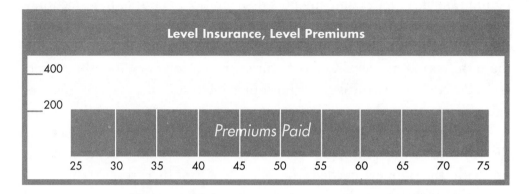

Level Term will have a level face amount and level premiums throughout the life of the contract. Since the "real" cost of insurance is less in the younger years, the company collects a double or triple premium in the early years of the policy. This extra money, with the interest it earns over those earlier years, helps to pay for the more expensive premiums as the insured grows older.

Advantages of Level Term. Since the premiums are level, they remain affordable during the later years.

Disadvantages of Level Term. The insured must make certain the policy stays in force without new evidence of insurability. If the company periodically requires new evidence of insurability, the policyholder must assume that risk. The premiums are higher than ART during the early years when younger people are likely to have less money to spend on insurance. Since level term has no cash value buildup, the owners must have the discipline to develop a separate savings program.

Deposit Term

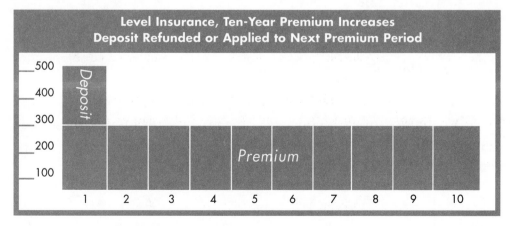

Deposit Term provides level term coverage for various periods such as five, ten, or fifteen years, the most common being ten years. The policy owner pays an additional deposit at the beginning of the contract period. The insurance company puts this additional deposit in a side fund to collect interest for the term of the contract. After the insured pays the first year's deposit and monthly premiums, the remaining premiums for the term period are level and, of course, much lower. When the period ends, the company returns the deposit plus interest to the insured, encouraging that it be used as a new deposit to buy insurance for another term.

Advantages of Deposit Term. At the end of the designated period, the "forced" savings through the required deposit makes it easier to come up with the money needed to renew for another term. The level premiums throughout the term make continued payments easier.

Disadvantages of Deposit Term. If the policyholder does not pay the annual premiums for the full term, he/she loses the entire deposit. Typically, the first-year deposit is usually double the annual premium, so this risk of loss is a significant disadvantage.

The premiums for all term insurance contracts buy affordable insurance coverage. There is no cash value buildup and no return for the money paid in. The premiums paid buy peace of mind. Their sole purpose is to protect the insured's beneficiaries against financial loss if the insured dies prematurely.

Permanent Policies

All forms of permanent insurance include a savings provision, or cash value, that comes from paying the higher premiums.

Types of Permanent Policies Include:
- Whole Life
- Modified Life
- Limited-Pay Life
- Single Premium Life
- Variable Life
- Universal Life

A definition of each policy plus the policies advantages and disadvantages follows.

Whole Life

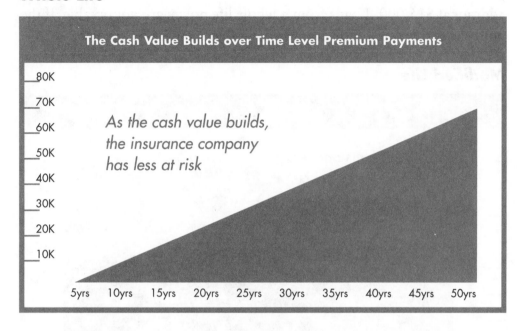

The Cash Value Builds over Time Level Premium Payments

As the cash value builds, the insurance company has less at risk

WHOLE LIFE contracts are permanent insurance. **The insurance company saves a portion of the premium in a side fund, which becomes the policy's cash value.** The side fund grows each year through compound interest earnings and additional payments made to the contract above the cost of insurance already built in to the premium. **The insurance company has more money at risk when the cash value is low.** Then, as the cash value builds, they have less money at risk since the face amount they pay includes the cash value. For example, with a $100,000 whole life policy that has a cash value of $30,000, the insurance company is at risk for the difference, or $70,000. **The cash value is always used to pay the face amount. So, as the cash value increases, the insurance company has less at risk in the policy.** The amount of coverage does not change unless the cash value exceeds certain limits. If this happens, federal guidelines require the face amount to also increase.

As long as the policy is in force, the cash value belongs to the insurance company. The insured must cancel the contract or borrow the cash value to receive it. In fact, if the policyholder borrows the cash value and does not pay it back, the insurance company subtracts the amount owed (principal plus interest) from the death claim paid to the beneficiary. For example, if a policyholder borrows $30,000 of their cash value at 5% interest from a $100,000 whole life policy, and does not repay the loan, the company will reduce the death claim by the $30,000 loan plus the accrued interest. At 5%, interest charges are $1,500 each year. So, in ten years, unpaid interest will reduce the face amount by an additional $15,000. Loans from a whole life policy are not taxable. If the policy is surrendered, however, the gain over deposits is taxable.

Modified Life

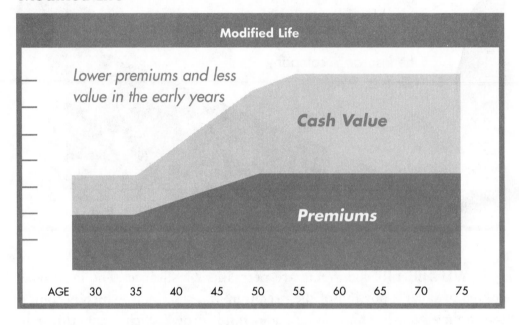

MODIFIED LIFE is a variation of the whole life contract. It has lower premiums and lower cash value during the earlier years. Then the premiums and, accordingly, the cash value increase during the "mid-earning" years when the owner's income is usually higher. This policy makes permanent insurance affordable for younger persons.

Limited-Pay Life

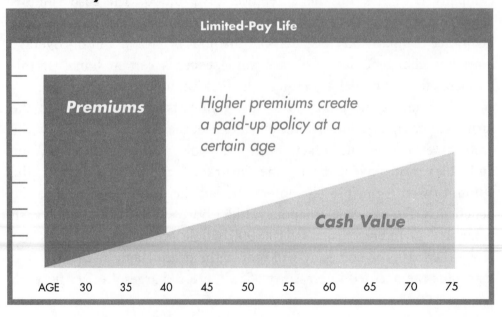

LIMITED-PAY LIFE is still another type of whole life. The policy-holder pays higher premiums for a certain number of years, such as fifteen or twenty, so the policy becomes "paid-up" at the end of the designated term. The insurance remains in force until death, with no further premiums due.

Single Premium Whole Life

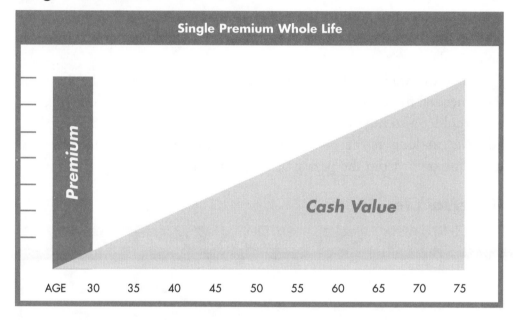

SINGLE PREMIUM WHOLE LIFE follows the same concept as limited-pay life. **The entire premium is paid in one lump sum to buy a certain amount of coverage until the policyholder dies.**

Variable Life

VARIABLE LIFE has exceptions to the basic rule that the insurance company must pay the face amount of the policy. **In this policy, the insured assumes the risk for the investments. Variable life invests the premiums into stocks and bonds, similar to a mutual fund.** The owner can take advantage of higher earnings but gives up a guaranteed cash value and a guaranteed death benefit. **The policy is worth what the investments earn minus the administrative fees and charges.** For example, a variable life policy could decline in value during a bear market (declining stock market). Should the insured die during this period, the beneficiaries would receive the policy's value, not the face amount

On the other hand, if the investments owned by the variable life policy do well, the contract will show considerable gains over the traditional fixed account. In such a case, the cash value is always available to the policyholder, and the insurance company always pays the full value of the policy to the beneficiaries.

Advantages of Whole Life. After several years of payments, the owner has a cash value in the insurance contract. If the policyholder stops paying premiums, the cash value must be paid to the policyholder or provided through equivalent benefits (covered later under nonforfeiture options). Whole life has a living benefit, which is the cash value available at termination of the policy or for borrowing. For those who don't have the discipline to save or invest, the whole life policy forces a savings plan.

Disadvantages of Whole Life. The premiums are much higher than those needed to purchase equivalent term insurance. With whole life, the policyholder also buys a savings plan. They do not own this savings plan, however, as long as the policy remains in force. To get their cash, they must borrow it from the policy or terminate the coverage.

Universal Life

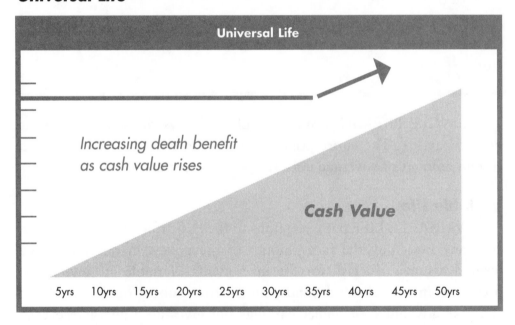

UNIVERSAL LIFE is the most flexible of permanent insurance contracts. Universal life became popular in the early 1980s when rising interest rates made a mockery of the low interest earnings on whole life policies. Because insurance companies traditionally invested in long-term bonds with fixed interest rates, the side funds of their whole life contracts could not compete with the prevailing short-term interest rates fueled by rising inflation. Cash values were earning 3% to 4%, while the going money market rates were 12% to 14% and higher! Obviously, people wanted the higher rates. This situation forced the insurance industry to develop new, more flexible products, or lose their whole life business.

Universal life became the new product, designed to compete in the current economic market. Universal life cash values were invested in short-term, less conservative investments allowing insurance companies to pay competitive interest rates. Variable universal life is also available for more aggressive investors.

Insurance companies designed universal life policies to be flexible so the policy could adapt to changing life situations. Although certain criteria must be met to be in compliance with federal tax guidelines, the policyholder can pay in more money, pay in less money, or even stop payments without canceling the contract.

Tax guidelines require that the death benefit and the cash values stay within certain limits. The law requires that the death benefit must also increase when the cash value reaches a certain level to maintain a certain ratio between the face amount of the policy and the cash value. **The insurance company must always have a certain percentage at risk for the proceeds to the beneficiary(ies) to be tax free.**

As with whole life policies, a universal life contract owner may take a loan from the policy. The basis can also be withdrawn, and it is also nontaxable since it is a return of your own money. Such a withdrawal will reduce the insurance in the contract to a proportionate amount. This is an important concept when the owner uses the policy to provide tax-free income.

Advantages of Universal Life. This contract has great flexibility and can be written to meet a policyholder's changing needs. The premiums can fluctuate with changes in income as long as enough is paid in to cover the "pure" cost of insurance and keep the coverage and cash account within the mandated guidelines. Companies invest the cash value, or side fund, in short-term investments that earn current interest rates. Many offer variable contracts with investments in stocks and/or bonds. Past performance of many of these funds has exceeded average interest rates. This may or may not be the case in the future.

With a sizable amount in the side fund, a policyholder can stop payments and let the side fund pay the premiums. This pays the premiums with pretax dollars, because the earnings on the side fund accumulate tax free. Another positive feature of universal life is the flexibility of the contract to raise or lower the death benefit to meet changing needs without switching to a new policy. This policy can also be used to supplement retirement income through policy loans and withdrawals from the policy.

Disadvantages of Universal Life. Deposits going into the "cash" fund have a sales charge. For example, on every $100 paid in, the company will deduct a certain percentage, such as 6%, or $6, as a sales charge, so only $94 gets credited to the policyholder's account. Also, the owner must keep a specified amount of insurance to meet certain cash value levels. If the cash value increases substantially, the owner will need to buy more insurance to match the new higher cash value.

Nonforfeiture Options

All permanent insurance policies have what the industry calls **NONFORFEITURE OPTIONS. This means, should the policy owner stop paying premiums, the company must make the cash value, or its equivalent in insurance options, available to the policyholder.**
The policyholder "elects" the options he/she prefers. The obvious choice is to surrender the policy for its cash value. Another alternative, however, is to **purchase REDUCED, PAID-UP INSURANCE.** You can instruct the insurance company to buy a single premium policy for a lesser amount with the cash value that has accumulated in your "lapsed" policy. Here, the insured will have a lesser amount of coverage paid to a certain age.

EXTENDED TERM is still another option. Here, the company uses the cash value to buy term insurance equal to the prior policy's face amount. The number of years the insured has coverage depends upon his/her age and the accumulated cash value of the lapsed policy.

If a policy with a cash value lapses due to nonpayment of premiums beyond the thirty-day grace period, the extended term provision automatically goes into effect unless the policyholder notifies the insurance company that he/she elects another option, such as taking the cash, or reduced paid-up insurance.

Policy Add-Ons: Riders

Additional coverage added to an original policy is called a rider. The premium increases with the addition of these riders, but often riders provide the least expensive way to get additional coverage. Riders can cover additional persons other than the insured. The company can add riders to any of the standard policies.

Term Rider

This adds an amount of level or decreasing term insurance to the policy. Policyholders often use this rider to purchase insurance for their spouse or other family members. To save premium dollars, add coverage for a spouse as a term rider.

Example:

If you want a $100,000 universal life or whole life policies on both a husband and a wife, have the agent write:

1) A $50,000 policy on the husband and add the wife with a $50,000 term rider, and

2) a $50,000 policy on the wife and add the husband with a $50,000 term rider.

This will give $100,000 coverage for both persons and save premium dollars.

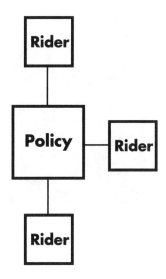

Children's Term Rider

This rider covers children, usually through age twenty-four, for amounts ranging from $1,000 to $20,000 per child.

Family Income Rider or Family Maintenance

Purchasing this rider guarantees a monthly income if the insured becomes disabled or suffers a major illness and is unable to work. The amount paid and the time period for the payments depends upon the details outlined in the rider.

Guaranteed Insurability Rider

This rider guarantees that the insured can purchase more insurance at designated ages without new proof of insurability. With most companies, this option expires at age forty-five.

Waiver of Premium Rider

If the insured becomes totally and permanently disabled, the policy remains in force with no further premiums due. The policy will pay double or triple the face amount of the policy if the insured dies from an accidental death.

Disability Income Rider

If the insured becomes permanently and totally disabled, he/she can receive regular monthly income from the insurance company.

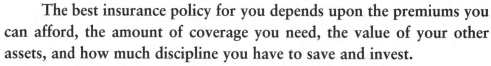

Permanent vs. Term: What Should You Buy?

The best insurance policy for you depends upon the premiums you can afford, the amount of coverage you need, the value of your other assets, and how much discipline you have to save and invest.

Decide the type and amount of coverage you want, then compare several policies. While "shopping," you may want to tell the insurance agent how much you can afford for premiums and see what he/she recommends. You need someone who will be objective in assessing your needs and making recommendations.

The biggest decision will be whether you buy term or permanent insurance. Pros and cons exist for each type of policy, as illustrated in the following case histories.

Two Case Histories: Permanent Insurance vs. Term Insurance

Two males, both age thirty and nonsmokers, with comparable incomes, bought $100,000 of insurance. Lee Johnson bought a WHOLE LIFE policy. Tom Allen bought ANNUAL RENEWABLE TERM and saved the difference between the whole life and the ART premium. Let's look at each of their situations twenty years later at age fifty.

Lee Johnson has paid premiums of $898 each year for his whole life policy. During the past twenty year period, his total outlay for premiums was $17,960. The guaranteed cash value in his policy now equals $21,215. He has had the advantage of $100,000 of insurance for twenty years and is ahead by $3,255 if he subtracts the premiums paid from the current cash value.

Lee has many options open to him: he can keep his coverage in effect by paying the same $898 annual premium and continue to build up his cash value until he retires; he can borrow the cash value; or he can terminate the policy and receive the $21,215 in cash. He can also take advantage of the nonforfeiture options by using the cash value to purchase a paid-up, extended term policy requiring no additional premiums, or a reduced, paid-up policy that will give him a lesser amount of coverage.

Tom Allen purchased annual renewable term insurance. Although he could afford the whole life policy, he did not want the insurance company to own his savings plan. Using the same dollar amount required to purchase a whole life policy, he bought the less costly ART and saved the difference. His first year's premium was only $127, compared to the whole life annual premium of $898, so he saved $771. By the tenth year, his ART premium had risen to $190, so he still saved $708 that year. By the twentieth year, he saved only $392 because his premium had grown to $506. Over the twenty years, Tom put the "excess premium" into an income fund that earned an average rate of 8%. By age fifty, he had $34,507 in this fund. Tom also had $100,000 of insurance coverage during the past twenty years.

Tom's income fund can't be compared to the cash value in Lee's whole life policy without considering the tax consequences. With Lee's whole life policy, he has paid no income taxes on his cash buildup since it is tax free. Tom, however, has paid additional taxes each year on the interest and dividends earned on his income fund. In fact, over the twenty years, he paid $9,413 in taxes on the fund's earnings. The after-tax value of his fund is therefore $25,094. Compare this to Lee's $21,215 whole life cash value.

Although Tom has full use of his income fund, he faces another problem that Lee does not have. His insurance premiums rise each year, so fewer "savings" dollars go into his income fund. By age fifty-seven, his premiums will be higher than the original $898 he planned to set aside. Since his insurance premiums increase each year and will be over $2,400 at age seventy, Tom most likely will let his policy lapse, and his beneficiary will lose out on the $100,000 death benefit.

Whether you should buy term or whole life insurance is a choice you will need to make. Pros and cons exist for each type of policy. If you are a disciplined saver and consistently put money aside that would other-wise be spent on premiums, you will come out ahead by buying term insurance and directly owning your savings plan. On the other hand, if you would not save or invest the difference in premiums between permanent and term insurance, owning a permanent policy gives you more options. Many people intend to invest the difference but actually don't. When this is the case, a permanent plan will serve you better because it forces a savings plan that you would not otherwise have. Also,

Pros and Cons Exist for Term and Whole Life Insurance

you must face the fact that as you get older, term premiums may become unaffordable. Unless you accumulate equivalent savings and investments, your survivors could be left with little or nothing.

Insurance companies continually design new life insurance policies, but the following gives a summary of the most common permanent and term insurance plans. All are explained in this chapter.

Table 12.1—Types of Insurance Policies

Term	Permanent Whole Life
Annual Renewable Term	Universal Life
Level Term	Variable Life
Decreasing Term	Single Premium Life
Deposit Term	Limited-Pay Life
	Modified Life

13

Health and Disability Insurance

HEALTH CARE COSTS have increased 266% during the past ten years. Chart 13.1 shows total U.S. health care expenditures since 1960.[1]

Chart 13.1—U.S. Health Care Costs (In billions of dollars)

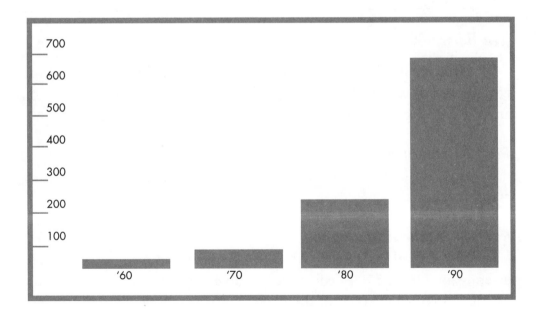

Sources for Health Insurance

Health care is so expensive today that without adequate coverage, a major accident or illness could easily wipe out all of your assets. Health and disability insurance can provide financial protection against such misfortune. Sources for health insurance include:

- Employer Group Plans
- Medicare
- Medicaid
- Health Maintenance Organizations
- Private Policies

Employer Group Plans

Most employers offer excellent group plans, often under a choice of policies. **Many employers pay all or a portion of the premium as employee fringe benefits.** Employers also contribute to a worker's compensation fund that will cover an employee's medical expenses should they get injured on the job.

Under C.O.B.R.A., a current federal law, if an employee loses their job, they can convert an employer provided policy to an individual policy with the same insurer. The premiums will be higher for the individual policy, but any preexisting conditions remain covered.

Medicare

Medicare is a health insurance program underwritten by the federal government. It is available for people age sixty-five and older or those of any age who are permanently disabled. Medicare has two parts:

Part A: Hospital Insurance

This hospital insurance pays for hospitalization and other associated costs.

Part B: Medical Insurance

The medical insurance pays 80% of all covered medical costs after meeting an annual $100 deductible. Eligible persons pay a low monthly premium that is taken out of their social security check.

Medicaid

Medicaid is a state program that is federally funded. It pays medical bills for low income people of all ages. Those who qualify for welfare automatically qualify for Medicaid. Eligibility and the extent of the paid medical expenses vary from state to state.

Health Maintenance Organizations (HMO's)

HMO's provide policies to groups and to individuals. **HMO's are usually a large group of doctors and other medical specialists operating out of a fully equipped medical facility to provide a full range of services.** These organizations offer total health care for a monthly fee. Services include doctor visits, hospitalization, prescriptions, physical therapy, vision, dental, emergency, outpatient, and home-care services. HMO's eliminate the paperwork of filing medical claims.

With HMO's, the quality of care varies in different locations and among different carriers. The insured must use one of the organization's member doctors and can only use certain authorized facilities. In many locations today, this limitation does not reduce the quality of the care received. In fact, an HMO may offer better care through streamlined diagnosis and doctor communication. For example, during your doctor's appointment, you might be sent to have x-rays and lab work. You walk to another part of the facility for these tests and wait for the results. Then, you report back to your doctor who analyzes the tests and gives you a prescription. Alternatively, the doctor may immediately refer you to a specialist or to another doctor for a second opinion, and you never leave the building. Thus, within one facility, you take care of all phases of your examination and health care needs and never file an insurance claim. Kaiser Permanente and FHP are two examples of popular extensive HMO's.

With HMO's, You Take Care of All Phases of Your Health Care Needs and Never File an Insurance Claim

Private Policies

If you cannot get coverage through your employer or through a federal or state insurance plan, you need a private policy. These are the same policies offered under group plans. Without the group's volume discount, you will pay more for equivalent coverage.

Other health policies cover only specific incidents and specific illnesses. These include:

- **Medigap.** Picks up benefits not covered by Medicare.
- **Dread Policies.** Covers cancer or another specifically named illness; only the named illness is covered.
- **Hospital Indemnity.** Covers only hospitalization; designed for supplementary coverage.
- **Long-Term Health Care.** Covers nursing home care not paid for by Medicare and Medicaid. Many policies include licensed nursing facilities as well as in home care.

Know the Policy Limitations for All Policies Covering Specific Incidents and Illnesses

Be cautious when applying for one of the specific policies not to duplicate coverage already included in another basic health plan in which you are already enrolled. Before you sign up, know what you are paying for, how much you are paying, and where the policy sets limits.

Major Medical

Basic health coverage gives protection for accidents, short-term illnesses, doctor and nurse visits, laboratory tests, and prescription drugs. Most policies have a DEDUCTIBLE that is paid every year. These deductibles range from a low of $50 to a high of $5,000. The most common are $100 and $250. If given a choice, one deductible that applies to an entire family will cost less money than a separate deductible for each individual family member.

Most policies have a COINSURANCE CLAUSE. After the insured meets the annual deductible, the insurance company pays a percentage and the insured pays the remaining percentage of all future claims within that year. The most common is an 80/20 split, with the insurance company paying 80% and the insured paying 20% of the medical bills. A different coinsurance amount, such as 50/50, often applies to vision and dental care if they are included in the policy.

Major medical is the most important medical coverage to own. It will pay most of the bills for a major illness or for extended hospital care. Practically all people can afford to pay for periodic visits to a doctor, but the costs associated with major illnesses such as cancer, heart disease, or kidney failure would bankrupt the average wage earner. Surgery, hospital care, medical specialists, and postoperative treatments can generate bills exceeding $350,000. If you can only afford one type of health insurance, select major medical.

The better policies pay 100% of all medical expenses once the expenses reach a certain limit, such as $5,000 or $10,000. To take advantage of this feature, your policy must have **a stop loss clause**. The insured's share of expenses stop after his/her out-of-pocket costs reach the stated limit. The policy explains the maximum you must pay before the stop loss clause goes into effect. From that point, the insured has 100% coverage for all continuing, approved expenses. **Also, major medical policies have a cap or policy limits on how much they will pay for each person covered under the policy.** Once the insurer has paid out this amount, they pay no more. For most situations, minimum coverage should be $250,000. Many policies set their limit as high as $1,000,000.

Better coverage for a major illness or accident comes from a lower stop loss clause (when the insurance company starts paying 100% of all medical costs), and from higher policy limits. The amount paid for the annual deductible affects premium's paid, not the extent of the coverage.

The insured pays a deductible each year. As mentioned, these amounts range from $50 to $5,000. **If you have a private policy, think of the deductible as the amount you can afford as "self-insurance" should a major illness affect you or a covered family member.** The higher the deductible, the lower the premiums.

The Insurance Company Pays 100% of All Covered Expenses Once a Policy Reaches the Stop Loss Clause

Policies Have Limits on How Much They Will Pay

Higher Deductibles Mean Lower Premiums

Summary

Deductible: The amount you pay each year.
Coinsurance: The insurance pays a percentage, you pay a percentage; i.e., 80% by insurance, 20% by you.
Stop Loss Clause: Insurance pays 100% once expenses reach this limit.
Policy Limits: Total amount the policy will pay.

Disability Income Protection

Disability occurs when you are not able to perform your regular job duties. How a policy defines disability is very important. It may be defined as:

- Unable to perform customary occupation.
- Unable to perform related occupation.

- Unable to perform any occupation.
- Total hospital or in-house confinement.

Unless the policy covers disability in your regular occupation (in some cases a related occupation is acceptable), you are wasting your premium dollars. If you are a dentist, a surgeon, a construction worker, or a piano player with a significant hand injury, you cannot perform your regular job duties. An inferior disability policy might say you can still work by running a mail order business from your home and not compensate you for the injury. Avoid policies with such restrictive definitions.

People often overlook disability insurance, but it is important protection to own. The ability to work and earn an income is a wage earner's greatest asset. **People have a greater chance of becoming disabled than of having their car destroyed in an accident or having their house catch on fire.** In fact, 3% of all mortgage foreclosures are due to death, but 48% are due to the mortgagee's disability.[2]

The Ability to Work and Earn a Living Is a Wage Earner's Greatest Asset

Statistics Show That Every Year:
- 1 out of 106 people die
- 1 out of 70 people have an automobile accident
- 1 out of 88 households catch on fire
- 1 out of 8 people suffer some extent of disability

If you have group health insurance where you work, you may be able to add a disability rider. This is the most cost-effective way to get disability protection. Some employers also offer separate disability policies.

A Disability Rider Is the Most Cost-Effective Way to Get Disability Protection

Although workers who are fully insured with social security have disability insurance, the definition is restrictive. Chances are much greater of becoming partially disabled, and social security pays only for total disability. If you are diagnosed as totally disabled, payments start six months after a doctor declares the total disability, and the payments will continue for the duration of the injury. The amount you receive depends upon your age and your current and past earnings (see Social Security Benefits, Appendix D) Workers who are injured on the job also have some disability coverage under the state worker's compensation fund.

The Social Security Definition of Disability Is Restrictive

Sources for Disability Insurance
- Group Health Insurance
- Riders to Health and Life Insurance Policies
- Social Security
- Individual Policies
- Worker's Compensation
- Veterans Administration
- Civil Service
- Unions

Most individual disability plans pay 60% to 70% of your current salary as long as you are disabled. Disability policies rate their premiums according to the insured's occupation and waiting period required before they must commence payments. More hazardous occupations require higher premiums. The waiting period is your choice. You can select when you want to start receiving payments: 30, 60, 90, 120, 180, or 365 days after you become disabled. **The longer waiting periods offer you an excellent opportunity to use self-insurance to reduce the premium.**

The Following Should Be Included in a Good Disability Policy:
- a definition that will pay you if you cannot perform your "regular" job,
- coverage of illness and accidents,
- payments that will continue for the duration of your disability and not stop after one year,
- payments that will be 60% to 70% of your present income (the policy limits rise with salary increases, and the premiums also increase proportionately), and
- partial payments for partial disabilities.

The risk of some form of disability is great, so make sure you have protection. **Partial disabilities are the most common and the least protected.** Your best option to save premium dollars is to add a disability rider to your health or life insurance policy. Only do so, however, if the policy's definition says it will pay if you cannot perform the functions of your regular job.

Medical insurance is important protection. Few people today can afford to pay out-of-pocket for 100% of their health care costs,

Most Individual Disability Plans Pay 60% to 70% of Your Current Salary as Long as You Are Disabled

especially if they suffer a major illness or accident. Premiums paid to insure or cover these potential costs are a wise investment. Likewise, a disability policy with a broad definition of disability is a wise purchase. It will provide income if you are unable to work, thus protecting your other assets.

Protect Yourself from Potential Financial Loss through Owning:
- major medical insurance, and
- disability insurance.

14
Property and Casualty Insurance

Homeowner's Policies

HOMEOWNER'S INSURANCE **protects you from financial loss should some disaster destroy all or a portion of your home, its surrounding buildings, or its trees and shrubbery.** If your home is totally destroyed, the insurance also pays for living expenses in a temporary location. Homeowner's policies can also provide protection against ice damage, theft, and broken water pipes. In addition, the liability portion covers accidents that take place on your property. If your cousin's child falls through your glass patio door and breaks an arm, a comprehensive homeowner's policy will pay the medical bills for the broken arm.

Dwelling

You should always insure your property for 80% of its replacement value (not the market value). As long as you have insurance for 80% of the replacement value, you are automatically covered for 100% of the loss. As the replacement value rises, so should your insurance. **Most policies have an inflation factor and adjust the replacement value automatically each year.**

Insure Your Property for 80% of Its Replacement Value

Generally, companies offer three types of homeowners policies: HO-1, HO-2, and HO-3. Table 14.1 shows the perils covered under each type of policy. HO-1 is the basic policy with the lowest premiums and fewest perils covered, HO-2 covers more perils, and HO-3 provides the most extensive coverage. The premiums increase with the perils covered.

Table 14.1—Perils Covered by Homeowner's Policies

		HO-1	HO-2	HO-3
1.	Fire or Lightning	XX	XX	XX
2.	Removal of Destroyed Property, i.e., cleanup after tornado	XX	XX	XX
3.	Wind or Hail	XX	XX	XX
4.	Explosion	XX	XX	XX
5.	Riot	XX	XX	XX
6.	Damage by an Aircraft	XX	XX	XX
7.	Damage by a Vehicle	XX	XX	XX
8.	Smoke	XX	XX	XX
9.	Vandalism	XX	XX	XX
10.	Theft	XX	XX	XX
11.	Glass Breakage	XX	XX	XX
12.	Damage from Falling Objects, i.e., branch falls from tree onto roof during hurricane		XX	XX
13.	Damage from Weight of Ice and Snow		XX	XX
14.	Building Collapse		XX	XX
15.	Hot Water System Heating Damage		XX	XX
16.	Damage to Water Pipes or Air Conditioner		XX	XX
17.	Frozen Pipes, Damage to Appliances		XX	XX
18.	Electrical Wiring and Fixtures		XX	XX
19.	All Perils Except Flood, War, Earthquakes, etc. (see exclusions in your policy)			XX

Source: Insurance Information Institute

If you live in a flood, hurricane, fire, or earthquake zone, your basic homeowner's policy will not cover these disasters. Furthermore, obtaining separate coverage for these catastrophes can be expensive. **Premiums for earthquake, fire, and hurricane insurance vary depending on where you live and your potential exposure. Check the exclusions of your policy so you know what is covered. Exclusions vary for different locations.**

If you live in a flood zone, you can qualify for more affordable federal flood insurance. This coverage is offered through the insurance company but guaranteed by the federal government. To qualify, you must live in the home 80% or more of the time.

Homeowner's policies have deductibles that range from $250 and up. That means you will always pay the first $250 for every claim, regardless of the extent of the loss or the number of claims you file in a year. Policies with higher deductibles have lower premiums. A higher deductible saves money in the long run, because homeowners generally do not file claims often. **Think of the deductible as the amount you can afford to pay for "self-insurance." The higher deductibles help keep your annual premiums low and still provide protection against major losses.**

You Pay Your Deductible with Every Claim Filed

Loss of Use

The amount stated on the policy is the maximum amount the insurance company will pay for temporary living expenses. Payment is normally for the shortest time required to repair or replace the home, or settle elsewhere.

If you rent all or a portion of your home, this coverage also includes payment for the fair rental value until the property is repaired or replaced.

Personal Property and Renter's Insurance

Personal property coverage is usually one-half of the total dwelling coverage. Rates do vary, so check your policy limits. Personal property includes appliances, clothing, furniture, rugs, jewelry and collectibles, etc. **Renter's insurance is basically personal property coverage.** It covers your furnishings and personal possessions within your apartment or condo.

Expensive jewelry, china, antiques, silverware, or furs should be covered separately. **Each insurance company sets a limit on how much they will pay for valuables. Usually the amount is around $2,500 total, with no more than $1,000 for each item unless you request and pay for additional coverage.**

Cover Valuables Separately if They Are Worth More Than $1,000 Each

Personal property is also insured when it is off premises. While traveling, your jewelry and clothing are insured. The coverage, however, is less. So, if you often travel with expensive items, contact your insurance agent and check the limits.

Liability

The liability portion of a homeowner's policy covers personal injuries to other people when these injuries take place on the property.

In some cases, the injured person sues the homeowner to collect their damages. The standard liability coverage on most homeowner's policies is $100,000. **In addition, most policies offer increased liability protection through an umbrella policy that will cover all personal liabilities up to $1,000,000. Such an umbrella policy is usually a very good buy.**

Filing a Claim

When damage occurs to a home or yard, or when you have items stolen, you need to file a claim. First, notify your insurance agent or the insurance company. They will send an adjuster to look at the damage and/or estimate the repair or replacement cost. If you have a theft, you need to file a police report and provide proof of the value of the stolen property.

When damages occur, do not attempt any repairs until the insurance adjuster estimates the harm and you both agree on the amount to be paid by the insurance company. The insurance company expects you to protect the property from further damage. So, if you must do emergency repairs before the adjuster arrives, take pictures of the damage before doing the repairs, and keep receipts of expenses.

Picture Inventory

Pictures of personal property, especially the expensive items, help prove their value to the adjuster if these items are destroyed or stolen. It is a good idea to take photos of all of your household belongings. If you own a video recorder, you can make a video tape. Also, you should separately appraise valuable works of art, collectibles, expensive jewelry, and furs to provide evidence of their worth. **Keep all appraisals and pictures of your personal property inventory away from your premises.**

They could be left with a trusted family member or neighbor. Many people use a safe-deposit box. Taking such an inventory is easy and will be invaluable if you ever have to prove a loss.

If you and the insurance adjuster cannot agree on the amount of loss for personal property, the company will hire an appraiser. You may also hire an appraiser, and the two sides will negotiate until they come to terms. **If you have evidence through appraisals or pictures of your valuables, proving your loss is far easier.**

Automobile Insurance

Automobile insurance offers three major types of coverage:

- **Liability.** Bodily injury your car does to others; property damage your car does to other vehicles and to personal property.
- **Collision.** Damage done to your car.
- **Comprehensive.** Glass breakage, theft, fire, damage from storms, etc.

Liability

Automobile insurance has two types of LIABILITY coverage:

- bodily injury, and
- property damage.

All Drivers Must Carry Bodily Injury Liability

Law requires all motor vehicle drivers to carry bodily injury liability insurance. The least amount of liability insurance you carry should be sufficient to cover your net worth. If your car injures or kills another person, the insurance company pays the damages up to the amount of the policy limits. If another person drives your car with your permission and has an accident, the injuries from this accident are also covered.

Policies show bodily injury liability in two parts, such as: 15/30, 50/100, 100/300. All numbers are understood to be stated in thousands. **The FIRST NUMBER is the maximum amount the insurance company will pay to ANY INDIVIDUAL in each accident, and the SECOND NUMBER is the maximum amount the insurance company will pay for ANY ACCIDENT regardless of the number of people hurt.**

The second type of auto liability insurance is for **PROPERTY DAMAGE.** This covers damage your car causes to another's property. The property includes other cars, fences, houses, posts, buildings, and so on. Again, your policy covers other drivers as long as they have permission to use the car.

Property damage is also stated in thousands and written as the third part of the liability coverage: 10/30/5; or 100/300/50. The amount of liability coverage for property damage in these examples are $5,000 and $50,000 respectively.

Liability Insurance

XX / XX / XX

Maximum Per Person/Maximum Per Accident/Maximum Property Damage

---

Collision

The third part of automobile insurance covers collisions. It pays for damage to your car regardless of who is at fault. Collision insurance has deductibles ranging from $100 to $1,000. The company will never pay more than the value of your car, so **if your car is worth less than $1,000, drop this coverage.**

If you don't have collision coverage and are in an accident that is not your fault, you must wait for the other person's insurance company to pay you for the damage. This process often takes months. You may need to hire a personal injury attorney to collect your damages. Without collision coverage, your insurance company has no responsibility to pay for repairs.

When you have collision coverage, your company will pay for the damage then collect from the other driver's insurance company if the other driver is at fault. Also, if you pay a deductible to get your car repaired, your insurance company will return this amount to you when they get reimbursed.

Collision Coverage Pays for Damage to Your Car

Comprehensive

COMPREHENSIVE is the third type of automobile insurance. It covers other accidents to your car except collisions with other vehicles. Some of these include glass breakage, theft, fire, vandalism, and damage from hail or storms.

Other Options

Other options that can be included in an automobile policy are for medical payments, uninsured motorists, and no-fault insurance (personal injury protection). Most people don't need any of these. If you have health insurance, you are already covered for medical payments, so don't duplicate the coverage. The uninsured motorist coverage takes care of medical payments for you and your family members for hit and run accidents and for injuries caused by uninsured motorists. Since companies don't make duplicate payments, you don't need this protection when you have health insurance. A standard health policy insures all medical injuries from whatever source.

If your state has adopted "no-fault" laws, your insurance company will pay up to a certain amount, generally $15,000, for your personal injury protection (PIP) and property damage claims from an accident no matter who is at fault. If your state has "no-fault" laws, you will pay an extra PIP premium for personal injury protection.

Automobile Insurance Includes:

- Bodily Injury Liability (Required)
- Collision
- Comprehensive

Premium Rates

Insurance companies decide the premiums they charge based upon:

- **Type of Car.** Luxury cars cost more to insure. The auto's crash resistance record also affects the premium rate. When shopping for a new car, get a quote from your insurance agent of the cost to insure the auto before you make the purchase.
- **Use of Car.** Whether the car is used mainly for business or mainly for pleasure affects the premiums. If you drive the car under ten thousand miles each year, you will pay a lesser premium.
- **Driving Record.** Good drivers with fewer tickets receive premium discounts for their good driving record.
- **Driver Classification.** Drivers are rated for premiums based on age, sex, and marital status. Those under twenty-five years of age pay higher premiums because they have a higher accident ratio. Since males under twenty-five years of age have more accidents, they are rated higher than females of the same age. Singles pay more than couples for the same coverage.

- **Rating Territory.** Those living in cities with higher population densities and more traffic pay more for their premiums than those who live in less-populated rural areas.

Premium Discounts

Most insurance carriers offer a reduced premium based on discounts. These premium discounts will reduce your overall premium outlay, so be sure to ask about them. Also, inform your agent when you qualify for one or more of the standard discounts. The most common premium discounts include:

- **Good driving record**
- **Driver education discounts** and/or students under age twenty-five with **good grades**
- **Student** living one hundred miles or more away from home listed as a driver on your policy
- **Multiple cars** insured with the same insurance carrier
- **Safety devices,** such as anti-theft devices, auto belting, air bags, anti-lock brakes
- **Nonsmoker** and/or **nondrinker**
- **Car pool**

To save premium dollars and still maintain adequate coverage, keep your insurance agent well-informed of all changes in your situation. Add your children under age twenty-five living at home as drivers on your policy. The cost is far less than them obtaining their own insurance. **Notify your agent if you qualify for any of the above discounts or if any of your covered children get married or move away from home.**

If you have deductibles of $500 or larger, you will pay much less for your insurance coverage. Also, the fewer claims you file, the better your rating with the insurance company. Never file a claim for less than your deductible. For damage under $1,000, consider not filing a claim. The extra you pay up-front to repair the car may save money in the long run. Most carriers will raise your rates when you file any claim, even when that claim is small.

For Damage under $1,000, Consider Not Filing a Claim

Part 5
The Self-Employed, p. 195

Part 5
The Self-Employed

THE SELF-EMPLOYED are people who work for themselves. Many have their own small businesses. Some are farmers or fishermen. Others are performing artists who work for a fee. Still others are experts in their field as tradesmen, consultants, or professional athletes. The varieties of self-employment are only limited by **their** imagination.

The challenges faced by the self-employed are unique. They are responsible for paying all their employment taxes, keeping proper books and records, and overseeing the daily operations of their particular business. They also have unique opportunities. A successful business, or the success of an individual, can reap handsome monetary rewards and provide much personal satisfaction. This section will help the self-employed understand their unique responsibilities.

15
Basics of Self-Employment

Criteria for Self-Employment

THE SELF-EMPLOYED **do not have an employer who tells them what to do or the hours they must work.** Being self-employed, they do not receive a salary that has federal, state, FICA, and Medicare taxes withheld from their pay. Instead, they perform services for others for a set fee or offer products for resale to the public for a certain price.

Self-employed persons have many descriptions. They include, but are not limited to: 1) professionals, such as attorneys, accountants, or veterinarians who have their own offices and employ others; 2) musicians who work different paid engagements (gigs) for a "fee"; 3) trade contractors who work for a general contractor; 4) experts in specific fields who have a product or service they offer to the public or professional athletes; 5) partners of a partnership; or 6) farmers, fishermen, and some truck drivers. The self-employed can work in an office or out of their home. **They do not receive a set wage weekly, biweekly, or monthly like salaried employees working for large or small companies. Instead, their income varies according to their "business success."**

The Self-Employed Pay for Their Insurance, Fund Their Retirement, and Pay All Employment Taxes

Because the income of the self-employed is "up" and "down" with no tax withholding, and because their employment does not include "fringe benefits," such as health insurance, life insurance, and company sponsored retirement plans, they face unique challenges. **They have to pay for their own insurance, fund their own retirement, and save ahead to pay their taxes.**

Self-employed persons also have many tax benefits. They can write off on their tax returns the business expenses they incur to generate their self-employed income. When they use their home or their car for business purposes, they can write off the "business" portion of these expenses. Also, they can deduct the cost of purchasing new equipment used in their business. More about business autos and business equipment is covered in chapter 17, Special Tax Considerations for the Self-Employed.

Considering Self-Employment

Before making a decision to become self-employed, know what your business undertaking will cost you to set up and to continue in operation month after month. Also, know your "market" and your competition, as these will help determine your chance for success. Ask yourself,

"Is there a need for my product or service?" or **"Can I offer it at a fair price, cover my expenses, and still make a profit?" Also,** ask yourself, **"How do I know this business will succeed?"** and **"Will I survive, given the competition?"** and finally, **"What do I have to offer that others need or want?"**

Discover Your Area of Excellence

Sometimes, financial growth is a stalemate because of a dead end job. People who dislike their work seldom advance. Therefore, equally important to having financial priorities is knowing your talents. Take care when assessing your potential not to overemphasize your limitations and understate your abilities. **Most people tend to dwell on what they don't do well instead of emphasizing their strong points. Your natural skills lead to your success.**

You have one talent that surpasses all others. You can identify it by what you love to do and what you do well. Developing this talent is most important; it is your area of excellence. Success here has less resistance and will positively influence all other facets of your life.

Ed

Ed never attained high grades in school. Yet, even as a boy, he could fix any tool or toy. Ed began working in construction as a cabinet maker. He was a good craftsman but never liked his job. What he did like was when the other workers asked him to help repair their broken equipment.

Eventually, Ed quit his construction job and took the risk of opening a repair shop for tools and small appliances. His enthusiasm for his work led to many referrals from satisfied customers, which made his business thrive. Soon, he had to hire people to work for him. Once Ed started using his natural abilities in his job, his income and confidence grew, and he was happier.

Jayne

Jayne loved all animals, especially dogs. Upon completion of high school, she had to leave the farm where she was raised and move to the city to work. Jayne went to secretarial school and eventually secured a good job with a large corporation. It took her several years before she realized that she disliked her work. In time, Jayne got involved with a group of people who bred and showed dogs. Through contacts in this group, she saw the potential of starting a dog grooming business.

Jayne launched her business part-time, working from her home. Soon, she had a steady customer list that kept growing. Before long, she quit her secretarial job to devote full-time efforts to her grooming business. She was happier doing what she loved. Her substantial increase in income was another reward.

If you find yourself in a dead end job that drains your enthusiasm, seriously consider a change. What is your area of excellence? Others can benefit from you developing this talent. Furthermore, as they benefit, you will be happy doing what you do best. Like Ed and Jayne, you will also probably earn more money—definitely a win-win situation.

Organizing Your Business

The U.S. Small Business Administration (SBA) offers numerous programs and services to small business owners. You can use their research resources to decide if you should go into business and to write a business plan. **They offer business loans and provide counseling and advice.** The SBA has offices in every city. In metropolitan areas, they are usually located in the federal building. Stop by and pick up some free brochures to learn about all of their services.

If you are on the Internet, you can reach the SBA home page at http://www.sba.gov. They have a U.S. Business Advisor on the Internet that can respond to written questions about small businesses. You can reach the Business Advisor at http://www.business.gov.

Many who have never been self-employed say they are going to leave their job and "go out on their own." For some, their job may end for one reason or another, and they consider self-employment as an alternative to working for another employer. Depending on the person and the circumstances, choosing self-employment could prove to be insightful or ill-advised. At the very least, someone considering self-employment should know what to expect and should know themselves well enough to determine if they can work on their own.

Self-employment is flexible because you are your own boss and have no one watching over you telling you what to do, but it can (and often does) stretch you to the limits. **You must be able to work well on your own, without supervision.** You must be a problem-solver and not get discouraged when you discover that running your own business is not as easy as it originally appeared. **Being on your own requires an extremely high level of discipline.** It is important that the work you must accomplish gets done and gets done on time just like it must when you work for someone else. Since you have no "boss," the temptation can be great to take time off to go to the movies, to play golf, or to play tennis. **Exercising the required discipline to complete a needed task is important for success.**

Equally important, you must realize that **your self-employment is a business that needs to be kept separate from your personal life.** This is even more important if you plan to work at home. **You need a separate work space where you can concentrate, plan, and carry out your business activities.** Whether you are selling products from your home, providing day care, providing a service for others, or doing freelance work, **people do not want to do business with a person who lacks professionalism.** If clients visit you in your home, wear appropriate clothing for your profession, keep accurate and neat records, and have your work area free of personal items, with the basic equipment of your profession clearly visible.

If you have a spouse and children at home where you are working, they need to understand that **you need to separate your home life and your business life.** Their support and encouragement is important. Share

The Self-Employed Need to Work Well on Their Own

Self-Employment Moves You out of the Comfort Zone and Stretches You to Reach Your Potential

Have the Basic Equipment of Your Profession Clearly Visible in Your Work Area

with them your goals and what you hope to achieve. After all, your work will affect them, so they need to be involved and understand your plan.

Making your business succeed can consume your personal life, which can be devastating. To be a happy, well-adjusted person, you will need to take time away from work to relax, have fun, be with family and friends, and exercise. Working twelve to sixteen hours a day, six or seven days a week, year after year is not healthy. **Your business may thrive while your personal life falls apart. What good is success if you drive away those close to you and they are not there to share in your prosperity?** Indeed, discipline is the number one criteria you need to make self-employment successful—the discipline to balance work with relaxation and **your business life with your personal life.**

Separate Your Home Life from Your Business Life

Forms of Doing Business

The legal form of your business determines how you report your income and expenses, the taxes you pay, the extent of your personal liability, and who makes the day-to-day business decisions. If you are going into business on your own, you can operate as a sole proprietor, you can incorporate, or you can form a limited liability company. If you are going into business with others, your choices are to operate as a partnership, to incorporate, or to form a limited liability company. A husband and wife who go into business together, who contribute jointly to the business and make joint business decisions, must form a partnership, a limited liability company, or incorporate. They cannot jointly operate as a sole proprietorship.

As a sole proprietor, you report business profit on your personal tax return. All other forms of business, including partnerships, require filing a separate business tax return. If you think you should operate under some business form other that of a sole proprietorship, it would be wise **to seek advice from a competent accountant or attorney who can explain the pros and cons of each business entity.** This explanation is beyond the scope of this book.

Sole Proprietors Report Business Profits on Their Personal Tax Return

Many who start out in business take on the expense of seeking legal advice and of forming a corporation before they experience justifiable business success. Once incorporated, they are inundated with forms from the IRS, forms from the state department of employment, and forms from the state tax commission. **If you do incorporate, know the**

advantages for doing so as well as the responsibilities of running a corporation. Corporations are easier to form than they are to dissolve.

For individuals who will be earning under $50,000 a year and who have little or no liability, a sole proprietorship is probably best business structure. Then, if the business expands and grows beyond this level, you can always consider the advantages of another legal form. **A sole proprietorship is the easiest business structure to set up and also to dissolve.** Increased tax write-offs are a poor reason to incorporate, simply because incorporation does not increase your write-offs. **Sole proprietors have similar benefits and deduct similar expenses as corporations.**

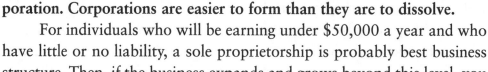

Independent Contractor or Employee?

Perhaps you are an employee but are treated as an independent contractor? Or, you might be an independent contractor and wonder if you shouldn't be an employee. Or, perhaps you are a business owner and plan to hire someone to work for you. Because of the many rules and laws regulating employees, **some business owners try to hire independent contractors and pay them an hourly fee, when they should be hiring employees.** The IRS devotes much time and money to this issue. Should the IRS reclassify an independent contractor as an employee, the employer suffers the consequences and becomes responsible for:

- Employment taxes that should have been withheld from the workers pay, such as FICA, Medicare, and federal and state income taxes.
- State and federal unemployment taxes.
- Penalties and interest for failure to file these taxes.

Furthermore, if the employer has a retirement plan and has workers reclassified from independent contractors to employees, the plan can be disqualified. When a plan is disqualified, vested benefits under the plan could become taxable to **all** plan participants.

The following guidelines are used by the IRS to determine employee status.

- The worker is required to follow instructions about when, where, and how the work is done.
- The worker is given training showing him/her how to perform the job in a particular manner. He/she has little discretion over how the job is done.

- The services provided by the worker are an integral part of the business operations.
- The worker has an ongoing relationship with the clients or customers of the business.
- The business hires an assistant to help the worker.
- The work is performed at a specific business location.
- The worker is required to turn in oral or written reports.
- The worker is paid hourly, weekly, or monthly (as opposed to being paid by the job).
- The worker's business and travel expenses are reimbursed, or the employer provides the worker transportation to and from the job site.
- The company furnishes the materials and tools of the trade for the worker.
- The worker works for one business rather than for several companies at the same time.
- The worker does not offer his/her services to the general public.
- The worker could be dismissed or fired for not performing the work satisfactorily.

The above is not the entire list used to determine if a employer-employee relationship exists, but it is enough to show you the guidelines. So take heed, and **if you need to hire an employee, hire an employee and file and pay your employment taxes.** Don't hire an "employee" and then try to "pay them under the table" and make them think they are an independent contractor so you don't have to deal with employee laws. Doing so could come back to haunt you when 1) the employee tries to collect unemployment benefits or 2) has to come up with the money they owe for paying their self-employment taxes and another person advises them that their "boss" should have helped them to pay. Such an employee could easily file a claim against you and win.

An independent contractor is one who does a job for a fee or commission. They are tradespeople or skilled in a certain area and hired to perform a certain skill. They have their own tools (and or talents) and do not need to be supervised or told how to perform their job. Those who hire independent contractors should have them sign an agreement stating that they are just that. The independent contractor should present an invoice to the business for the job or services performed.

Since an employee gets an hourly wage, when the job lasts longer than expected, he/she makes more money, especially if overtime is

When You Have an Employee, Treat Them as an Employee, Not an Independent Contractor

Independent Contractors:

Perform a Certain Skill

Work for a Fee

Have Their Own Tools and Equipment

Need No Training

Invoice Their Clients

involved. In contrast, when an independent contractor's job takes longer than expected, the profit margin is less. **To the self-employed, time is money.**

Legal Requirements

The SBA in your area can help you in this area. Small businesses must comply with federal, state, and local laws. Be sure to check with your state department of labor and your city or county government. Legal requirements will include:

- A business license from the city, county, or state where you work.
- A sales tax number if you resale to the public.
- A separate business bank account.
- Compliance with federal and state laws that govern employees and employee withholding.

Business or Hobby?

An individual with a bona fide business intends to make a profit. If for some reason business expenses exceed business income, the business is allowed to write off those losses. **To determine if you have a business, the "profit" motive is very important.** If a profit is not made in at least three out of five years or if profits are small in the three profit years and losses are large in the two loss years, the IRS can recategorize the business as a hobby if they can prove there is no profit motive. **Once a business is recategorized as a hobby, it can write off expenses only up to income.** It can no longer deduct "losses" (expenses that exceed income).

A Bona Fide Business Can Write Off Its Business Losses

Some of the criteria used by the IRS to prove "Profit Motive" are:

- The manner in which the owner carries on the activity. **Does he/she conduct himself or herself as a professional engaged in a business activity?** This could include owning or renting the appropriate equipment, invoicing clients, and advertising to increase business activities.
- **The expertise of the owner.** Does he or she have the knowledge and experience necessary to offer services to others?

- **The time and effort spent in making the business succeed.** Is this an activity that the owner runs consistently, or does he/she engage in the activity sporadically.
- If the business involves owning and selling assets, does the expectation exist that these assets will appreciate in value over time?
- Has the owner had success in doing similar or even dissimilar activities?
- **What is the history of income or loss** with respect to the activity? Is the owner "writing off the business" primarily to offset other income?
- **What is the amount of occasional profits?** Are they small and seemingly unjustified when compared to the business losses?
- **What is the financial status of the owner and his/her spouse?** Are the profits from this business needed to help pay for living expenses, or as mentioned earlier, is the main motive of the "business" to generate tax write-offs that will offset other income?
- Does the business contain elements of personal pleasure or recreation? If so, **does the owner engage in the "business" activities primarily for recreation or primarily to make money?**

The above list gives you an idea of how the IRS thinks when they make the determination whether or not a business has a profit motive. Everyone realizes that many businesses are not profitable when they start out. It takes two to three years for a business to grow. After that amount of time, however, you can expect the IRS to look closely at the profit motive of the business.

Deducting Expenses of Looking for a New Business

You may incur preliminary expenses for travel, accounting, or legal advice before deciding to go ahead with a business venture. These expenses cannot be deducted directly but must be taken (amortized) over five years (sixty months). Once the business opens and you are in a position to make a profit, you can then deduct all business expenses.

Start-Up Expenses Must Be Deducted over Five Years

Example:

Sally wants to leave her job and start her own business. She is currently a legal secretary and has some ideas about how she could start a company that would offer services to attorneys, such as locating records and delivering them to the attorney, filing court documents, and computer services. Sally paid a fee to her accountant to talk about the bookkeeping system required and the rules she would need to follow when she hired employees. She also paid a legal fee to an attorney to discuss whether or not she should incorporate. Sally also had travel expenses because she wanted to check out the available services and similar companies in several areas. All together, over her year of searching, she paid out $2,500 in expenses. Sally decided to open the business in her hometown. She opened for business on July 1. Since the $2,500 she had already paid out was done before July 1, she must amortize these expenses over a five-year period. She will be able to deduct $500 each year for five years. Once Sally opens the door for her business, she can then deduct all legitimate operating expenses.

Summary

Self-employment has its responsibilities, risks, and rewards. You have the responsibility to make the business work, the responsibility to advertise and to promote your skills, and if you hire employees, the responsibility to pay and report their salary(ies) and your share of employment taxes.

With a salaried job, you have a set amount of income you can count on taking home each pay day for the work you perform. With self-employment, most people experience lean times as well as times when there is more than enough money. For most, income is up and down. **You must learn to save during the abundant times to see you through when deals get canceled and you have no money coming in.** Sometimes your personal finances are on the line, which creates additional stress when all does not go as expected. **The risks are great, but if you succeed, you can also reap greater rewards.**

It is possible that you can run a business that will provide more money and more free time than you would receive if you did the same type of work for an employer. With self-employment, you are in charge. No other person can tell you how to run your business or when and how you should complete your work. Also, you don't need to worry about

The Income of Self-Employed People Is Often Up and Down

layoffs, company buyouts, and being phased out of your job. You are the one in control, and you are building your future.

16
Building Your Business

Your Professional Image

THE FOLLOWING are essentials to starting a business:

- A separate checking account specifically for your business.
- A separate work space specifically for you to work.
- Separate bookkeeping systems for your business finances and your personal finances.
- The tools, equipment, and supplies necessary for you to complete your job and conduct your business.

A professional business image is important for success. All of the following will enhance your professionalism:

- A separate business telephone line, complete with telephone and answering machine. The answering machine is especially important if you are starting out without a secretary. People needing your services want to know they are dealing with a legitimate business.
- A "firm" or personal brochure that describes your talents, products, and/or services.

- Business cards, business stationery, business envelopes, and an invoice that you will use to bill clients. If possible, place your business logo on all these documents.
- Note cards and/or thank-you notes, again with your logo or business card. Clients appreciate receiving notes and thank-you cards.

Continue to Build Your Professional Image

Look at the money you have available. **If you do not have enough resources to pay for everything when you start out, set priorities about what is most important.** Then, as your finances improve, continue to build your professional image. Consider designing a logo and coming up with a business name and/or a catchy phrase that describes what you do. You might need to hire someone to help you with the logo.

Where to Work

Some businesses, such as construction work, house and window cleaning, house painting, yard work, snow removal, and freelance work for artists, musicians, writers, and actors can operate efficiently from most home offices because the work is located at another site. Occupations that are labor intensive do not involve meeting clients regularly and are perfect for a home office. Generally, the owner goes out to the job with or without help from others.

You must know your business and where you want to work. For some, a home office is used minimally. It is a place to keep records, use the telephone, and line up work for the next day, week, or month. For others, their "home office" is where they keep and practice musical instruments or write their books. Then, there are those whose home office is a place where they regularly meet with clients. Most home offices are set up with standard office equipment, such as a desk, file cabinets, bookshelves, chairs, a computer, a fax machine, a telephone, and a copier. **Your office and work area must contain all the equipment and supplies you need to keep yourself organized and to be able to produce your work.**

Working at home has its advantages. It is less costly than renting an office space, it is convenient to "be home" and "be at work" at the same time. If you are not seeing clients, you don't have to "dress up," and you can work in sweatpants or shorts. To find something to eat, you only need to go to the refrigerator. You can double up on chores and do laundry, care for a small child, or supervise teenagers while you work.

Then, if you can't sleep, you can get up in the middle of the night and work for a couple of hours. Some can even work while they watch a movie or listen to music.

Working at home also has its disadvantages. You never leave your job. It is with you all the time, twenty-four hours a day. Accordingly, it is most important that you learn to separate your business and your personal life. Family and friends can easily interrupt you, which can be a serious problem. Working at home, isolated from other people, can get discouraging, so you need to **make it a priority to regularly meet with others who do similar work.** When you work alone and have no one to share ideas or talk over cases, make certain you attend the meetings held by your professional organization(s). **It is important to be around others who are in the same line of work. You can share successes and frustrations, discuss business trends, and get good pointers.**

With a Home Office, It Is Difficult to Separate Your Business Life from Your Personal Life

Renting an office has its advantages also. Although more expensive, **the office is often more accessible to clients.** Because you need to go there to do your work, you tend to keep regular business hours. Clients will just drop by an office with a question or to say, "hello," but they often will not drop by your home for the same reason. If your work is client intensive and your home not easily accessible, having an office in a good business location makes it possible for you to see more clients. Although it isn't true, some clients often think that someone working in an office outside the home is "more successful."

Expenses are the biggest detriment to renting an outside office. Many sole proprietors haven't reached the point that they can hire a secretary or an assistant, so they do everything. **It is a challenge to be the boss, the secretary, and the mail clerk for a growing business.**

Business Investment

Keep enough money in your business so you have the funds available to continue to make it grow. When you take out profits to pay essential living expenses, still keep enough money in your business to pay for promotion and advertising. Don't spend all of your profit. Promotion and advertising are essential.

Keep Enough Money in Your Business to Pay for Continued Promotion

Especially in the early years of developing your business, you may not have the money to build your personal investments via mutual funds, retirement plans, etc. Your business takes it all and then some. **Remember that your business success is your investment. When you**

Your Business Success Is an Investment

succeed at building your business, you can make as much money or more than you would in outside investments. Your business might even grow to the point that others will want to invest in it. Then someday, you may be able to sell it for a handsome profit.

What Kind of Benefits Should You Buy?

If you do not have health insurance from another source, purchasing it should be your number one priority. Secondly, look at disability and life insurance. Then when profits allow, work on funding your retirement.

Health Insurance

Health insurance can be expensive, especially for a family. Be aggressive in seeking the best possible rates. Check out possible coverage through professional organizations to which you belong. Group rates are far less expensive than individual rates. Congress realized that many self-employed persons often go without medical insurance. Consequently, they designed the new Medical Savings Plan that offers many benefits for the self-employed.

Medical Savings Plans

The New MSP Offers Many Benefits for the Self-Employed

To qualify for a Medical Savings Plan, you must be self-employed (or an employee of a small business with fifty or fewer employees) and have a high deductible insurance policy. A high deductible policy means a minimum deductible of at least $1,500 but not more than $2,250 for individual coverage, and $3,000 but not more than $4,500 for family coverage. In addition, paid medical expenses cannot be more than $3,000 for individual coverage or $5,500 for family coverage. The second and greatest challenge is to find an insurance carrier who offers Medical Savings Plans. Insurance companies are dragging their feet in offering these policies. Golden Rule, a carrier in most states, helped push this bill through Congress and does offer qualifying high deductible coverage. Once you find a carrier providing the coverage, you then deposit the deductible into a Medical Savings Plan, herein referred to as a MSP. **When you file your tax return, you take a deduction for your MSP contribution.**

- Deduct 65% of the MSP contribution for individual coverage, and
- 75% of the MSP contribution for family coverage.

At Tax Time, You Must Take a Deduction for Your MSP Contribution

The deduction to your MSP account is an adjustment that reduces your gross income dollar for dollar just like a contribution to any retirement plan. **You can then withdraw the money from the MSP to pay for medical expenses. Covered medical expenses include all of those that the IRS allows you to deduct, such as doctor and hospital visits, prescription drugs, vision care, dental care, etc. So, the money you withdraw from your MSP that pays for these qualified medical expenses is tax free.** Should you make a withdrawal and spend the money for something other than medical expenses, you will pay taxes and a hefty 15% penalty on the amount withdrawn.

You Withdraw Money from Your MSP Account to Pay for Medical Expenses

If you do not spend all that you contribute in one year, it will carryover to the next year to pay for future medical expenses. Each year that you deposit into your MSP account the amount of your insurance deductible, you can generate the tax write-off for this deposit. **If you don't use all of the money, it will continue to grow until you reach age sixty-five. At that time, you can withdraw any excess and pay taxes on what you withdraw, just like an IRA**

Health insurance premiums are not covered expenses. You must pay for these, but you get to take the health insurance deduction. Self-employed persons can write off a percentage of what they pay for insurance premiums as an adjustment to income. This deduction gives a dollar to dollar write-off. The percentage allowed is shown below:

Money Not Used in a MSP Can be Withdrawn at Age Sixty-Five Just Like a Traditional IRA

Table 16.1—Self-Employed Deduction for Health Insurance Premiums

Tax Year	Percentage
1997	40%
1998 & 1999	45%
2000 & 2001	50%
2002	60%
2003–2005	80%
2006	90%
2007 & thereafter	100%

Premiums for Long-Term Care Can Be Paid from an MSP Account

Keep in mind that the premiums for high deductible insurance are much less than those offered for the standard $250 deductible. An added bonus with the MSP account is that **premiums to pay for long-term care can be paid out of MSP funds.** This means you could purchase a long-term care policy and pay for the premiums from your MSP account. You save both ways.

An individual becomes ineligible for an MSP when covered by any other health plan. Exceptions include insurance for a specific illness, medical coverage under an auto insurance policy, a hospitalization policy for a fixed sum, and Medicare supplements.

The MSP account is an experiment by Congress to provide affordable health care for the self-employed. Only around 18,000 accounts had been opened by the end of 1997, while the law preapproves up to 750,000 of these accounts. After the year 2000, they may or may not be available. They are a great plan for those who qualify.

Jeff

Jeff is self-employed and pays premiums of $400 per month for health insurance coverage for his family. These premiums amount to $4,800 per year. Since Jeff's gross income is around $80,000, he cannot take a medical deduction on his tax return. To be deductible, medical expenses need to exceed 7.5% of adjusted gross income, so he would have to incur over $6,000 of expenses before he has a deduction.

Jeff signed up for a MSP account with a deductible of $4,500, the highest allowed for family coverage. During the year, the family had $2,800 of medical expenses, and Jeff withdrew $2,800 to pay for these expenses. The $1,700 not spent remained in his MSP account to be used another year and to earn tax deferred interest.

The best news is that the MSP created a $3,375 tax deduction, which saved Jeff and his wife approximately $1,181 in taxes. The prior year, he paid $400 a month for health insurance premiums, but with his MSP, his premiums have dropped down to $200 per month.

Considering the money saved in taxes, Jeff's real cost for the MSP contribution is $3,319. This is $1,481 less than he paid before opening the MSP, and he has money (balance of $1,700) growing in his account to use for future expenses, to pay for long-term care, or to withdraw after age sixty-five.

Disability and Life Insurance

The particulars about disability and life insurance are covered in chapter 12, Life Insurance, and chapter 13, Health and Disability Insurance. A consideration applicable to business owners is "key man" insurance for the person(s) essential to your business operation. The business can purchase a life insurance policy to cover the "key" person's life. If the key employee or owner should die prematurely, the business would receive the proceeds from the policy. **Such insurance will help protect a business when there is an unexpected death of a pivotal employee. Proceeds from the policy can provide the resources to replace the talent and expertise of the deceased key employee.**

Key Man Insurance Covers the Persons Essential to Your Business Operations

Retirement

All retirement plans, including those available for the self-employed are covered in chapter 10, Retirement Plans. **SEP IRA's and Keogh Plans are designed specifically for sole proprietors** (partners in a partnership can also contribute). In addition to contributing to the SEP or Keogh, sole proprietors can also contribute to an IRA, either the traditional IRA or the new Roth IRA. The traditional IRA is subject to income limitations. **With the Roth IRA, there is no deduction, but all of the proceeds are tax free upon withdrawal.** The Roth IRA is subject to a contribution limitation based on income; the phaseout starts at $95,000 for singles and at $150,000 for married couples.

Hiring an Employee

When your business begins to enjoy a modicum of success, you may want to hire help to expand this success and to divide your work load. You can place a want ad in a newspaper to advertise the position you want to fill. You can also contact your local employment office and tell them about the position. Specify required business skills, and the employment office will test for those skills before sending the candidate to you for an interview. **Interview as many candidates as possible, even if the first one who shows up seems perfect for the job.**

Rely on more than your intuition and business sense when making such an important decision as hiring an employee. If you do not go through the employment office, you can design a competency test or secure such a test from job services, a community college, or even a local

Test the Skills of Your Potential Employee before You Hire

high school. One way or another, make certain that you test the skills of your potential employee before you hire.

Have all candidates fill out an employment application. Have them list references, and call to check those references. Before you hire, write a job description, and list the job responsibilities. Specifically explain in writing what you expect of the employee in this job and the wage you are willing to pay. Outline the expected pay advances over time. **Once hired, take the time to train your employee.** Don't expect them to guess what needs to be done and how you want it done, then get mad when they don't know what "you're thinking." **Be up front with what you expect.** It is much better to start out tough and then loosen up than starting loose and trying to tighten the strings later. **Let your employee know that they are expected to be to work on time.** Tell them when they can take breaks and how long they have for lunch. Should you ever offer more than forty hours of work per week, know your state employment rules for overtime. If you need to familiarize yourself with your state employee laws, your state department of employment can help. They have numerous bulletins and pamphlets that outline the regulations for hiring, evaluating, and firing employees. **Many state employment departments (also called departments of labor) offer free seminars for small business owners.**

Before you hire the employee, know how and when you will evaluate their work. **Give them a written review.** This is especially important if they are not performing up to expectations and you foresee that you might have to replace them. **When you know that an employee is not working out or is not right for your business, let them go.** The sooner you cut the strings and hire someone new, the better for you and for them.

Once hired, you need to pay your employee a regular and fair salary. There are numerous rules regarding employment taxes. You can hire an accountant or bookkeeper to do the payroll for you or attempt to do it yourself. If you do it yourself, know what you are doing. The IRS has a service for small businesses called S.T.E.P. It includes a video tape and instructions on how to "make payroll." Making payroll includes paying the employee and withholding the proper amounts, then sending the withheld taxes, along with the employer's share, to the right place on time. The educational branch of the IRS also offers an informative, free, one-day seminar. These seminars usually involve presentations by the State Department of Employment and the State Tax Commission. This seminar covers "making payroll" as well as state employee requirements.

Specifically Explain in Writing What You Expect of the Employee and the Wage You Are Willing to Pay

Another option to familiarize yourself with the rules is to rely on your accountant to help you. **Paying a bookkeeper, accountant, or payroll service to do your payroll is money well-spent.** Such a service is a bargain for the headaches relieved and the time freed to make you more productive. Employment law and employment taxes are complicated and confusing for the novice. Don't be afraid to ask questions and seek help.

When you pay an employee, you withhold their federal and state income taxes and their FICA and Medicare taxes. These taxes are entrusted to you to be paid by the due date. **You must not use this money to meet other business obligations.** This "tax liability" should immediately be separated, since most of it is the "employee's money" or money withheld for their benefit.

You, the employer, will pay a matching FICA and Medicare tax on all wages. Currently, the FICA tax is 12.4%, one half comes from the employee (6.2%) and the other half comes from you, the employer (6.2%). **For 1998, FICA tax is due on the first $68,200 of earnings.** The Medicare tax is 2.9%, 1.45% from the employee and 1.45% from the employer. **The Medicare tax is assessed against all wages, there is no cap.** In addition, each quarter you will send in withheld taxes to your state tax commission (assuming your state has a state income tax). You may also need to send in local taxes. You will also pay a percentage of the employee's salary to the State Department of Employment. (They have different names in each state, i.e., Department of Labor, Department of Unemployment, Job Services, etc.) This "contribution" works similar to an insurance premium to pay for unemployment benefits for employees. You will be charged a standard rate based on past claims filed in your business category. **Finally, you are required to carry worker's compensation insurance. If an employee is injured on the job, you are not personally liable, since they are covered through worker's compensation. Without the insurance, you could be sued directly by your employee for injuries that occur while they are working and take a substantial penalty for being uninsured.** As you can see, the rules are complex and many, so seek competent advice and help from a bookkeeper, your accountant, or a business attorney.

The reports you must file include:

- Form 941, filed quarterly, showing federal withholding, employee and employer FICA, and Medicare taxes. Deposits for these taxes are made with a local bank when the employer owes $500 or more. Payments under $500 are made quarterly and paid to the IRS with Form 941.

Withheld Employee Taxes Must Be Held in Trust and Not Used to Pay Other Business Expenses

You Are Required to Carry Worker's Compensation Insurance

- Payment and reporting document filed quarterly to your state tax commission for state withholding tax.
- Payments to your State Department of Employment for unemployment insurance. These are filed and paid quarterly.
- FUTA, federal unemployment insurance, is filed annually on Form 940 and 940EZ. Deposits are made with a local bank when the liability reaches $100.

You might consider using a temporary agency for employment help if you don't need assistance on a regular basis. They take care of the payroll, the insurance, and pay all the taxes. You pay an hourly wage or fee for the employee's time. Basically, you "lease" an employee with qualified skills. Although you pay substantially more, you have no employer responsibilities and no permanent commitment. **You can hire such an employee for a day, a week, a month, for a production task or job, or for whatever time you need them.**

Promoting Your Business

Try to think at least six months ahead. Where would you like to be in six months, in a year? What will make that happen? What can you do to make it happen? **Advertising and marketing must always be on your mind.** How do you get new clients/customers? Once you have a client/customer base, ask them for referrals. People referred come to you with positive expectations. **To make your business grow, you must continue to advertise your business, even when you are the busiest, and even when funds are low.**

The amount of promotion you can do may depend upon the money you have available. Even with minimal funds, you can:

Advertising and Marketing Help a Business Grow

- Design flyers and have them distributed to Post Office boxes. Have them delivered to houses with bulk mail, or place the flyers with businesses. Some cities have a welcome wagon package that they distribute to all new home owners. Including your brochure or flyer as a part of that package is an inexpensive way to advertise. You can also place ads in civic and church bulletins or your local newspaper, all for a nominal fee.
- Join your local Chamber of Commerce. They often sponsor job fairs and help to promote the businesses of their members. Some cities have a Web site where they list all of the participating

businesses by category. The cost for membership varies but will be around $200.
- You should have a listing in the white pages in the business section of your local telephone directory. This is usually included with your business telephone line.

Remember that continued advertising is necessary for business growth. If funds permit, consider the following:
- Take out an ad in the yellow pages of your local telephone directory.
- Place an ad in a local newspaper and/or a larger newspaper in your area that has wider circulation. Generally, the larger the circulation, the more expensive the ad.
- Place an ad in trade magazines or journals appropriate for your business.
- Have an ad placed on a billboard.
- If certain of increased profits, consider television or radio advertisements. They are both expensive but may be very effective.

Businesses grow by word of mouth when you provide excellent service to your clients. A job well done often means a repeat performance with a new and bigger audience. If your skills and talents warrant, keep your fees in the upper third of the standard for your industry. People don't like to pay too much, but they also like a good deal. **Correct pricing on your part is important.** Keep in mind that if your fee is too low, many people will think they got an inferior product or budget service rather than a good deal.

Correct Pricing Is Important

Madeleine

Madeleine runs a bridal shop. She had twenty dresses that she wanted to move, so she placed them on sale, slashing the already low prices by 60%. She got a very good deal on the dresses because she bought them in quantity. They were high quality dresses, purchased at a bargain price. Madeleine intended to pass these savings on to her customers. After two days, she only sold one of the dresses. She then doubled the price and marketed the dresses not as "sale" or "budget" items but as quality dresses that were 30% off. They all sold in a day.

If you believe in yourself and believe in your service or product, your business has a good chance for survival. Your goal should be to go beyond "survival" and experience business success. **Be aggressive in pursuing your goals, but don't overextend.** The number one cause of business failure is expanding too quickly. **If you do your homework and "pay your dues," you will reap long-term benefits from your self-employment.** Never forget that you are the one responsible for the success of your business. Others may contribute, but you make it happen.

17
Special Tax Considerations for the Self-Employed

SELF-EMPLOYED PERSONS not only need to promote their business and stay motivated but also have responsibilities to keep records, pay taxes, and purchase and maintain their business equipment. This chapter will tell you some about requirements as well as give you some tips on how to cut your tax bill.

Record Keeping

The business books should show all sources of income. Depending on how thorough your records, it could also be important to keep your billing invoices and deposit slips. If you don't keep invoices, then note the source of income on each deposit slip. **Keep your business and personal accounts separate.** If you are audited and have made personal deposits to your business account and have no records to show the source of this money, the IRS may consider it income to the business.

The business books should also support all expenses or deductions. **Pay for most of your business expenses with checks so you have the canceled check as proof of the expenditure.** Along with the canceled check, you need to keep sales slips, invoices paid, and copies of bills. When possible, staple the invoice or receipt to the appropriate canceled check.

Save the sales receipts for all equipment you purchase. The date and amount are needed to set up depreciation schedules. Keep the support for your income and deductions for at least six years after the tax return for that year is filed.

Schedule C

The sole proprietor reports income and expenses on a tax form called "Schedule C." Self-employed farmers report their business activities on Schedule F. These forms are filed along with others that comprise your personal federal tax return. **If you have employees or a Keogh plan, you are required to have an FEIN number (Federal Employer Identification Number).** This is a special number given to businesses and serves the same purpose as a social security number. **If you are not required to have an FEIN number, you can use your social security number.**

To get an FEIN number by phone:

- Complete Form SS-4, which you can obtain from the IRS or the Social Security Administration either directly at their local offices or off of their Web sites on the Internet. Sole proprietors must sign and mail this form to the IRS after they are given their FEIN number by telephone.
- Call one of the numbers listed below. These numbers only issue FEIN's and should not be used for any other purpose. The operator will give you the FEIN number and tell you where to mail the completed SS-4.

Table 17.1—FEIN Numbers by Telephone

Andover, MA	(508) 474-9717
Atlanta, GA	(404) 455-2360
Austin, TX	(512) 460-7843
Holtsville, NY	(516) 447-4955
Cincinnati, OH	(606) 292-5467
Fresno, CA	(209) 452-4010
Kansas City, MO	(816) 926-5999
Memphis, TN	(901) 365-5970
Ogden, UT	(801) 620-7645
Philadelphia, PA	(215) 574-2400

Accounting Methods

An accounting method tells how you report your income and expenses. Once you use an accounting method, you must keep that same method. **It should clearly reflect the true income of the business.** To change from one accounting method you have used to another, you must first get consent from the IRS. This is done on Form 3115, Application for Change in Accounting Method.

Cash. The cash method **reports income when money is received** and **deducts expenses when they are paid.**

Accrual. The accrual method reports income when earned, even though payment hasn't been received. **Expenses are deductible when incurred,** even if payment hasn't been made. **The accrual method must be used to account for all inventory purchases and all inventory sales.**

Hybrid. The hybrid method is a combination of the CASH and ACCRUAL methods. The most common uses the CASH method to report income and expenses, and the ACCRUAL method to account for inventory purchases and sales.

Your Accounting Method Should Reflect the True Income of the Business

Income and Expenses

Income and expenses show inflow and outflow of money; money received and money spent. Gross receipts or income are reported in Part I of Schedule C (or Schedule F). **Include in income all cash receipts and all bartering transactions.** Bartering is trading done with others without money changing hands.

Example:

A lawyer might give free legal advice to an auto mechanic in exchange for the mechanic fixing the lawyer's car. They must both include the fair market value of goods and/or services received as income.

The income section includes a carryover from Part III, Cost of Goods Sold. Cost of Goods Sold reports purchases and expenses of inventory.

All expenses (except those associated with inventory) are reported in Part II. Common expenses include but are not limited to:

Advertising	Pension and Profit Sharing Plans
Bad Debts	Rent or Lease
Auto Expenses	Repairs and Maintenance

Commissions and Fees	Taxes and Licenses
Depreciation	Travel
Employee Benefits	Meals and Entertainment
Interest	Utilities
Legal and Professional Advice	Wages
Office Expenses	Home Office Expenses

Self-Employment Tax

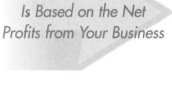

Your Self-Employment Tax Is Based on the Net Profits from Your Business

Self-employment tax is FICA and Medicare tax that is due from all sole proprietors who have a profit from their business. You calculate and pay this self-employment tax when you file your personal tax return. **The rate is 15.3% on net profits from your business.**

For example:

If your net profits were $22,000, your self-employment tax would be $3,366 (15.3% of $22,000). **As a self-employed person, you are both the employer and the employee** and must pay FICA tax (6.2%) and Medicare tax (1.45%) for the employer and the employee. This amounts to 15.3%.

Employee FICA	6.2%
Employer FICA	6.2%
Employee Medicare	1.45%
Employer Medicare	<u>1.45%</u>
TOTAL	15.3%

Estimated Tax Payments (Quarterlies)

Because the self-employed do not have any taxes withheld on the profits they earn from their business, they must send in quarterly tax payments based on their prior year's income. To avoid penalties, each year the self-employed are required to pay in, via a quarterly estimated tax payment, 90% of the tax due or an amount equal to what they owed in tax the prior year.

Example:

If a person owed $6,000 in regular tax and self-employment tax for tax year 1997, then their estimated tax payments would be $1,500 each quarter, ($1,500 x 4 = $6,000) or $6,000 annually. Even if they owed $10,000 in tax for 1998 and had paid in the $6,000, they would owe no penalty because they paid in an amount equal to what they owed the prior year. (For more detailed information, see chapter 6, Personal Income Taxes: Withholding and Tax Estimates.)

Business Auto

You can deduct the costs of buying and operating a car used for business, however, many restrictions apply. Auto expenses are deducted on Schedule C or Schedule F. **Eligibility to deduct automobile expenses requires that you keep a travel log for each business trip.** The log should include: date, miles traveled, client or customer visited, or business purpose. Keep this "log" in your daytimer or calendar or in a special auto expense log that can be purchased at a stationery store. Each day, enter the business miles traveled for each business trip during that day. Stationery stores have inexpensive simple automobile logs to help you keep track. You can also use your daytimer or calendar. Without this log, the IRS can disallow your auto expenses.

Two Choices for Deducting Auto Expenses

You have two choices for deducting automobile expenses. You make that decision the first year that you place your car in "business" service. **One choice is to take the standard mileage allowance ($.32$\frac{1}{2}$ for 1998 tax returns).** If you use the standard allowance, you need to keep track of all business miles traveled and keep the travel log explained above, but you do not need to keep track of all of your actual auto expenses, such as gas, oil, repairs, etc. **Once you choose a method, you can't change.**

The second choice is to take depreciation on your car plus the actual operating expenses. Since you can only deduct the business portion, you must know both how many business miles you traveled and how many total miles you drove during the year. It is necessary to **write down your odometer reading on the first and last day of the year so you know how many miles you traveled during the year. Total miles traveled during the year is then divided by your business miles to come up with a business percentage. This business percentage is then used to calculate your actual auto expenses.**

You Are Required to Keep a Travel Log for Business Trips. The log should show:

Date

Miles Traveled

Business Purpose

You Have Two Choices for Deducting Automobile Expenses:

Standard Mileage Allowance, or

Actual Expenses Plus Depreciation

Example:

Susan put 15,600 miles on her car during the year. 11,300 of those miles were for business. Her business percentage is 74.2% (11,300 divided by 15,600 = 74.2%)

If you choose to use actual expenses, you must also keep track of all operating expenses for the automobile. This includes:

- Registration Fees
- Interest Paid on Car Loan
- Insurance
- Gas and Oil
- Tires, Batteries, and Other Necessities
- Repairs
- Safety Inspections
- Washing, Waxing, etc.

Example:

Assume Susan's operating expenses during the year were $4,000. She can deduct 74.2% of $4,000 or $2,968 as auto expenses on her Schedule C.

In addition to the expenses of operating an auto, the IRS allows the business owner using the "actual" method to also depreciate the car. All automobiles are written off over a five-year period. The IRS limits the amount of depreciation that can be taken on all automobiles that are not heavy duty vehicles with a specific business purpose. For tax year 1997, this depreciation ceiling was $3,160.

The IRS has more than one method of depreciation. MACRS allows larger write-offs during the first two years of operation, then they are reduced. Straight line depreciation is the same percentage each year. **Regardless of the method of depreciation you choose, you are subject to the depreciation ceiling.** Purchasing the car during the last quarter will reduce the amount allowed. Also, you must use the straight line depreciation method if the business use of your car is less than 50% of the total use.

Susan's new car, purchased mid-year in 1997, cost $23,000. The straight line depreciation percentage gives her $4,600, but the IRS ceiling is $3,160, so she must use the lower ceiling amount. She can deduct $2,345, which is her business percentage of 74.2% times the maximum allowable, or $3,160.

All Automobiles Are Written Off over a Five-Year Period

If Susan chose to take the actual costs, she would be able to deduct the business portion of her operating expenses (gas, oil, repairs, etc.), or $2,968, plus the business portion of her depreciation, $2,345, for total car expenses of $5,313. The actual expense approach requires more bookkeeping, but it will usually generate larger write-offs during the first two or three years of operation if the car is new. After five years, when the car is fully depreciated, Susan can only deduct the business portion of her actual operating costs. She cannot keep driving this car and switch to the standard allowance and take the cents per mile because it would give a higher deduction.

If Susan uses the standard mileage allowance, she could take $.32½ per mile on her 11,300 business miles, or $3,560. She could then use this same rate each year that she owns the car and would not have to keep track of all business expenses. However, she would still be required to keep her travel log.

Buy or Lease?

Circumstances, available money, and lease terms are more important considerations than tax savings when you decide whether to buy or lease. Leasing an automobile generally has lower monthly payments and a smaller down payment than buying. When you lease, however, you never "own" the car, you just rent it for the term of the lease. **The business portion of your lease is fully deductible** (in Susan's case it would be 74.2% of her annual lease payment), **plus the actual operating expenses.** The following considerations may help you decide whether to lease or buy.

Reasons to Buy:
- **You intend to keep the car for more than four years** or until it falls apart.
- **You drive more than 15,000 miles per year.** (Most lease contracts have a 15,000 annual mileage limit. When you go beyond the annual mileage permitted under the lease, you will pay a premium on the extra miles, sometimes as high as $.20 to $.25 per mile.
- **To use the standard mileage allowance** for all business miles for as long as you own the car. (Remember, it requires less record keeping. You can't use the standard allowance for a leased car.)

Reasons to Lease:

- **Little or no money down and smaller monthly payments.**
- If you **like to drive a new car,** you can trade in the car every two or three years without tax consequences.
- Leasing is usually **less expensive than borrowing money** to finance a car.
- When you are ready for a new car, you don't have to worry about trading in your old one or selling it.
- Writing off the business lease is simpler than taking depreciation. When you depreciate a car, there are tax consequences upon its later sale or trade. **When you turn in a leased vehicle, there are no tax consequences.**

Business Use of Home

The IRS allows certain deductions for the use of your home as a business office. **To deduct home office expenses, you must have a specific area or part of the home set aside for business.** More importantly, you must show that you use the home office (the room or area set aside for business) exclusively and on a regular basis either to:

- meet with patients, clients, or customers in the normal course of your business, or
- to work there, generating most of your business income from this location.

If a self-employed contractor spends forty hours per week working out of the home on jobs, he/she does not qualify to deduct a home office, although a specific room is set aside in which to keep books and records, calculate bids, and write out invoices for customers. **To deduct a home office, it must be your primary work area.**

Congress liberalized the home office rules for tax year 1999. **Under these more liberal rules, a home office qualifies as a principal place of business as long as it is used to conduct administrative activities and you have no other place to work.**

For Tax Years 1999 and after, Congress Liberalized the Home Office Rules

Day Care

People engaged in day care can deduct certain expenses associated with running their business. **Licensed day care providers do not have to meet the "exclusive use area" test.** They only have to use an area on a regular basis to tend and care for children or others. **The area used for day care is divided by the total square footage of the home to come up with the home office percentage. Similarly, the total hours spent in day care can be divided by the total hours in a year to come up with the business percentage.**

Example:

Nancy runs a day care center from her home. The square footage of her home is 2,800 feet, and her business area is 350 square feet. Her business percentage is 12.5%, using the square footage method (350 feet divided by 2,800 feet). During the year, Nancy tended children for 1,575 hours. There are 8,736 hours in a year, so her business percentage using the hourly method is 18%. Nancy should use the hourly method because it gives her a larger percentage.

Deductible Home Office Expenses

When you have a home office, you can deduct numerous expenses that are indirectly related to the home office space. You can deduct the business percentage of:

- Mortgage Interest
- Taxes
- Homeowner's Insurance
- Utilities
- Cleaning and Yard Maintenance
- Depreciation on the Home
- Depreciation for Improvements That Benefit the Entire Structure.

The business percentage is calculated by taking the square footage of the home office and dividing it by the square footage of the entire home.

Example:

Marilyn has a home office that is 270 square feet. Her home has 2,800 square feet. Marilyn's home office is 9.6% of the entire structure.

Therefore, she can deduct 9.6% of all the above listed expenses on her tax return.

The basis, or cost of the home, minus the value of the land is used to figure the depreciation that can be taken on the home office.

Example:

Marilyn paid $150,000 for her home several years ago. Her tax bill shows that the value of the land is 18% and the value of the structure is 82%. $150,000 x 82%, or $123,000, is the cost or basis of the structure. 9.6% of this $123,000, or $11,808, becomes the basis for the home office. It must be depreciated over thirty-nine years, so this leaves Marilyn with a depreciation deduction of $291 per year for a full year.

Deductions for the business portion of insurance, utilities, mainte-nance, and depreciation cannot exceed business income. The "overage" on these expenses will carry over to the next year or indefinitely until the home business generates enough income to allow for the full deduction.

Example:

Marilyn's profit from her business was $2,000. Her deductions for the costs of the home office for the year were $2,600. Her entire home office deduction is limited to $2,000. She can carry forward into the next year her $600 of operating expenses that she couldn't take this year.

Net Operating Loss

Businesses can and do experience unprofitable years for one reason or another. **A net operating loss occurs when business loss(es) exceeds income from all sources.**

A casualty or theft loss, even when the property was used for per-sonal purposes, can be included in the figures used to arrive at a net oper-ating loss. Other inclusions are moving expenses for job relocation, deductible employee job expenses, your share of a partnership or an S-Corporation loss, and the loss on the sale of small business stock.

Example One:

Assume you are self-employed and have a $20,000 business loss, and your only other income is wages of $15,000 earned by your spouse. You would have a business loss of $5,000. This is the amount that exceeds all other income.

Example Two:

On the "loss side" is a business loss of $2,000, moving expenses for job relocation of $6,000, and a casualty loss from a fire of $60,000 that has no insurance coverage, for total "losses" of $68,000. On the income side is a net capital gain of $5,000 and wages of $35,000, for total income of $40,000. After offset by positive income, the net loss is $28,000.

Other non-business deductions, such as most itemized deductions and the personal exemption further reduce the loss. In example two, assume the itemized deductions were $6,000 and the personal exemption was $2,600. The $28,000 "loss" will be reduced by another $8,600, leaving a net operating loss of only $19,400.

A net operating loss was designed to help those who lose much of what they owned through a business failure or a catastrophe such as a flood or fire. The net operating loss can be carried back to the third prior tax year to receive an immediate refund of taxes paid. This reimbursement of "old" taxes paid can help the business owner get started again.

Example:

Use the $19,400 net operating loss explained above. The loss occurred in 1997, so it can be carried back to 1994 (the third carryback year). If the business owner had taxable income of $24,000 in 1994, this '97 loss could reduce the '94 taxable income to $4,600. ($24,000 - $19,400 = $4,600). This could mean a refund to the business owner of nearly all the taxes paid for 1994, or approximately $3,600. The business owner need only apply for this by filing the appropriate tax forms.

If the loss is not completely absorbed in the third carryback year, it is carried forward to the next tax year and then the next year until it is completely absorbed.

This section does not attempt to show you how to figure a net operating loss but rather to explain the concept of a net operating loss. You need to know they exist so you can receive a refund of prior taxes should you or your business ever experience a year when your total losses exceed your total income. Seek competent tax advice if you ever have occasion to file one; net operating losses are much more complicated than shown here.

Tax Saving Tips

Employ your child and save on social security tax.

Parents who have an unincorporated business can employ their children who are under the age of eighteen. The child could earn as much as $4,250 in 1998, and it will not be subject to any employment taxes, such as FICA, Medicare, or federal and state withholding. The child's wages can be deducted as wages by the business 1) as long as the child actually does work for the business, 2) the wages given to the child are reasonable for the work done, 3) payments are actually made to the child, and 4) the work is related to the parent's trade or business.

Employ your spouse and save on medical expenses.

Sole proprietors can deduct as a business expense all medical insurance premiums and all medical reimbursement costs incurred under an accident and health plan that covers all employees. If the sole proprietor's spouse is also an employee, the sole proprietor can be covered under the plan as the spouse of the employee.

The employer can deduct the amounts paid to the employee-spouse under the plan, and this amount is not included in the income of the employee-spouse 1) as long as the money is a reimbursement for medical expenses, and 2) the business has a written medical reimbursement plan.

New Business Equipment

For qualifying business equipment purchased in 1998 (each year the amount may change), a business owner can deduct the cost of such equipment up to a maximum limit of $18,500 per year. This election, called first-year expensing, is limited to tangible business property purchased for business use, such as machinery, office equipment, office furniture, computers, cars, or trucks.

This election taken up front can help to reduce profits when business is booming. It takes the place of regular depreciation that must be deducted over the life of the asset. Should you sell the equipment early, you will have to recapture as income some of the cost that you deducted.

Part 6
Financial Planning

THIS SECTION HELPS you assess your finances and come up with the specific actions needed to implement your goals. Chapter 18, Financial Inventory, has you look at your cash flow and your net worth so you can see what you bring in and, what you spend, and what assets you have working for you. Chapter 19, Know What You Want to Achieve with Your Money, uses a financial pyramid to evaluate risk. It also looks at the objective of numerous savings and investment choices. Chapter 20, Planning, shows how to figure out how much money you need to meet specific goals and how to plan for retirement. This chapter also covers the basics of estate planning. Finally, chapter 21, Implementing Your Plan, shows you some ways to find the money to fund your goals.

18
Financial Inventory

Overview

A FINANCIAL INVENTORY shows you where you are now. **You need to know your starting point to reach your destination. Assessing your current position shows what resources you have working for you.** How much money do you earn? How much do you spend? What do you own, and how much do you owe on those assets?

The cash flow and net worth statements discussed in this chapter are tools for taking a financial inventory. They show you where you are and help you find ways to get to where you want to be. **A close scrutiny of these statements will uncover weaknesses in your finances and help you overcome these weaknesses by implementing new strategies.**

Many who have sought professional financial planning say the planning session was valuable because they took the time to:

- look at their assets and liabilities,
- look at their income and expenses, and
- discuss financial goals with family members.

Analyzing on paper what happens to your money takes time but gives you important information. It provides working tools to improve your cash flow and initiate a healthy, growing net worth.

Cash Flow

Cash Flow Statement

A cash flow statement shows your inflow and outflow, that is, what you bring in and what you spend. It can be simple or detailed. The more out-of-control your spending, the more itemization and inquiry needed toward your income and expenses.

The cash flow statement compares money earned to money spent. The numbers are specific, gleaned from pay stubs, checks, and bills. If, like most people, you need everything you earn and then some just to meet your expenses, don't get discouraged. Eventually, you will learn how to find "hidden pockets" that can free extra money to work for you.

After looking over the sample cash flow statement in Table 18.1, take a sheet of paper and follow its format: at the top, write CASH FLOW and today's DATE. On the left, write INCOME; on the right, EXPENSES. Using Table 18.1 as a guide, you will need to put down the income and expense headings that fit your situation.

Cash Flow	
Date	
Income	Expenses

Table 18.1—Cash Flow Statement

Inflow:		Outflow:	
Fixed		**Fixed**	
Salary 1	_____	Federal Taxes	_____
Salary 2	_____	FICA Taxes	_____
Other:	_____	State Taxes	_____
Other:	_____	Health Insurance:	_____
Variable	_____	401(k) Contribution	_____
	_____	Mortgage / Rent	_____
	_____	Auto Payment (s)	_____
	_____	Auto Insurance	_____
		Variable	_____
		Auto Service / Gas	_____
		Food	_____
		Household Expenses	_____
		Other	_____
		Other	_____
		Savings	_____
Total Inflow _____		Total Outflow	_____

Net Income after Expenditures

_____

Get your data by looking at a typical month's income and expenses. If possible, use the most recent month. You will need copies of pay stub(s), bills, check book register(s), and a calculator. **If your employer pays you weekly or biweekly, convert these amounts to a monthly gross income.**

Begin by listing gross income from all income sources, such as salary(s), pension(s), tips, alimony, child support, and social security. If you have income that varies, such as tips, bonuses, commissions, or royalties, go back six months to get an average (add the total income for six months, then divide that total by six). Use that average as the month's income for this projection.

After finishing with all your income, list your expenditures. Some of these will be fixed monthly expenses. That is, they remain the same each month. Start with the amounts taken out of your pay for federal, state, and employment taxes (FICA and Medicare). Then look at other payroll deductions, such as retirement contributions, health and life insurance, loan payments, and savings plans. Next, list mortgage or rent payment(s) and car payment(s), then all other fixed payments, such as insurance. **If you pay insurance or other expenses annually or quarterly, convert your payment to a monthly expense.**

Variable expenses include amounts that change from month to month, such as charge card payment(s), food, recreation, and clothing. When payments vary, take a six-month average. Education contributions and child care could be either a fixed or a variable expense. Write down what you contribute each month to a 401(k), IRA, or savings account.

Paycheck
Expenses:
Federal Tax $_____
State Tax $_____
FICA $_____
Medicare $_____
Insurance $_____
Loans $_____
Retirement Plan $_____

When you have written down all of your monthly expenses, total both your income column and your expense column. The final step is to see how much income you have left after paying your expenses. Table 18.2 shows a completed monthly cash flow statement for a family of four. The averages are based on studies by the U.S. Bureau of Labor Statistics.

Table 18.2—Completed Monthly Cash Flow Statement Showing Percentages

Income:			Expenses:		
Fixed		%	**Fixed**		%
Salary 1	$3,200	69%	Federal Taxes	$288	7.0%
Salary 2	$ 978	31%	FICA Taxes	$320	7.6%
Other:			State Taxes	$174	4.2%
Other:			Health Care:	$111	2.7%
Variable			Housing	$993	24.0%
			Transportation	$705	17.0%
			Insurance/Pensions	$466	11.0%
			Variable		
			Entertainment	$165	4.0%
			Food	$459	11.0%
			Education	$ 49	1.0%
			Contributions	$159	3.8%
			Clothing/Personal	$247	6.0%
			Miscellaneous	$ 4	.7%
Total Income	$4,178	100%	**Total Expenses**	$4,140	$100.0%

Net Income after Expenses

$38

Analyzing Your Cash Flow

- **What percentage of total monthly income goes toward total monthly expenses?** If total income is $1,500 and total expenses are $1,400, expenses are 93% of income. Divide monthly expenses by monthly income ($1,400 ÷ $1,500 equals 93%)—7% is left after expenses.

- **What percentage is each expense item?** If total expenses are $1,400 and you spend $450 for rent, then rent is 32% of total expenses. Divide each expense item, such as rent, by the expense total, such as $1,400 ($450 divided by $1,400 equals 32%). Know what percentage you pay for taxes, food, auto repairs, installment debt, etc.

- **Do some expense areas surprise you?** Are they greater or smaller than you expected? What are these areas? Why are you surprised?
- **What expenses will reduce or end in the future?** (They may be car loans or other debt when paid off.) When do they stop, or when will they be reduced?
- **Do you have money going into some type of retirement plan, savings, or investments?** What percentage?
- **What expenses, if any, can you reduce?**
- **Do you have too much installment debt?** What would your situation look like without it or with a smaller percentage of debt?

Your completed cash flow statement, with percentages by each expense items, is a tool. It will help you take charge of your finances instead of "wants" directing you. If you are not pleased with your cash flow, try to channel more money into areas that are important to you, and cut back on ones that aren't.

Take time to do this cash flow analysis. To work, it must be written and put down in the format discussed. A completed cash flow analysis gives you specific information that will help you take charge of your money. **Solutions are not possible until you know the problem.**

Net Worth

Net Worth Statement

A net worth statement is the second important tool for taking your financial inventory. It is a personal balance sheet showing the value of your assets and the balance of your debts. **Basically, it reveals the assets you have working for you and how much equity (ownership) you have in them.**

Again, on a piece of paper, write NET WORTH at the top and, under it, write today's date. Divide the paper in half; on the left, write ASSETS and on the right, LIABILITIES. Under assets, list the market value of each asset you own. On the right, list the balance owing on all of your loans. When finished, total the amounts for both columns. Your NET WORTH is your ASSETS minus your LIABILITIES. Use Table 18.3 as a guide.

Be sure to list the total market value for all major assets and the balance owing on all loans or credit cards. If you own a home and it is

A Net Worth Statement Shows What You Own and What You Owe

worth $120,000, list the full market value as an asset under "Home." If you owe $80,000 on the mortgage, list the $80,000 loan as a liability under "Home Mortgage." Your home equity is $40,000, the difference between the market value and the balance on the loan. **Equity adds to your net worth.**

Table 18.3—Net Worth Statement

Assets: List Market or Cash Value		Liabilities: List Total Balance	
Checking	_____	Mortgage	_____
Savings	_____		
Life Ins. Cash Value	_____	#1 Car Loan	_____
Stocks	_____	#2 Car Loan	_____
Mutual Funds	_____	Credit Card	_____
Annuities	_____	Credit Card	_____
Pension (Vested)	_____	Credit Card	_____
Residence	_____	Loan Balance 1	_____
Automobiles	_____	Loan Balance 2	_____
Rec. Vehicles	_____	Loan Balance 3	_____
Furniture	_____		
Valuables	_____		
Total Assets	_____	**Total Liabilities**	_____
Net Worth (Assets Minus Liabilities)			
_____			

Analyzing Your Net Worth
What Is Your Net Worth?

- Identify the assets that are growing in value each year.
- Identify the assets that are decreasing in value? (i.e., cars, home furnishings, etc.)
- **What assets can you easily liquidate,** such as savings accounts and money market funds? **Do you have sufficient liquid assets to cover an emergency?**
- **Compare liquidity with non-liquidity.** Some people today are "asset poor." They have too much money tied up in real estate, pension plans, or hard assets and works of art that can not be

sold easily if cash is needed. Their net worth looks great on paper, but they have nothing in the bank to see them through an emergency and are often "cash" poor.

- **Is your net worth growing fast enough to keep ahead of inflation and taxes?** If you have large amounts of equity with little growth, consider freeing the equity so it can better serve your needs. This means selling the asset or borrowing against it. Such repositioning can also create greater liquidity and possibly provide some tax relief. The two case studies given in chapter 21, Implementing Your Plan: What Others Have Done, will give you some ideas.

A primary financial goal should be having a net worth that grows each year. Net worth increases by acquiring more assets, by increasing the value of assets, or by reducing liabilities. **The higher your net worth, the more money you have working for you.**

The Higher Your Net Worth, the More Money You Have Working for You

Summary

Your cash flow statement can help you improve your net worth, and your net worth statement can help you improve your cash flow. Study them together, and look for solutions in the one that seems to have the lesser problem. Often, the solution to a poor cash flow can be found through analyzing net worth, and the solution to a poor net worth can be found through analyzing cash flow.

For example, your net worth statement may reveal you have a large amount of equity in your home. Your cash flow statement shows you have two car loans and several credit card balances, all with high interest charges. A home equity loan at a lower interest rate might help you reduce your monthly payments, reduce your taxes, and free some money for savings.

Your cash flow statement might show you have money left after meeting necessary expenses, but none of it is going into savings. If this is the case, you could start increasing your net worth by getting a handle on money spent unnecessarily.

Continual scrutiny of your cash flow and net worth helps you use more of your income to accumulate assets that grow in value and also have enough liquidity to meet unexpected expenses.

19

Know What You Want to Achieve with Your Money

Financial Pyramid, Risk and Objective

A FINANCIAL PYRAMID is an illustration tool that puts your savings and investment choices into categories according to investment purpose. This chapter uses information from other areas of this book to give you a comprehensive summary. The first step is to evaluate the risk and objective of saving and investment choices then put them on the levels of the pyramid. **The broad base at the bottom of the pyramid consists of the basics, or foundation.** These basics include insurance, savings plans, and home ownership. The levels above the basics, or foundation, are investment choices to make your net worth grow. As the pyramid progresses upwards, it shows choices that assume more risk. **The middle levels have low to moderate risk, while the choices on the upper levels have moderate to high risks.**

If the pyramid is "top heavy," without widespread support at the base, it can topple. For example, those who invest in commodities, undeveloped land, or stock options when they have inadequate insurance coverage and no savings take unnecessary chances and could lose everything. A financial pyramid is shown in Table 19.1.

This Chapter Uses Information from Other Areas of This Book to Give You a Comprehensive Summary

Table 19.1—Financial Pyramid

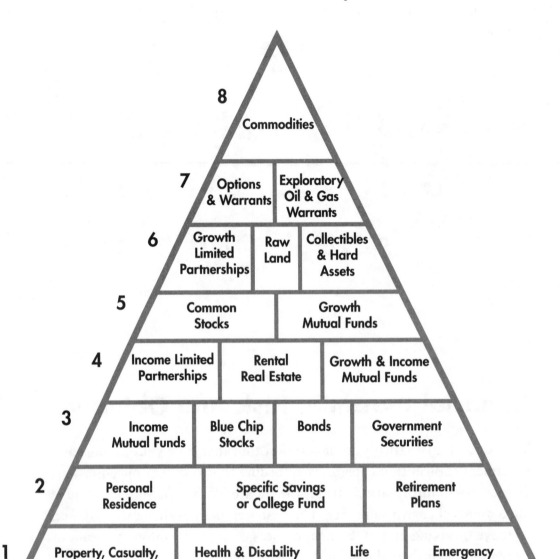

The Basics—Foundation

A solid financial plan starts with the basics that appear on the first two levels of the pyramid then progresses upward. **A strong foundation reduces exposure to unforeseen events and unplanned expenses, thereby strengthening one's ability to accumulate assets. The basics include:**

- Sufficient **savings** to cover unanticipated emergencies.
- Adequate **automobile and homeowner's insurance.**

- Sufficient **life insurance or other assets** to provide for dependents should the provider die early.
- Purchase of a **personal residence.**
- Funds to help **educate your children.**
- Sufficient **investments and savings to cover retirement** so those years are free from financial worry.

Property, Casualty, and Liability Insurance

Purchasing and maintaining a home and/or automobile(s) requires you to spend many hours working just to make the payments. These assets could be destroyed in an accident, fire, flood, or other disaster. **Proper insurance prevents a major accident or disaster from bringing financial ruin, because the insurance compensates you for the damages.** Unexpected lawsuits, which you lose, could also cause you to lose your assets. Liability protection, via your homeowner's policy, provides adequate protection for most commonplace incidents.

Health and Disability Insurance

A major illness suffered by you or an immediate family member can be extremely expensive. Don't put yourself in the position of having to sell your assets to raise the money needed to care for yourself or a loved one. An extended illness, without health insurance, can deplete everything you own and still cost more money. Health insurance helps preserve your assets and provide the money to pay for major illnesses.

In most cases, group health and disability plans offered through employers are the least expensive. Many organizations offer group insurance to their members. When some type of group plan isn't possible, you will need to find an independent source.

The chances of becoming disabled are much greater than most people realize. Yet, **disability insurance** is the most misunderstood of insurance policies. If you are a breadwinner and are unable to work for an extended period, who pays the bills when your wages stop? Disability policies provide income during an extended illness not covered by sick pay.

Disability Policies Provide Income during an Extended Illness Not Covered by Sick Pay

Life Insurance

Life insurance protects the earning power of the major wage earner(s) in a family. Should income suddenly stop due to an unexpected death, life insurance provides the needed funds to care for dependents. Although adequate coverage is essential, don't over-insure. Your dollars can earn more in other places.

Emergency Fund Savings

Everyone needs enough money in a liquid, "safe" savings account to cover unexpected expenses. Then, if you must make a sudden trip to attend a funeral, your car breaks down, or your home needs a repair, you will have the money to pay for these items without relying on credit cards with their expensive finance charges.

Different situations call for various amounts in an "emergency" account. A single person does not need as much savings as a family. A rule of thumb is to save an amount equal to three to six months' living expenses. Then, if you ever lose your job or have emergency expenses, this fund will see you through. Incidentally, after dipping into your emergency fund, be sure to replenish it as soon as possible. And, if it grows beyond what you need, move the extra funds to a higher level on the pyramid where they will earn a better rate of return.

Personal Residence

Owning your own home is a win/win situation. It creates a tax savings that helps to free other money. Be aware that the location, the climate, and the job market of a particular area will affect the market value of your home. Homes can go down in value as well as up. Additionally, if you have a variable interest rate on your mortgage, the payment will fluctuate.

Specific Savings or College Fund

If you have a particular goal, it is important to set money aside to achieve it. Keep in mind that the sooner you start saving, the fewer dollars you will have to put away.

Retirement Plans

Contributions to most retirement plans are deducted from gross wages or gross income **before taxes.** The deduction reduces taxable income dollar for dollar, providing tax relief. Included are: **IRA's, Keogh's, SEP IRA's, 401(k) plans, ESOP** (employee stock option plans), **deferred compensation, profit sharing, and 403(b)** plans for non-profit organizations. **Retirement plans offer several advantages. The earnings accumulate free of tax, making it possible to save much more.**

These plans become even more attractive if an employer matches a percentage of the employees contribution. The low interest loans that may be available with many 403(b) and 401(k) plans are an added feature. The loan option allows the contributor to feel comfortable saving

A Political Risk Does Exist with Pension Plans, Because Congress Frequently Changes the Tax Laws

larger amounts, because he/she has access to the money without penalty through the loan provision. A **political risk** does exist with pension plans, however, because Congress frequently changes the tax laws. Additionally, these plans are **not liquid until age fifty-nine and one-half** without a 10% tax penalty.

Income

Once you cover the basics, use the investment choices shown on the mid-pyramid levels to fund your financial goals. The choices you select will depend on your age, your objective, your risk tolerance, and the number of years you expect to invest the money.

Bonds and Government Securities

Municipal bonds, corporate bonds, and **government securities** offer a **consistent income** but are subject to an **interest rate risk.** They can provide higher rates of return than money market accounts, certificates of deposit, or bank savings accounts, but the principal will fluctuate. When general interest rates rise or fall, the bond's principal will decrease or increase in value.

The Principal of a Bond Fluctuates

Income Mutual Funds and Blue Chip Stocks

Income **mutual funds and blue chip stocks** (including many utility stocks) are subject to market risks but offer fairly consistent dividends with some potential growth of principal. Income mutual funds may hold both stocks and bonds in their portfolio, or only stocks, or only bonds. They offer the same advantage as the underlying investment but with better diversification.

Income Mutual Funds and Blue Chip Stocks Offer Consistent Dividends with Potential Growth of Principal

Growth and Income

Rental Real Estate

Real estate rentals offer **direct tax advantages** for those who **manage their own properties.** The risk varies according to the type of property owned, the amount of rent received, and the payment due on the mortgage. Higher mortgages carry higher risks, because when tenants move out, the owner(s) still must cover the mortgage payment. Nevertheless, well-selected real estate offers **equity buildup and tax write-offs.**

Mutual Funds and Limited Partnerships

Growth and income mutual funds provide consistent dividends with the potential of an increasing principal. They are subject to both an interest rate risk and a market risk. They often hold a mixed portfolio of stocks and bonds, with an emphasis on quality blue chip stocks. **Income limited partnerships** vary in value and risk because they can have investments in income-producing oil wells, income-producing real estate, or other income investments.

Growth

In general, growth investments pay little or no income but can increase in value over the years. They assume more risk because their future value is unknown.

Common Stocks and Growth Mutual Funds

In the past, common stocks have proven to be an excellent inflation hedge. Growth mutual funds, like all mutual funds, offer diversification and professional management. They come in many varieties, with some having the objective of aggressive growth. Growth mutual funds invest primarily in common growth stocks.

Growth Limited Partnerships, Hard Assets, and Land

An assortment of **growth limited partnerships** exists. These partnerships can invest in storage containers, movie rights, raw land, oil wells, or commercial real estate. A major risk of any limited partnership is the quality of management offered by the general partner. Also, fees and charges paid by the limited partners affect profits.

Collectibles and hard assets include paintings, works of art, a sundry of valuable collections, gold, silver, and other precious metals. Since no open market exists for these investments, to sell, an owner must find a willing buyer. Moreover, if forced to hire a middleman, the commissions charged by dealers and brokers are quite expensive.

Speculative Growth

Stock options and warrants, exploratory oil, and gas and commodities are all high risk investments. They are for those who have covered their bases in the other areas and have extra dollars to "gamble." Much money can be made here. However, these investments are very volatile, and losses often exceed their earnings.

Investment Purpose

Along with evaluating risks and objectives, as shown on the financial pyramid, you also need to identify your investment purpose. Investment purposes vary according to a person's age and income. Those who are young with money to invest will probably benefit the most from growth investments that offer a hedge against inflation. The middle-aged also need growth but have less time, so they should take a more conservative approach. Retirees, or those close to retirement, usually want a dependable income, so look to those "safe" accounts that generate consistent interest or dividends. Incidentally, even in retirement, some growth is necessary to offset inflation.

Know what you want to achieve with your money. Is it for an emergency fund savings, for long-term savings, or do you need to live on some of the income? An emergency fund savings needs both safety and liquidity. **Purpose leads you to the appropriate choices. No ideal investment exists that has "all" features. Everything is a trade-off. You must give up some liquidity for tax advantages or give up guarantees to have growth. Consider:**

- Safety
- Liquidity
- Income
- Tax Advantages
- Growth (Inflation Hedge)

Safety

A "safe" investment may or may not be guaranteed. The federal government guarantees bank accounts up to $100,000 for members of banks covered by FDIC insurance. The federal government also pledges their credit to cover the different issues of U.S. Government Securities. Other investments are secured by the assets of the company or issuer. Such investments include annuities, life insurance contracts, and bonds. Mortgages are secured by a deed on the property.

The quality of an institution's assets and investment portfolio are extremely important. They reflect the overall "safety" of the money you "loaned" to the institution. For example, if an insurance company owns large amounts of overappraised real estate or junk bonds, those assets could lose value or become worthless, leaving investors with nothing backing their money.

Liquidity

Normally, accounts that offer high liquidity have other disadvantages, such as lower yields or no tax advantages. **Bank passbook accounts** are easily converted to cash. This liquidity convenience, along with their safety, is the main appeal. All **certificates of deposit** have a penalty for early withdrawal, so depending on their maturity, you will lose some liquidity but may gain a greater yield than with a passbook savings account. As a rule, **money market accounts** offered through mutual funds pay the highest possible yields that maintain instant liquidity. Although these accounts are considered low risk, they are not "guaranteed" with FDIC insurance.

Other accounts also offer liquidity, though not with the same convenience. **Insurance policies** with loan provisions have low interest loans, often at 5% or 6%. **Most annuities** offer a 10% (or more) free withdrawal each year, without a contract penalty, before the policy matures. In both these cases, the owner will usually have a check within one to three weeks after submitting the paperwork. **Mutual funds, stocks,** and **bonds** can all be cashed out within five business days upon receipt of the proper form/certificate and signature guarantee. Most mutual funds allow shares to be sold through a telephone request. **The main drawback when liquidating stocks, bonds, and mutual funds is that they are subject to market or interest rate risks. If the account value is down when you need your money, you lose. As a rule, these investments require TIME to build their value.**

Income

Bonds pay a consistent income that can be taxable or tax free. The income remains consistent for the life of the bond. If interest rates rise, the bond principal will lose value, but their interest payments remain constant. **Certificates of deposit** and **money market funds** also generate a fixed rate of return, but the amount paid fluctuates to reflect current interest rates. **Blue chip stocks** and **utility stocks** generally pay consistent dividends to their stockholders. **Income mutual funds** are a combination of all of the abovementioned investments. They also have a history of steady payments. Finally, some **limited partnerships** that invest in producing oil wells or unleveraged rental properties will pay an income stream to their limited partners.

Income Mutual Funds Have a History of Steady Payments

Tax Advantages

Retirement plans offer a tax write-off for the contribution, plus tax free earnings on the principal. When the tax is deferred during accumulation, all moneys are fully taxed when withdrawn. These taxable withdrawals must begin by age seventy and one-half to avoid a 50% penalty. **Municipal bonds** provide tax free income. In addition, all **U.S. Government Securities** are free from state taxes. Many **mutual funds** invest only in municipal bonds or U.S. Government Securities, so they offer the same advantages with more diversification. Actively managed **rental properties** allow tax write-offs from depreciation and expenses that help offset the income. Numerous **limited partnerships** offer rental properties or tax credits to help those in higher income brackets. Be careful of the many risks inherent in limited partnerships.

Growth (Inflation Hedge)

Growth investments typically generate little or no income but concentrate on increasing their principal. Instead of paying dividends, these companies take their "earnings" and reinvest them back into the company to make it grow and become financially stronger. **Common growth stocks** and **growth mutual funds** (comprised of common growth stocks) are typical investments. Many investors have found that well-located **real estate,** purchased at the right price, also offers appreciation. In all these investments, the principal has potential for growth. Investments that offer appreciation are inflation hedges, because their value increase often exceeds the annual inflation rate.

Summary

Whatever purpose you select for your investment dollars, you can't have all benefits in one investment. Different purposes require different investments. For example, growth investments that are good inflation hedges produce little income and are not immediately liquid for a profit. They need TIME to make them valuable. Fixed income accounts that pay steady interest have no growth of principal and thus are poor inflation hedges. Investments that offer tax advantages often lack liquidity. Savings that provide safety and liquidity are poor inflation hedges. **Everything is a trade-off, so above all, know what you give up, and know**

Know What You Value, and Take the Time to Implement Those Values

what you want to achieve with your investment dollars. Financial priorities take thought and time—thought to know what you value, and time to implement those values.

20
Planning

AFTER YOU HAVE taken a financial inventory (covered in chapter 18) and basically know what you want to achieve with your money (covered in chapter 19), it is time to get more specific. This chapter will show you how much you need to save or invest to reach a certain goal. It will also give you information to help you plan your future by looking at retirement planning, tax planning, and estate planning.

Saving for Specific Goals

A specific savings goal might be a child's education, a down payment for a home, a vacation, or an assessment coming due. **Estimating how much you need to save to have a certain number of dollars later requires knowing the rate of return the "saved" money will receive for the time it is saved.** Tables 20.1 and 20.2 show how much you need to put away now to have a certain future sum. To allow for a wide range of savings and investment options, the periods range from five to twenty years, and the compound earnings range from 3% to 12%.

Table 20.1 shows the **LUMP SUM** (one time investment) needed to equal $1,000.

Table 20.2 shows the **ANNUAL INVESTMENT** needed to equal $1,000.

Follow instructions at the bottom of each table to figure amounts other than $1,000. Knowing the numbers you need can make a goal reality, especially when the amount needed is less than you thought.

Table 20.1—Lump Sum Needed to Equal $1,000

Years	5%	6%	7%	8%	9%	10%	11%	12%
20	377	312	258	215	178	149	124	104
19	377	331	270	232	194	164	138	116
18	416	350	296	250	212	180	153	130
17	436	371	317	270	231	198	170	146
16	458	394	339	292	252	218	188	163
15	481	417	362	315	275	239	209	183
14	505	442	388	340	299	263	232	205
13	530	469	415	368	326	290	258	229
12	557	497	494	397	356	319	286	257
11	585	527	475	429	388	350	317	287
10	614	558	508	463	422	386	352	322
5	784	747	713	681	650	621	593	567

For larger amounts, such as:

$ 5,000   multiply table amount by 5
$ 7,300   multiply table amount by 7.3
$25,000   multiply table amount by 25

Table 20.2—Annual Investment Needed to Equal $1,000

Years	5%	6%	7%	8%	9%	10%	11%	12%
19–20	33	30	27	24	22	20	18	16
17–18	39	35	32	30	27	25	22	20
15–16	46	43	40	37	34	31	29	27
13–14	56	53	50	47	44	41	38	36
11–12	70	67	63	60	57	54	51	48
9–10	91	87	83	80	77	74	71	68
8	105	101	97	94	91	87	84	81
7	123	119	116	112	109	105	102	99
6	147	143	140	136	133	130	126	123

> **For larger amounts, such as:**
>
> $ 5,000   multiply table amount by 5
> $ 7,300   multiply table amount by 7.3
> $25,000   multiply table amount by 25

Ten Years or Longer

With time on your side, you can consider growth investments. If you have ten years or longer to achieve your financial goal(s), select your investments by determining how comfortable you are with varying degrees of risk.

For many who are not completely comfortable investing and want to minimize risk, a mutual fund with a well-established, long-term track record is a safe choice. Several available growth and income funds and balanced funds have averaged a compound rate of return between 12% and 15% for money invested with the fund ten years or longer. The portfolios of these funds have a mixture of quality stocks and bonds that maintain value under changing market conditions. They are often not the years "hottest" funds but funds with a proven history of performance. They grow in "up" markets and hold their value in "down" markets.

Another investment choice is **zero coupon bonds.** A zero coupon bond is bought at a discount, then the interest accumulates until the bond matures. **You can plan the maturity date for the time when you will need the money.** These bonds can be used to accumulate a specific amount of money. A disadvantage is the bond's sensitivity to interest rates, especially for bonds with a longer maturity time. For example, a $1,000 bond with twenty years to maturity will drop in value from $372 to $307 when interest rates rise from 5% to 6%. If you hold the bond until it matures, you will always get its full value. An advantage is the lower out-of-pocket cost at purchase. A $1,000 bond earning 6% with ten years to maturity costs $554. **Table 20.3 shows what you would pay for a zero coupon bond for various maturity dates and yields.**

Table 20.3—Value Per $1,000, Zero Coupon Bond

Years to Maturity	Yield to Maturity on $1,000 Bond			
	5%	6%	7%	8%
20	$372	$307	$253	$208
18	411	345	290	244
16	454	388	333	285
14	501	437	382	333
12	553	492	438	390
10	610	554	503	456
8	674	623	577	534
6	744	701	662	625
4	821	789	759	731
2	906	888	871	855

You buy U.S. Government **Series EE Bonds** at a discount. At maturity, the redemption value is double the issue price. The interest rate paid determines how many years until the bond matures. If you cash in the bonds early, you will receive a reduced interest rate. You can pay income taxes on the interest earnings when you cash in the bond, or you can elect to pay the tax annually. **If purchased after 1990, Series EE Bonds are tax free when used to pay for education.** Many trade and technical schools qualify, along with colleges and universities, for this tax free advantage. To receive the full tax free status, the following conditions must apply:

- The bond purchaser must be twenty-four years of age or older.
- The bonds used for a child's education must be in the parent's name(s) and redeemed by the parents.
- The bond proceeds must be used for tuition and fees for dependents, spouse, or bond owner. (Room and board and books do not qualify.)
- The year's educational expenses must exceed or equal the value of the bond. If the bond is worth more, the "tax free" interest is prorated.
- For married couples filing jointly, their taxable income must be under $62,900. For singles and head of household filers, their taxable income must be under $41,950.

Table 20.4—Series EE Bonds

Issue Price	Face Amount
$ 25.00	$ 50.00
$ 37.50	$ 75.00
$ 50.00	$ 100.00
$ 100.00	$ 200.00
$ 250.00	$ 500.00
$ 500.00	$ 1,000.00
$2,500.00	$ 5,000.00
$5,000.00	$10,000.00

Under Ten Years

With only five to ten years to invest, it is wise to take less risk with your investments. Select returns you can count on. This could be stock from well-established corporations that show a history of profits, short-term corporate bonds, short-term government securities, or fixed interest accounts. Due to the shorter time period, your investment is subject to a loss through interest rate risk, market risk, and even political risk. If you have to liquidate when the value is down, you will lose some money.

Retirement Planning

While earning money, you need to adequately plan for the time your paychecks will stop. If you don't, frustration, or even hardship, could result. This is especially true since life expectancies keep rising and the cost of living keeps increasing every year. Being prepared for living longer and for higher prices requires extra money. **What you are able to save and invest during your working years decides if your retirement will be a time of travel and leisure or a time of scrimping and confinement.**

Table 20.5 shows how many years actuaries expect the average person to live after retiring.

Table 20.5—Unisex Life Expectancy Table

Age	Life Expectancy
55	23 More Years
60	20 More Years
65	16 More Years
70	13 More Years

Future Dollars Needed

Those retiring at age fifty-five need adequate income for twenty-three years or longer. Will your future pension benefits, savings and retirement plans, and social security be adequate to cover your future expenses? To answer, you need to know:

A. An estimate of monthly income
    (in today's dollars) that you
    will need when you retire: $_____

B. The number of years from today
    until you plan to retire: $_____

Next, you need to convert today's dollars to the dollars needed for your future. Every year, the dollar loses value because of inflation, and that loss must be considered for future projections in order to maintain the same buying power. Average inflation rates in the past have been:

- 10 Years = 3.66%
- 15 Years = 4.94%
- 20 Years = 5.73%

You need to estimate what you think the inflation rate will be for the number of years until you retire. (Don't use less than the averages.) Then, multiply the estimate of monthly income needed in today's dollars (Part A) by the inflation factor from Table 20.6 for the number of years until you retire (Part B).

C. The monthly income you will need
     converted to future dollars: $_____

   "**A**" times Inflation Factor for "**B**".
   (See Table 20.6)

Example:

Lloyd, age forty, decides he needs $1,500 per month in today's dollars to live on when he retires. He plans to retire in twenty years at age sixty. He expects inflation to be 4% during that time period. So, he multiplies $1,500 by 2.191, the factor found under 4% and across from twenty years. This calculation, 2.191 x $1,500, reveals that in twenty years, Lloyd will need $3,286 per month in future dollars to equal today's $1,500.

Table 20.6—Inflation Impact Table

Years	3%	4%	5%	6%
5	1.159	1.217	1.276	1.338
6	1.194	1.265	1.340	1.419
7	1.230	1.316	1.407	1.504
8	1.267	1.369	1.477	1.594
9	1.305	1.423	1.551	1.689
10	1.344	1.480	1.629	1.791
11	1.384	1.539	1.710	1.898
12	1.426	1.601	1.796	2.012
13	1.469	1.665	1.886	2.133
14	1.513	1.732	1.980	2.261
15	1.558	1.801	2.079	2.397
16	1.605	1.873	2.183	2.540
17	1.653	1.948	2.292	2.693
18	1.702	2.026	2.407	2.854
19	1.754	2.107	2.527	3.026
20	1.806	2.191	2.653	3.207
25	2.094	2.666	3.386	4.292
30	2.427	3.243	4.322	5.743

What Will You Receive?

The next step calculates what you expect to receive from all your retirement benefits. This includes your employer's pension plan, your social security benefits, and your private retirement funds, such as IRA's, 401(k)'s, etc., plus cash value life insurance, and/or other savings and investments.

D.   Monthly income expected from
company pension plans: $_____

Monthly income expected from
social security: (See Appendix D,
Social Security Benefits) $_____

Monthly income expected from
all other sources: $_____

Total monthly benefits expected: $_____

Next, compare your expected benefits to the future dollars you will need. If you are short, start planning now for ways to supplement your retirement income.

E. Monthly income you will need
    (From Part "C") $_____

    Monthly benefits expected
    (From Part "D") $_____

    Dollars Short (Monthly) $_____

Dollars Short

The following will help you calculate what you now need to begin saving in order to maintain your current lifestyle in retirement. Take your monthly dollars short from Section "E" and multiply it by twelve to get the annual dollars short.

F. Annual Dollars Short $_____

    How many years you are
    expected to live after retiring
    (See Table 20.5) $_____

    Total amount needed to cover your
    retirement (Line 1 x Line 2) $_____

Part "F" gives the total dollars short for the number of years you can expect to be retired, based on unisex life expectancy tables.

Example:

Sandy plans to retire in five years at age fifty-five and is now projected to be $200 short per month at retirement, or $2,400 annually. At age fifty-five, her life expectancy is twenty-three years (Table 20.5). $2,400 (annual amount short) x 23 (life expectancy at retirement age) equals $53,200. Sandy needs to save $53,200 during the next five years to have a secure retirement and not change her lifestyle. Once Sandy does retire, her money needs to earn a break-even rate of return each year for her to maintain current purchasing power. (Break-even rate of return is discussed later in this chapter.)

Sandy's advance planning is not good news for her. She may have to work two or three years longer than she planned just to save the extra money she will need. She is glad, however, that she discovered the amount short now rather than after she retires. At least now she can do something about it.

How Much Do You Need to Save?

The final step shows what you need to start saving to make up the projected dollars short. Tables 20.7 and 20.8 help you calculate what you need to save. These tables give a monthly or lump sum investment needed for the number of years to retirement. Use the total amount needed to cover your retirement from part "F". The information at the bottom of each table tells how to covert the $100,000 table amount into larger or smaller sums.

Example continued:

Sandy is short $53,200. The factor she would use from table 20.7 is .532 (53,200 ÷ 100,000 = .532). Assuming she expects to earn 6% on her money, she needs to start saving $766 each month to have the required sum in five years ($1,439 x .532 = $765.55—see Table 20.7 for five years @ 6%).

Had she looked at her situation five years earlier, with ten years to retirement, the amount she needed to save would have been only $374 per month. With more time for the money to work, she could also have increased her rate of return, thereby reducing the needed monthly savings even more.

Table 20.7—Monthly Investment Required to Have $100,000

	5 Years	10 Years	15 Years	20 Years	25 Years	30 Years
3%	1,547	716	441	305	224	172
4%	1,508	679	406	273	195	144
5%	1,475	648	378	246	171	120
6%	1,439	615	349	221	148	100
7%	1,405	585	321	197	128	82
8%	1,371	555	296	176	110	67
9%	1,338	527	273	157	95	55
10%	1,306	500	251	139	81	44
11%	1,275	475	231	124	69	36
12%	1,245	451	212	110	59	29

Divide the total dollars short by $100,000. This factor times the appropriate table amount will give you the sum you need to save monthly to reach your retirement goal.

Examples:
Dollars short = $52,000; $52,000 ÷ 100,000 = .52. With ten years to retirement and expected earnings of 6%, save $320 monthly (615 x .52 = 319.80).

Dollars short = $225,000; $225,000 ÷ 100,000 = 2.25. With twenty years to retirement and expected earnings of 11%, save $279 monthly (124 x 2.25 = 279).

All rates of return are compound annual rates.

Table 20.8—Lump Sum Investment Required to Have $100,000

	5 Years	10 Years	15 Years	20 Years	25 Years	30 Years
3%	86,261	74,409	64,186	55,368	47,761	41,199
4%	82,193	67,556	55,526	45,639	37,512	30,832
5%	78,353	61,391	48,102	37,689	29,530	23,138
6%	74,726	55,839	41,727	31,180	23,300	17,411
7%	71,299	50,835	36,245	25,845	18,425	13,137
8%	68,058	46,319	31,524	21,454	14,602	9,938
9%	64,993	42,241	27,454	17,843	11,597	7,537
10%	62,092	38,554	23,939	14,864	9,230	5,731
11%	59,345	35,218	20,900	12,403	7,361	4,368
12%	56,743	32,197	18,270	10,367	5,882	3,338

Divide the total dollars short by $100,000. Use this factor to multiply the amounts in the table. This will give you the correct sum you need to save monthly to reach your retirement goal.

Dollars short = $52,000; $52,000 ÷ 100,000 = .52. With ten years to retirement and expected earnings of 6%, you would need to save $29,036 ($55,839 x .52 = $29,036).

Dollars short = $225,000; $225,000 ÷ 100,000 = 2.25. With twenty years to retirement and expected earnings of 11%, you would need to save $27,907 now to have $225,000 in twenty years ($12,403 x 2.25 = $27,907).

All rates of return are compound annual rates

Social Security

Social security alone will not be adequate income for future retirees. The system was always designed to be supplemental, and truly, it will be just "a supplement" in the future. As the baby boomers (those born between 1946 and 1964) reach retirement age and begin to "take" from the system, retirees will dramatically outnumber contributing workers.

In 1935, when social security originated, each retiree had forty workers paying employment taxes. By the year 2010, when the first of the baby boomers reach age sixty-five, only two workers will be paying taxes for each retiree. Given these facts, and the staggering FICA tax increases already imposed upon current workers, benefits are likely to decrease.

Table 20.9—Social Security Workers and Retirees

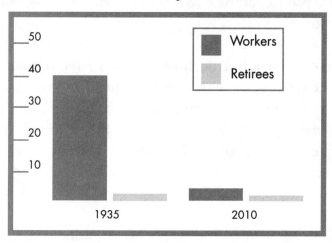

Tax Planning

Tax Bracket

To make wise investment decisions, you need to know your tax bracket. Consider your tax bracket when looking at investments expected to generate tax write-offs or add to taxable income. **Currently, all income is taxed by the federal government at 15% until it reaches a certain level. Then it moves to the higher brackets: 28%, 31%, 36%, and 39.6%.** Each year, the dollar amount of these brackets change (see Appendix C for the 1998 federal rates). To the federal taxes, you then add the percentage from your state. To get this percentage, see Appendix C, Tax Bracket: State Tax Rates.

(federal %) + (state %) = tax bracket

If you multiply your tax bracket by any additional income (interest, dividends, bonuses, capital gains, etc.), you will know the percentage you will pay in taxes and, correspondingly, the percentage you get to keep.

Example:

If you are in a 35% tax bracket (28% federal, plus 7% state), while you remain in this bracket, 35% of any additional income goes to taxes, and you keep 65%. That means, when you earn $2,000 in taxable interest, $700 goes directly to tax ($2,000 x 35% = $700), leaving you with a $1,300 profit. A raise of $100 leaves you with $65 after the 35% is taken out for taxes.

On the other hand, deductible expenses have a lower "real" cost due to the tax savings. Expenses, such as qualified pension plan contributions, alimony, mortgage interest, charitable contributions, etc., actually cost less than their dollar value because they also reduce your taxes. A deductible expense multiplied by your tax bracket shows an estimate of your tax savings.

A Deductible Expense Multiplied by Your Tax Bracket Shows Your Tax Savings

Examples:

For the same 35% tax bracket, a contribution of $5,000 to a SEP IRA has an out-of-pocket cost of $3,250. The balance, or $1,750, comes from tax savings ($5,000 x 35% = $1,750). You reduce your taxes by $1,750 due to the $5,000 contribution.

If your mortgage interest is $900 a month, or $10,800 a year, and your tax bracket is 35% (28% federal + 7% state), you will have a $3,780 tax reduction due to the mortgage interest paid ($10,800 x 35% = $3,780). Considering the $3,780 in taxes saved, the net cost of the mortgage is $7,020.

Break-Even Rate of Return

To get ahead, you must earn more than the amount lost through inflation and taxes. The following shows the net return on $100. The conditions are:

- 5% interest earnings,
- 4% inflation, and
- a 35% tax bracket (28% federal + 7% state).

Example:

If $100 earns 5% interest, at the end of the year, it is worth $105. The $5.00 in earnings is fully taxed. In a 35% tax bracket, you will pay $1.75 in taxes, which leaves net earnings of $3.25, or a total of $103.25. The 4% inflation rate then reduces the purchasing power of $103.25 to

$99.12. In other words, the $100 that grew by $5.00 in one year is worth $99 at year's end after inflation and taxes take their bite.

Your dollars shrink every year that they don't break even. A formula used to figure a **break-even rate of return,** or the minimum you must earn to keep up with taxes and inflation, is:

$$\frac{\textbf{Inflation Rate}}{\textbf{(100) - (Tax Bracket)}} = \textbf{Break-Even Rate of Return}$$

If the inflation rate is 4% and your tax bracket is 35%, you need to earn 6.15% just to break even! With the same 35% tax bracket, if the inflation rate rises to 6%, your break-even point becomes 9.2%.

$$\frac{4\%}{100\% - (35\%)} = 6.15\%$$

A standard rule of thumb used by many investors is: you need to receive a net 2% return after inflation and taxes. **THAT MEANS 2% ABOVE YOUR BREAK-EVEN RATE OF RETURN.**

Annual Tax Projection

Estimating your annual taxes can help you have the correct amount withheld or paid in through estimated payments. When an event changes your finances, you will know what you can expect to pay in taxes. **Such advance planning leads to better management of your money.** It could mean higher monthly take home pay and/or no surprises at tax time.

Use the Annual Tax Projection form to estimate what you will owe anytime one or more events change your financial situation. You will need to refer to the current year's tax rates or estimate by using last year's tax bracket. An estimate using last year's rates will be close enough if the current year is not subject to major tax reform. Use annual figures for all entries.

Some circumstances that will change your taxes are:

PERSONAL CHANGES	INCOME	EXPENSES
change in marital status	increase in salary	buying a home
losing a dependent	decrease in salary	a business "loss"
gaining a dependent	unexpected income	loss from sale of an investment
	increase in interest	paying alimony
	increase in dividends	change in state taxes paid
	large state tax refund	increase in tax deferred
	receiving alimony	retirement contributions
	bonus	increase in charitable
	gambling winnings	contributions
	gain from sale of an	medical expenses exceeding
	investment	7.5% of AGI
	gain from sale of a home	business expenses exceeding
	(if taxable)	2% of AGI
	increased business profits	qualified child care expenses
	taxable fringe benefits	

Worksheet—Annual Tax Projection

GROSS INCOME
  Salary   _____
  Salary   _____
  Other   _____
  Other   _____

A. Total Income $_____

  DEDUCTIONS FROM INCOME
  B-1   Deductions from Worksheet I (see below)   _____
  B-2   Deductions from Worksheet II   _____
        Exemption Credits
        Standard Amount x Each Dependent   _____

B. Total Deductions $_____

C. Taxable Income (Line A minus Line B) $_____
Tax Due on Line C
   (from tax tables/schedules/estimates) $_____

Worksheet I
   Medical Expenses (must exceed 7.5% of AGI) $ _____
   State Income Taxes Withheld $ _____
   Additional State Taxes Paid $ _____

Property Taxes Paid $ _____
Personal Property Tax (automobiles, etc.) $ _____
Home Mortgage Interest $ _____
Charitable Contributions $ _____
Business Expenses Exceeding 2% of AGI $ _____
Deductible Casualty or Theft Losses $ _____
Other $ _____

Total 1   Total Itemized Deductions $_____
Total 2   Standard Deduction (From Tax Tables) $_____
    Take the Higher of Total 1 or Total 2 to Line B-1

Worksheet II
    Alimony Paid $ _____
    Deductible Contributions to Retirement Plans $ _____
    Other Adjustments to Income $ _____

    Total (Take to Line B-2) $_____

The amount of tax you will owe will be the tax due on line C minus any credits, such as child care credits. Refer to chapter 6, Personal Income Taxes for more information about credits, deductions, and taxable income.

Estate Planning

A good estate plan assures that a deceased person's assets pass to his/her beneficiaries as intended. It also helps to keep property out of the probate court. This is done by having assets pass to heirs directly as named beneficiaries on trusts, on life insurance and annuities, or on property held in joint tenancy with right of survivorship. Avoiding extensive probate cuts down on delays and reduces fees and taxes, thereby leaving more to the heirs.

Probate is a legal process supervised by the probate division of the state court. It passes ownership of property from a deceased person to others. **The probate court also approves wills, values assets, pays off creditors, files estate taxes, directs an estate trustee, and oversees the administration of property left to minor children.** The probate court follows the instructions in a will whenever it can under the law. Without a will, state law directs the distribution of property and appoints guardians for minor children.

The first step in estate planning is to know the value of all assets. If the value is under $625,000, a will and property set up to pass directly to heirs is probably sufficient. The exemption level of $625,000 allowed for 1998 will increase each year until it reaches $1,000,00 in 2006. Currently, estates valued under $625,000 are not subject to federal estate tax.

Gifting

"Gifting" helps to reduce the taxable estate. This means giving property or money early to potential heirs. Each person can gift up to $10,000 each year ($20,000 per couple) with no gift tax due. The beneficiary will only pay tax on the earnings from their "gift." The amount given is not taxable. Gifting transfers assets to family members and removes these assets from the taxable estate. After 1998, the $10,000 allowed per person will be indexed to the inflation rate and increase each year.

Taking Title

The way title is held on jointly-owned property (two or more persons) affects how the property is handled when one party dies.

- **JOINT TENANCY WITH RIGHT OF SURVIVORSHIP:** This form of title denotes **equal** ownership and can be held by two or more persons, who are often referred to as tenants. If three people own the property, each has a one-third undivided interest. If two own the property, each has a one-half undivided interest. When one tenant dies, the property passes automatically to the other tenant(s) outside the will, thus avoiding probate.
- **TENANTS IN COMMON:** This form of title allows for **unequal** ownership and unequal distributions. One person may own 70% and the second person 30%. No right of survivorship exists. A deceased tenant's ownership rights would pass under his/her will.
- **COMMUNITY PROPERTY:** Currently, nine states are community property states; the remaining states are called "common-law" states. Under community property rules, all property acquired during a marriage, except gifts, inheritances, and income derived from these, belongs equally to both spouses, regardless of who purchased or earned the property. Furthermore, how the property is titled is irrelevant. In cases of

divorce and death, the spouses share 50/50 in all assets accumulated during their marriage. In common-law states, property from divorce and death pass to beneficiaries and heirs as titled or through a will.

Wills

Joint ownership with a right of survivorship by itself cannot be regarded as an "estate plan." A will defines many additional ways property can be divided and allows for more options. Equally important, a will appoints guardians for younger children and an administrator for the estate.

For those who die without wills, the state decides who receives their property, who becomes guardian(s) for their minor children, and who administers their estate. Under certain circumstances, the state can even take the property. Understandably, any additional administration adds to probate costs, reducing the final amount received by heirs.

For couples with minor children, a will is a must. Joint ownership with right of survivorship does not settle the matter of guardianship for the children should both parents die on or about the same time. Neither does joint ownership appoint a person to distribute the estate assets or file the final tax return. A will, however, can provide these tools.

Wills require legal language drafted by attorneys who are familiar with applicable state and federal laws. Small technicalities, unknown to laypersons, can make a will invalid. Individuals often make the mistake of writing in dollar amounts, which can quickly become outdated, or the estate may not have enough money to pass on the intended sum. **Percentages work much better because they require fewer changes.**

Another common error by people who write their own will is asking a beneficiary to be a witness. This action can void all gifts left to that beneficiary. **People also make a mistake when they write over or cross out an item in the will.** This can make the will invalid. Generally, wills should be formally amended. A codicil is an amendment to a will that can be used instead of redrafting the entire document. It can add new provisions and change or delete existing ones.

Furthermore, wills have little use if they are not kept current. As family and financial situations change, wills should be updated. Changes in federal and state laws, as well as births, deaths, marriages, and divorces within one's family, can make a will's provisions obsolete.

A WILL

Offers Many Options for Dividing Property,

Appoints Guardians for Minor Children, and

Appoints an Administrator for the Estate

For Couples with Minor Children, a Will Is a Must

To Be Effective, Wills Must Be Kept Current

If you have a computer, you can purchase software (designed by attorneys, for an approximate cost of $60) to draw up your own will. Most software considers the particular laws of each state and comes with a complete instruction manual. Although the software doesn't save much over the initial attorney fees to draft a will, it has the advantage of allowing you to do your own updates and changes with ease.

Probate

Having a will does not avoid probate. The will merely gives instructions to the probate court on how the deceased wishes to have his/her estate handled. Without a will, all property is distributed according to state laws.

Probate is expensive and time consuming. Avoiding probate is not illegal, but wise estate planning.

To avoid probate, do not leave property to minor children without creating a trust for their benefit or appointing an adult as their guardian. For example, if life insurance proceeds are left directly to minor children with no provision for a guardian or trustee, then the court must decide who will manage those funds for the benefit of the children. The court usually appoints a bank that will charge an annual administrative fee. Without a will, the court also decides who will take care of the children. Although unlikely, it could be someone unknown to the deceased's family.

Granting the executor of an estate the power to settle will disputes and sell estate property if needed can help to reduce probate costs. **Another wise move to save potential probate costs is to have as much property as possible pass directly to heirs. This can be done when they are named beneficiaries on life insurance policies, retirement plans, and annuity contracts, or when they hold title to property as joint tenant with right of survivorship.** Right of survivorship simply means the other owner(s) directly inherits the deceased's share of the property.

Life Insurance

Life insurance proceeds create an instant estate. The proceeds also protect an existing estate from losing money, since the policy can cover probate costs and estate taxes. The advantage of life insurance is that the proceeds pass directly to heirs with no taxes due.

Be sure to name primary and secondary beneficiaries in all policies. A primary beneficiary is the first in line to receive the proceeds. A

Avoiding Probate Is Wise Estate Planning

Granting the Executor of an Estate the Power to Settle Will Disputes and Sell Estate Property if Needed Can Help to Reduce Probate Costs

secondary beneficiary is the second in line and only receives the proceeds if the primary beneficiary is not living. Again, do not name minor children as primary beneficiaries unless you also set up a trust to manage the funds for the benefit of the children. Minor children cannot receive proceeds; they need a guardian to manage the money.

Stepped-Up Basis

If you own appreciated assets, such as real estate or securities, you can hold them in joint tenancy with a beneficiary. Upon your death, ownership passes to the beneficiary at its current market value. **This is called a "stepped-up" basis, because beneficiaries inherit property at the current market value, NOT the purchase price.** The "stepped-up" basis has a big tax advantage for beneficiaries should they decide to sell the asset. The only taxable gain will be the difference between the inherited market value and the sales price. Whereas, if you, as owner, sell an appreciated asset, your taxable gain will be on the full difference between the market value and the original purchase price.

Example:

A mother holds several stock certificates in joint tenancy with her daughter. The stock has a market value of $80,000. The purchase price was $12,000. When the mother dies, the daughter inherits the stock at its current market value on the day of death, or $80,000. If the daughter immediately sells the stock for $80,000, she has no taxable gain because the basis and selling price of the stocks are the same. If the daughter sells the stock one year later for $82,000 she would have a $2,000 taxable gain, the difference between the inherited value and the selling price. Had the mother sold the stock immediately before her death, she would have had a taxable gain on $68,000, the difference between the $12,000 cost and the $80,000 sales price. This example holds true for all appreciated assets, including real property.

Trusts

Seek competent advice from an estate planning attorney if the value of all of your assets exceeds $625,000 in 1998. $625,000 is the exemption allowed before assets become taxable. Remember, this exemption amount will increase each year until it reaches $1,000,000 in 2006. Included in the estate's value are: the market value of all real property, the market value of all securities, the cash value of life insurance, the value of all retirement plans, plus the value of all other assets. **Setting up a trust can avoid many unnecessary taxes, which is no small matter since estate taxes are considerable, ranging from 37% to 55%. Without proper planning, estate taxes can greatly reduce an estate, and heirs will receive much less than intended.** If an estate is worth more than $625,000, it is subject to federal estate taxes and needs to file an estate tax return nine months after the death.

Trusts are complicated and come in many varieties, so make certain you see an attorney who specializes in estate planning. Trusts are created by a person called the trustor (grantor) and administered by a trustee for the benefit of a third party, or beneficiary. The trustor can give specific directions to the trustee on how to disperse and manage the assets. In some cases, the trustor can also be the trustee.

A living trust avoids probate and allows total flexibility for the person(s) making the trust. Also, it can take the place of a will. A **testamentary trust** is created as part of a valid will. It does not come into existence until the death of the will maker. Before the death, the testamentary trust can always be canceled or changed. Some non-testamentary trusts can be changed, others cannot, and they all have various tax consequences.

Overall, trusts allow for tax savings, management of investments, transfer of assets to minors, and minimum probate costs. When established, they become their own taxable entity and must then file a separate "trust" tax return.

Once again, if your estate is valued over the exemption amount ($625,000 in 1998), see an estate planning attorney. This is true even if you plan to pass everything to your spouse and avoid estate taxes with the $625,000 marital deduction. It is important to note that the majority of taxes become due not when the first spouse dies but when the second spouse (primary beneficiary of first spouse) dies.

Many people give little priority to estate planning. Yet, without it, an untimely death can leave much unfinished business for survivors. Take the time to seek competent counsel to draft a will, a trust, or both. If you have minor children, own a home, or have assets worth more than the exemption level ($625,000 in 1998), estate planning is imperative. Otherwise, taxes and expensive probate costs can eat away at your estate until little is left for intended heirs.

Trusts Allow for Tax Savings, Management of Investments, Transfer of Assets to Minors, and Minimum Probate Costs

Summary

Tax and investment planning stops surprises and helps you take control of your finances. Also, in many cases, knowing what you need to save to reach a future goal becomes the impetus to start saving. Estate planning allows you to provide for your heirs and determine who you want to benefit from your assets. As long as future needs remain "vague" and "out there," they will give you cause to worry. Recognizing and dealing with the facts: how much money you need, what it will take to get that money, what you will owe in taxes, and who you want to benefit from your assets when you die gives you a "track to run on."

Whether you plan for a child's education, a trip, a down payment, your retirement, or your estate, knowing what you need helps you to make decisions. Priorities and planning go hand in hand. Neither are easy, but both are necessary to be in charge of your finances.

21
Implementing Your Plan

Finding the Money to Fund Your Goals

THE FINAL STEP is to implement your plan. You should have an idea now of what you want to achieve with your money and what it is going to cost you to cover the important basics of financial planning and also attain your ambitions. Reaching your goals won't happen by itself. You need to be committed to making your net worth grow. **This chapter will give you some ideas on finding the money to fund your goals.**

To improve your net worth, make a commitment to get some money working for you. If you wait until you have money "leftover" to start building a nest egg, time will pass, and then it will be too late. **Take your savings and investment dollars off the top, and pay yourself first before you start spending.**

If we had no withholding, how many people would be in trouble on April 15 because they wouldn't have the money to pay their income taxes? State and federal taxing agencies know that they need to take their revenues out of gross pay before citizens take it home. Do the same for yourself. Save some money off the top before you take it home. Pretend this savings is a tax increase that reduced your take home pay. Aim to

Aim to Save 10% of Your Gross Pay

save 10% of your gross pay. If this is too much, start with a smaller percentage, and increase the amount as quickly as you can.

If your cash flow shows you need every dime, hope still exists. Three "pockets" could be holding some extra money for you. They are:

- Tax Savings
- Expense Reductions
- More Income

Tax Savings

Look at last year's tax return. **Did you get a large refund? If you did, you are having too much withheld.** You can start investing or saving that refund money each month, and you benefit from the earnings instead of giving Uncle Sam free use of your money. Form W-4, used by employers, decides the amount of withholding taken out for taxes. Most importantly, you have some control over the amount your employer sends in on your behalf. Tax law says that taxpayers with taxable incomes under $150,000 only need to pay in an amount equal to their previous year's taxes, or 90% of their current year's tax bill, whichever is less. Staying within these limits avoids all penalties. At the same time, do careful estimates, and don't make the mistake of underpaying and then owing taxes in addition to penalties on April 15. Such poor planning can ruin your attempt to get ahead. **You must have a legitimate refund due to decrease your withholding and use that extra money throughout the year.**

You control your withholding by the filing status and the number of exemptions you claim on the W-4. If you are single and claim "married with ten dependents" on your W-4, it's OK. However, you must claim your correct filing status and correct number of dependents on your tax return. The purpose of Form W-4 is to decide a withholding amount. If you claim more than ten exemptions, the IRS may ask you to justify your deductions.

Many people judge their taxes by their refund, not by what they pay. This thinking needs to be reversed. **Parking "extra" money with Uncle Sam gives you no earnings, and your money isn't accessible until your refund check arrives.**

Any event that saves you taxes allows you to decrease your withholding. Some of these events include: adding a dependent, buying a new home, having a deductible capital or ordinary loss, contributing to

Have Withheld from Your Pay 90% of What You Expect to Owe, or What You Owed Last Year, and No More!

You Control Your Withholding by the Filing Status and the Number of Exemptions Claimed on Form W-4

Any Event That Saves You Taxes, Allows You to Decrease Your Withholding

a tax deferred savings plan, and many others. Reducing taxable income usually means a refund, and that refund allows you to decrease your withholding.

As often as needed, do an annual tax projection calculating what you expect to owe in taxes. Most libraries keep copies of the current year's tax rates and withholding tables. After doing the projection, divide the expected tax by your number of yearly pay periods, such as twelve, twenty-six, or fifty-two. Then, use the current withholding tables to figure out how many exemptions you need to claim to have the amount you expect to owe, and nothing more, taken out of your paycheck. The extra money is yours to save or invest now.

Annual tax projections are not difficult. Refer to chapter 6, Personal Income Taxes, and the annual tax projection form in chapter 20, Planning. Get in the habit of doing a tax projection when some event may change the amount of tax you will owe. If you are uncomfortable with the tax projection process, call a tax professional for help and advice. Accountants have software that makes this process easy, but you must supply the correct data.

Cutting Expenses

Will you have any loans that will soon be paid off? If so, this expense reduction can have the effect of raising your income. The increased cash flow becomes an excellent source for new savings.

If excessive consumer debt is putting you under, take steps to reverse the situation. **Consider bill consolidation through a home equity loan or an alternative source to reduce your outflow and give you more available cash.** Sometimes, this is the only way to get out from under the huge monthly payments that tie up all your money. If you do this, you must stop ongoing credit card charging and unnecessary spending. Trading "bad" debt for "good" debt won't work if you keep adding to the balance of the "bad." The amount paid for finance charges and interest is money you put directly into the pockets of someone else. **Cut or reduce your finance charges, and use this same money to fill your own pockets.**

More Money

If tax savings and cutting expenses won't help, then you need to look at bringing in more money. Can you take an extra job? Can you start a part-time business? Can you work overtime? Can your spouse work part-time or in the evening? **You must be creative and optimistic about finding ways to get some extra money.**

What Others Have Done

The following two cases illustrate how an appropriate action can help you fund your goals with little change in "spendable" income.

Case One: Carl

Carl, thirty-six years old and single, earns approximately $45,000 a year as a foreman for a utility company. Two years ago, he purchased a condominium for $135,000. He put $10,000 down and assumed a $125,000 mortgage at 8% interest. His mortgage payment is $1,050 a month, $915 for the loan and $135 for the impound account for insurance and taxes. Prior to buying the condo, he was paying $800 a month for rent. For the past two years, Carl has received tax refunds of approximately $4,000. The first year, he used this money to help furnish the condo, the next year, he used his refund money to take an extended vacation. Table 21.1 shows Carl's expenses before and after the condo purchase. The figures show that he had $1,821 more spendable income after purchasing the condo and assuming the larger monthly payment (24,012 - 22,191 = 1,821).

Table 21.1—Expenses before and after the Condo Purchase

Before	Expenses	After
$ 8,195	Federal Tax	$ 4,569
2,775	State Tax	1,580
3,442	FICA	3,442
9,600	Rent/Mortgage Payment	12,600
$24,012	Total Expenses	$22,191

The home mortgage interest and property tax deductions on **Schedule A, Itemized Deductions** helped reduce his total federal and state tax bill by $4,821 (8,195 - 4,564 = 4,821). Table 21.2, Carl's Taxes before and after the Condo Purchase, shows the tax breakdown.

Additionally, having the mortgage payment now allows Carl to deduct other expenses, such as state taxes and charitable contributions that he could not take before as a "renter." While renting, Carl claimed the standard deduction for single persons, and for that year, it was $3,800. After buying the condo, his itemized deductions totaled $16,566. The larger itemized deductions reduced his taxable income.

Table 21.2—Taxes before and after the Condo Purchase

Before	Expenses	After
$45,144	Income	$45,144
-(3,800)	Standard Deduction	0
0	Itemized Deductions	-(16,566)
-(2,450)	Personal Exemption	-(2,450)
38,894	Taxable Income	26,128
8,012	Federal Taxes	4,442
2,775	State Taxes	1,580

Since Carl has $3,600 in savings but no investments, he decided to invest most of next year's anticipated $4,000 tax refund. Since Carl preferred to receive his "refund" early, he changed his withholding on Form W-4 to have $300 less taken out of his pay each month for federal and state taxes ($3,600 annually). He used this money to start his investment program. He started contributing $100 a month to his employer's 401(k) plan. In addition, he opened a check-o-matic plan with a mutual fund for $200 a month. After taking this action, Carl's spendable monthly income remained the same, but he received much smaller tax refunds, approximately $400 per year.

The purchase of the condo became the catalyst that got more assets working for Carl. By reducing his taxes, he had an extra $300 each month to invest. As Table 21.3 shows, Carl's net worth grew substantially in ten years. The condo only appreciated 2% a year. The mutual fund earned an average compound rate of 12.8%, and the 401(k) plan earned 8%, tax deferred. His savings account grew by 3%. Notice that the market value of the condo has increased, and the mortgage balanced has declined; the difference adds to Carl's personal net worth. This equity buildup is a benefit of home ownership that cannot be realized by renting.

Table 21.3—Net Worth

Carl's Net Worth Year of Condo Purchases			
Savings	3,600	Mortgage	125,000
Condo*	135,000		
Assets	$138,600	*Liabilities*	$125,000
Net Worth = $13,600			
*Market Value			

Carl's Net Worth Ten Years Later			
Savings	4,838	Mortgage	109,468
Mutual Fund	46,294		
401(k)	18,866		
Condo*	164,500		
Assets	$234,498	*Liabilities*	$109,468
Net Worth = $125,030			
*Market Value			

Case Two: Phil and Mary

Phil and Mary Piper both work, are in their late thirties, and have four children. They purchased a home several years ago. Although their joint incomes are above average, they can't keep up with their expenses. They are in a 35% tax bracket: 28% federal, and 7% state. Their taxable income for the past year was $48,000, and they owed more taxes in addition to their withholding. They want to get ahead, but nothing has worked yet.

Although they jointly earn $3,765 each month, they always spend more than they earn. Phil and Mary try not to charge, but things come up that they need for the children or the house, and they seldom have the extra cash to pay for it. Over the past three years, their charge card balances have grown. They also realize that taxes take a larger and larger bite each year. They want to pay off their credit cards to free some extra money but don't have enough left over at the end of the month to make any additional installment payments. Their biggest problem is a negative cash flow. This is due to a large amount of consumer debt. Following are their annual cash flow and net worth statements:

Table 21.4—Cash Flow Statement before Refinancing

Cash Flow Statement (Annual)			
Income		Expenses	
Salaries (Gross)	62,100	Federal Tax	5,630
		State Tax	2,400
		FICA	4,752
		Insurance	2,160
		Mortgage	12,228
		Car Loan #1	4,980
		Car Loan #2	3,192
		Credit Cards	7,200
		Food	8,000
		Clothing	2,400
		Household\Yard	900
		Auto Maintenance\Gas	3,433
		Misc. and Children	6,000
Total Income	**$62,100**	**Total Expenses**	**$63,275**
Net Income after Expenses -($1,175)			

Table 21.5—Net Worth Statement before Refinancing

Net Worth Statement (Annual)			
Assets		Liabilities	
Home (Market Value)	185,000	Home Mortgage	97,000
Retirement Plan	32,000	Auto Loan #1	12,500
Cars (Value)	15,000	Auto Loan #2	7,000
Savings	200	Credit Cards	14,000
Total Assets	**$232,200**	**Total Expenses**	**$130,500**
Net Worth $101,700			

Their net worth statement shows that they only have $200 in liquid assets (savings account). Their only investment is Phil's retirement plan. Their largest asset is the $88,000 equity in their home.

Their original mortgage was for 10.5%, and rates are now at 7.5%. They feel the only way they can get ahead is to refinance their home and use the money to pay off their credit cards and car loans. They qualify for a loan of $148,000, which is 80% of $185,000, their home's market value (most lending institutions will loan this 80% to value on home mortgages). They discussed the pros and cons of refinancing and considered different loan amounts. They decided to take the maximum.

The refinancing increased their home mortgage from $97,000 to $148,000. Their monthly mortgage payment changed from $915 to $1,035. The payment only increased by $103, because their interest rate dropped from 10.5% on the old loan to 7.5% on the new loan.

Refinancing Information

Total Loan Proceeds	148,000			
Minus		New Monthly Payment	1,035
Points & Fees	-(2,960)	Insurance & Taxes	231
Pay Off Old Mortgage	-(97,000)	Total	1,266
Pay Off Credit Cards	-(14,000)		
Pay Off Auto Loan #1	-(12,500)		
Pay Off Auto Loan #2	-(7,000)	New mortgage of $148,000 @ 7.5% interest has monthly payments of $1,035.
Balance Left	**$15,540**	No change in insurance and taxes.

They used most of the $14,540 balance from the loan proceeds to start the funding of their financial goals. They spent the money as follows:

Money Market Fund	5,000
Bank Savings Account	2,000
Mutual Fund	5,000
Universal Life Policy	2,500
Total Invested	**$14,500**

Their new cash flow statement looks much brighter, and their new net worth statement shows possibility for more growth. The new loan reduced their taxes and paid off their nondeductible consumer debt, thus reducing their overall expenses. After refinancing, their cash flow and net worth statements reflect the following:

- Their joint salaries remain the same.
- Their mortgage payment is higher.
- Their federal and state taxes are now lower due to more deductible home mortgage interest.
- They purchased needed life insurance, paying $1,800 annually for the policy.
- They have no consumer debt.
- They have an extra $11,614 each year after paying all expenses.
- Their net worth decreased due to refinancing and assuming a higher mortgage, but overall, it shows more potential for future growth.

Table 21.6—Cash Flow Statement after Refinancing

Cash Flow Statement (Annual)			
Income		Expenses	
Salaries (Gross)	62,100	Federal Tax	5,149
		State Tax	2,500
		FICA	4,752
		Insurance	2,160
		Mortgage	15,192
		Food	8,000
		Clothing	2,400
		Household\Yard	900
		Auto Maintenance\Gas	3,433
		Misc. and Children	6,000
Total Income	$62,100	Total Expenses	$50,486
Net Income after Expenses $11,614			

Table 21.7—Net Worth Statement after Refinancing

Net Worth Statement (Annual)			
Assets		Liabilities	
Home (Market Value)	185,000	Home Mortgage	148,000
Retirement Plan	32,000		
Cars (Value)	15,000		
Savings	2,200		
Money Market Fund	5,000		
Mutual Fund	5,000		
Total Assets	$244,200	Total Expenses	$148,000
Net Worth $96,200			

By repositioning their assets, they now have extra money working for them. Now, instead of one large asset (home equity), they have several more liquid assets growing at a higher rate of return. In addition, their home value continues to increase at 2% each year. After refinancing, Mary and Phil were able to stay out of debt. They had the extra money to start investing $750 monthly. They decided to put this money into two mutual funds. They added $350 monthly to Fund A, which they had already established. Then, they opened another fund and made contributions of $400 monthly. Ten years later, their net worth statement showed the value of paying off their consumer debt and consistently contributing to their growing assets.

Table 21.8—Net Worth Statement Ten Years after Refinancing

Net Worth Statement (Annual growth rate is shown by each asset)				
Assets			Liabilities	
2.0% Home (Market Value)	230,024		Home Mortgage	133,507
8.0% Retirement Plan	68,800			
3.0% Savings	2,200			
5.0% Money Market Fund	8,144			
11.9% Mutual Fund A ($5,000 plus $350 monthly for ten years)	96,382			
12.3% Mutual Fund B ($400 monthly for ten years)	93,654			
Cash Value Life Ins.	27,127			
Total Assets	$527,088		Total Expenses	$133,507
Net Worth $393,581				

Summary

As you can see from reading the two cases, once you put money to work, the miracle of compounding takes over. With enough time, even small amounts create future fortunes with income you won't be able to outlive. The key to financial security is taking the time to look closely at how you spend/invest/save what you have.

It can't be said enough. To make money, you must get money working for you. Use your creativity to find a way to save a portion of all you earn. This will provide for yourself (and your family) a secure financial future. The following charts will provide further incentive.

Table 21.9—Personal Savings Rate of U.S. Citizens

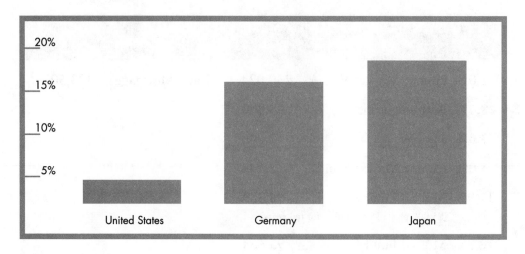

Table 21.10—The Realities of Inflation

	20 Years Ago	Today	In 20 Years
Average Car	$ 3,742	$ 16,692	$ 74,458
One Year Public College	1,621	4,852	14,523
Average Home	24,910	100,299	403,849
Bag of Groceries	5	13	33

Sources: U.S. Bureau of the Census, WEFA Group, U.S. Dept. of Education: Digest of Education Statistics, The College Cost Book, 1991, U.S. Bureau of Labor Statistics, U.S. Dept. of Commerce. Future prices estimated at same rate as they grew over the last twenty years. Of course, there is no guarantee that past inflation trends will continue in the future. As of 12/31/91.

Table 21.11—Long-Term Saver's Guide—Average Rates of Return

Years	Stock Market	Treasury Bonds	Money Market	Inflation
64	10.3%	4.6%	3.6%	3.1%
10	17.3%	12.6%	9.5%	4.8%
5	17.7%	12.0%	7.0%	3.8%

Source: Ibbotson Associates, *U.S. News & World Report*

Table 21.12—The Benefits of Long-Term Investing

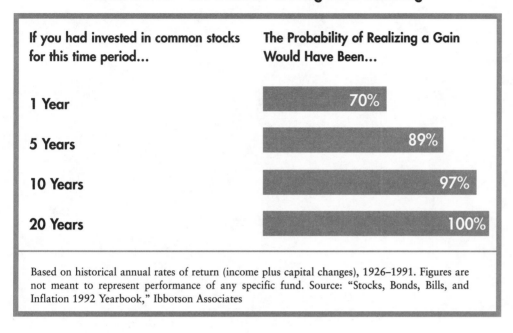

If you had invested in common stocks for this time period...	The Probability of Realizing a Gain Would Have Been...
1 Year	70%
5 Years	89%
10 Years	97%
20 Years	100%

Based on historical annual rates of return (income plus capital changes), 1926–1991. Figures are not meant to represent performance of any specific fund. Source: "Stocks, Bonds, Bills, and Inflation 1992 Yearbook," Ibbotson Associates

Table 21.13—Time Is Your Greatest Ally

Procrastination Is a Deadly Enemy		
Investments of:	$ 20 Monthly @ age 25	Produces Same
	$ 60 Monthly @ age 35	Results at Age 65
	$200 Monthly @ age 45	
	$850 Monthly @ age 55	

In Closing

Information presented throughout this book has two primary goals:

- To help you get more of your money working for you.
- To show you the importance of saving and investing a portion of everything you earn.

Use this book often as a reference, to answer questions, to look up information, and to put your hard-earned money to its wisest use.

Appendix A
Federal Reserve Banks and Branches

TREASURY ISSUES can be purchased directly from any of the twelve Federal Reserve Banks and their branches through the government's treasury direct program. Before purchasing, write to the nearest bank and ask for the necessary forms. Submit the completed form along with your payment to purchase any treasury offering. By purchasing directly, you will save the fees charged by local commercial banks and by brokers. Call your nearest Federal Reserve Bank or any of their branches for more information, or call the Bureau of the Public Debt (202) 874-4000. The Federal Reserve banks are in bold.

Table A-1—Federal Reserve Banks and Branches

ATLANTA	104 Marietta Street NW, Atlanta, GA 30303 (404) 586-8500
BALTIMORE	P.O. Box 1378, Baltimore, MD 21203-1378 (410) 576-3300
BIRMINGHAM	P.O. Box 830447, Birmingham, AL 35283-0447 (205) 731-8708
BOSTON	600 Atlantic Avenue, Boston, MA 02106 (617) 973-3000
BUFFALO	P.O. Box 961, Buffalo, NY 14240-0961 (716) 849-5000
CHARLOTTE	P.O. Box 30248, Charlotte, NC 28230 (704) 358-2100
CHICAGO	230 South LaSalle Street, P.O. Box 834, Chicago, IL 60690 (312) 322-5322
CINCINNATI	P.O. Box 999, Cincinnati, OH 45201 (513) 721-4787, Ext. 334
CLEVELAND	1455 East Sixth Street, P.O. Box 6387, Cleveland, OH 44101 (216) 241-2800
DALLAS	400 South Akard Street, Station K, Dallas, TX 75222 (214) 651-6111
DENVER	P.O. Box 5228, Denver, CO 80217-5228 (303) 572-2470

DETROIT	P.O. Box 1059, Detroit, MI 48231 (313) 964-6157
EL PASO	P.O. Box 100, El Paso, TX 79999 (915) 544-4730
HOUSTON	P.O. Box 2578, Houston, TX 77252 (713) 659-4433
JACKSONVILLE	P.O. Bo 2499, Jacksonville, FL 32231-2499 (904) 632-1179
KANSAS CITY	925 Grand Ave., Federal Reserve Station, Kansas City, MO 64198 (816) 881-2000
LITTLE ROCK	P.O. Box 1261, Little Rock, AR 72203 (501) 324-8272
LOS ANGELES	Attn.: Marketable Securities, P.O. Box 2077, Los Angeles, CA 90051 (213) 624-7398
LOUISVILLE	P.O. Box 32710, Louisville, KY 40201 (502) 568-9236 or 9238
MEMPHIS	P.O. Box 407, Memphis, TN 38101-0407 (901) 523-7171, Ext. 423
MIAMI	Attn: Treasury Direct Unit, P.O. Box 520847, Miami, FL 33152-0847 (305) 471-6497
MINNEAPOLIS	250 Marquette Ave., Minneapolis, MN 55480 (612) 340-2345
NASHVILLE	301 Eighth Ave., North, Nashville, TN 37203 (615) 251-7100
NEW ORLEANS	P.O. Box 61630, New Orleans, LA 70161 (504) 593-3200
NEW YORK	33 Liberty Street, Fed. Reserve P.O. Station, New York, NY 10045 (212) 791-5000
OKLAHOMA CITY	P.O. Box 25129, Oklahoma City, OK 73125 (405) 270-8652
OMAHA	2201 Farnam Street, Omaha, NE 68102 (402) 221-5636
PHILADELPHIA	100 North Sixth Street, P.O. Box 66, Philadelphia, PA 19105 (215) 574-6000
PITTSBURGH	P.O. Box 867, Pittsburgh, PA 15203-0867 (412) 261-7802
PORTLAND	P.O. Box 3436, Portland, OR 97208 (503) 221-5913
RICHMOND	701 East Byrd Street, P.O. Box 27622, Richmond, VA 23261 (804) 643-1250
SALT LAKE CITY	P.O. Box 30780, Salt Lake City, UT 84130-0780 (801) 322-7882
SAN ANTONIO	P.O. Box 1471, San Antonio, TX 78295 (210) 978-1303 or 1305
SAN FRANCISCO	400 Sansome Street, P.O. Box 7702, San Francisco, CA 94120 (415) 544-2000
SEATTLE	P.O. Box 3567, Seattle, WA 98124 (206) 343-3605
ST. LOUIS	411 Locust Street, P.O. Box 442, St. Louis, MO 63166 (314) 444-8444
WASHINGTON, D.C.	Capital Area Servicing Center, 1300 C Street SW, Washington, D.C. 20239-0001 (202) 874-4000

Appendix B

How Long Will Your Money Last?

TABLES A-2 AND A-3 show how many years a sum lasts at various withdrawal rates and various rates of return. Apply a certain withdrawal rate and the expected annual rate of return to a total sum you think you need. Then, lower or raise the amount until it fits the needed annual income.

For example, $100,000 earning 8% per annum will provide $8,000 annually, or $667 monthly, and never reduce the principle. $100,000 earning 8% if withdrawn at 15% will provide $15,000 annually or $1,250 monthly for nine years.

The interest rate and the withdrawal rate determine how many years the sum will last. Note: when the rate of return is low, more money is needed to maintain a certain monthly income; or, the total sum will last for fewer years. $100,000 at 8% provides $667 monthly, but $100,000 at 5% provides $417 monthly. Anytime the interest earned is less than the payout rate, the money will last fewer years.

Table A-2—How Long Will Your Money Last?

Withdrawal Rate	Annual Growth Rate of Fund									
	5%	6%	7%	8%	9%	10%	11%	12%	13%	14%
5%										
6%	36									
7%	25	33								
8%	20	23	30							
9%	16	18	22	28						
10%	14	15	17	20	26					
11%	12	13	14	16	19	25				
12%	11	11	12	14	15	18	23			
13%	9	10	11	12	13	15	17	21		
14%	9	9	10	11	11	13	14	17	21	
15%	8	8	9	9	10	11	12	14	16	20

Number of Years Money Will Last

Table A-3—How Long Will Your Money Last?

Payout Rate %	Annual Growth Rate of Investment									
	1%	2%	3%	4%	5%	6%	7%	8%	9%	10%
10%	10	11	12	13	14	15	17	20	26	
9%	11	12	13	14	16	18	22	28		
8%	13	14	15	17	20	23	30			
7%	15	16	18	21	25	33				
6%	18	20	23	29	36					
5%	22	25	30	41						
4%	28	35	46							
3%	40	55								
2%	69									
1%										

Number of Years Money Will Last

Appendix C

Tax Bracket

Table A-4—Federal Tax Rates—1998 Tax Year

Beginning of	Single	Married Filing Joint	Married Filing Separate	Head of Household
15%	0	0	0	0
28%	25,350	42,350	21,175	33,950
31%	61,400	102,300	51,150	87,700
36%	128,100	155,950	77,975	142,000
39.6%	278,450	278,450	139,225	278,450

Tax Year 1998

Personal Exemption:	$2,700
Standard Deduction:	
Single	$4,250
Married Filing Joint	$7,100
Head of Household	$6,250
Married Filing Separate	$3,450

State Tax Rates

Add the state tax rate to your federal tax rate for your true marginal tax bracket.

For Example: If your state tax rate is 6% and your federal tax rate is 28%, your combined tax bracket would be 34% (6% + 28% = 34%)

You can use your tax bracket to make financial planning decisions. The calculation will be close, but not exact, because of variables such as tax credits and state taxes that are deductible on a federal return. Also, taxpayers in the higher brackets are subject to phaseout limitations of itemized deductions and personal exemptions.

Table A-5—State Tax Rates

	Taxable Income Brackets		
State	Tax Rates in %	Lowest Amount under:	Highest Amount over:
ALASKA	No State Income Tax		
ALABAMA	2.0 – 5.0	$500	$3,000
ARKANSAS	No State Income Tax		
ARIZONA	3.8 – 7.0	$10,000	$150,000
CALIFORNIA	1.0 – 11.0	$4,374	$100,000
COLORADO	5% of Modified Federal Taxable Income		
	1.5	Flat Rate	
DELAWARE	3.2 – 7.7	$2,000	$40,000
District of Columbia	6.0 – 9.5	$10,000	$20,000
FLORIDA	No State Income Tax		
GEORGIA	1.0 – 6.0	$750	$7,000
HAWAII	2.0 – 10.0	$1,500	$20,500
IDAHO	2.0 – 8.2	$1,000	$20,000
ILLINOIS	3	Flat Rate	
INDIANA	3.4	Flat Rate	
IOWA	0.4 – 9.98	$1,060	$47,700
KANSAS	4.5 – 5.95	$27,500	$27,500
KENTUCKY	2.0 – 6.0	$3,000	$8,000
LOUISIANA	2.0 – 6.0	$10,000	$50,000
MAINE	2.1 – 9.89	$4,150	$37,500
MARYLAND	2.0 – 6.0	$1,000	$3,000
MASSACHUSETTS	5.95 – 12.0	Flat Rate	
MICHIGAN	4.6	Flat Rate	
MINNESOTA	6.0 – 8.5	$13,620	$44,750
MISSISSIPPI	3.0 – 5.0	$5,000	$10,000
MISSOURI	1.5 – 6.0	$1,000	$9,000

Taxable Income Brackets			
State	Tax Rates in %	Lowest Amount under:	Highest Amount over:
MONTANA	2.0 – 3.5	$1,600	$57,600
NEBRASKA	2.37 – 6.92	$1,800	$27,000
NEVADA	No State Income Tax		
NEW HAMPSHIRE	Limited Income Tax		
NEW JERSEY	2.0 – 3.5	$20,000	$75,000
NEW MEXICO	1.8 – 8.5	$5,200	$41,600
NEW YORK	4.0 – 7.88	$5,500	$13,000
NORTH CAROLINA	6.0 – 7.75	$12,750	$60,000
NORTH DAKOTA	2.67 – 12.0	$3,000	$50,000
OHIO	0.74 – 6.9	$5,000	$100,000
OKLAHOMA	0.5 – 7.0	$1,000	$9,950
OREGON	5.0 – 9.0	$2,000	$5,000
PENNSYLVANIA	2.1	Flat Rate	
RHODE ISLAND	27.5% of Federal Tax Liability		
SOUTH CAROLINA	2.5 – 7.0	$2,070	$10,350
SOUTH DAKOTA	No State Income Tax		
TENNESSEE	Limited Income Tax		
TEXAS	No State Income Tax		
UTAH	2.55 – 7.2	$75	$3,750
VERMONT	28 – 34% of Federal Income Tax Liability		
VIRGINIA	2.0 – 5.75	$3,000	$17,000
WASHINGTON	No State Income Tax		
WEST VIRGINIA	3.0 – 6.5	$10,000	$60,000
WISCONSIN	4.9 – 6.93	$7,500	$15,000
WYOMING	No State Income Tax		

Appendix D
Social Security Benefits

TO BE ELIGIBLE for social security benefits, a person must have credit for work under social security. Credits are earned by working in employment covered by the law after 1936, and working in self-employment covered by the law after 1950. A working person can earn a maximum of four credits per year. No benefits are payable if employment ends before earning enough credits to qualify.

For a worker and his/her dependents to be eligible for most benefits, the worker must be fully insured. The wages earned during the eligibility time helps determine the amount of benefits paid. A person who reaches age sixty-two after 1991 must have forty credits or ten years of service to be fully insured.

Maximum Earnings

The maximum earnings in any one year that count toward social security is set by law.

The following table shows the maximum eligible earnings for each year since 1975.

Table A-6—Maximum Social Security Earnings

Year	Annual Maximum	Year	Annual Maximum
1975	$14,100	1987	$43,800
1976	$15,300	1988	$45,000
1977	$16,500	1989	$48,000
1978	$17,700	1990	$51,300
1979	$22,900	1991	$53,400
1980	$25,900	1992	$55,500
1981	$29,700	1993	$57,600
1982	$32,400	1994	$60,600
1983	$35,700	1995	$61,200
1984	$37,800	1996	$62,700
1985	$39,600	1997	$65,400
1986	$42,000	1998	$68,400

Benefit Estimate Statement

An eight page document called "Earnings and Benefit Estimate Statement" can be ordered from the Social Security Administration to show what you have paid in to date. Based on your current earnings, they will project what you will receive in retirement benefits, disability benefits, and survivor benefits. Call 1-800-772-1213 and ask for Form SSA-7004 or download the form from their Web site at: http://www.ssa.gov/

Age Full Benefits Begin

For a person born in 1937 or earlier, the normal retirement age is age sixty-five. For all persons born after 1937, they must be over age sixty-five to collect full benefits. The following table shows at what age a person can collect full benefits.

Table A-7—Age Full Social Security Benefits Begin

Year Born	Age Full Benefits Begin
1938	65 years, 2 months
1939	65 years, 4 months
1940	65 years, 6 months
1941	65 years, 8 months
1942	65 years, 10 months
1943–1954	66 years, 0 months
1955	66 years, 2 months
1956	66 years, 4 months
1957	66 years, 6 months
1958	66 years, 8 months
1959	66 years, 10 months
1960 & Later	67 years, 0 months

When Is a Person Disabled?

To be considered disabled, according to social security law, a person must have a physical or mental condition which:

- Prevents the worker from doing any gainful, substantial work, AND
- Is expected to last (or has lasted) for twelve months, or is expected to result in death.

Medical evidence from a physician must show that the worker is prevented from working. If he/she can do any job that is substantial and gainful, he/she is not considered disabled under social security law.

When a person receives social security disability, monthly benefits can also be paid to certain dependent family members.

- Unmarried child under age eighteen.
- A child disabled before age twenty-two who is over the age of eighteen.
- A spouse who cares for the disabled worker's child who is under age sixteen, or a child disabled before age twenty-two.
- A spouse who is sixty-two or older.

Work Credits Needed for Disability

The work credits needed depend upon the age of the worker when he/she became disabled.

- **Before Age Twenty-Four**—Six credits in the three-year period ending when the disability starts.
- **Ages Twenty-Four through Thirty**—Credit for working half the time between age twenty-one and the age of disability.
- **Age Thirty-One or Older**—Same number of credits as needed for retirement benefits.
- **Blind Person**—One credit for each year since 1950, or since becoming age twenty-one if that is later.

Approximate Social Security Benefits

The approximate benefit assumes the worker has had 6% pay raises each year through 1997. The calculations also assume the worker's current earnings will stay the same until the normal retirement age.

Tables A-8 and A-9 show projected benefits for retirement, death, and disability.

Table A-8—Approximate Social Security Benefits

Approximate Benefits For Workers Earning $16,000–35,000 in 1997					
Year Born	AIME (Average Indexed Monthly Earning)	Current Annual Income			
		$16,000 to $20,000	$21,000 to $25,000	$26,000 to $30,000	$31,000 to $35,000
1935	Retirement	$1,224	$1,564	$1,904	$2,228
	Death	$1,200	$1,533	$1,867	$2,182
	Disability	$1,187	$1,517	$1,848	$2,159
1936 to 1940	Retirement	$1,258	$1,608	$1,957	$2,294
	Death	$1,211	$1,547	$1,884	$2,204
	Disability	$1,198	$1,531	$1,864	$2,180
1941 to 1945	Retirement	$1,321	$1,688	$2,055	$2,415
	Death	$1,228	$1,569	$1,911	$2,240
	Disability	$1,214	$1,552	$1,889	$2,214
1946 to 1950	Retirement	$1,368	$1,748	$2,128	$2,505
	Death	$1,246	$1,593	$1,939	$2,277
	Disability	$1,231	$1,573	$1,915	$2,248
1951 to 1955	Retirement	$1,411	$1,803	$2,195	$2,586
	Death	$1,265	$1,617	$1,969	$2,316
	Disability	$1,243	$1,589	$1,935	$2,275
1956 to 1961	Retirement	$1,458	$1,864	$2,269	$2,674
	Death	$1,296	$1,656	$2,016	$2,375
	Disability	$1,261	$1,612	$1,963	$2,310
1962 to 1967	Retirement	$1,497	$1,913	$2,329	$2,745
	Death	$1,365	$1,745	$2,124	$2,503
	Disability	$1,286	$1,644	$2,002	$2,359
1968	Retirement	$1,500	$1,916	$2,333	$2,750
	Death	$1,457	$1,862	$2,267	$2,672
	Disability	$1,304	$1,666	$2,028	$2,391

Table A-9—Approximate Social Security Benefits

		Approximate Benefits For Workers Earning $36,000–55,000 in 1997			
Year Born	**AIME** (Average Indexed Monthly Earning)	**Current Annual Income**			
		$36,000 to $40,000	$41,000 to $45,000	$46,000 to $50,000	$51,000 to $55,000
1935	Retirement	$2,522	$2,783	$3,034	$3,273
	Death	$2,457	$2,693	$2,921	$3,136
	Disability	$2,422	$2,646	$2,862	$3,065
1936 to 1940	Retirement	$2,605	$2,891	$3,178	$3,452
	Death	$2,495	$2,754	$3,002	$3,237
	Disability	$2,462	$2,708	$2,944	$3,166
1941 to 1945	Retirement	$2,750	$3,081	$3,429	$3,772
	Death	$2,537	$2,813	$3,108	$3,386
	Disability	$2,505	$2,771	$3,051	$3,314
1946 to 1950	Retirement	$2,858	$3,222	$3,588	$3,951
	Death	$2,575	$2,876	$3,196	$3,508
	Disability	$2,540	$2,830	$3,145	$3,450
1951 to 1955	Retirement	$2,960	$3,346	$3,732	$4,109
	Death	$2,617	$2,945	$3,275	$3,593
	Disability	$2,567	$2,881	$3,200	$3,511
1956 to 1961	Retirement	$3,073	$3,477	$3,881	$4,283
	Death	$2,696	$3,045	$3,393	$3,722
	Disability	$2,612	$2,946	$3,279	$3,590
1962 to 1967	Retirement	$3,161	$3,577	$3,993	$4,409
	Death	$2,883	$3,262	$3,642	$4,021
	Disability	$2,681	$3,030	$3,377	$3,712
1968	Retirement	$3,166	$3,583	$4,000	$4,416
	Death	$3,077	$3,481	$3,886	$4,291
	Disability	$2,725	$3,083	$3,442	$3,795

Table A-10 Retirement and Survivor Benefits

Match nearest AIME from Tables A-8 and A-9

Retirement and Survivor Benefits					
AIME (Average Indexed Monthly Earning)	Retired Worker[1]	Retired Worker Age 62	Surviving Spouse (under age 60) 1–2 children[2]	Surviving Spouse Age 60	Maximum Family Benefit
4,800	1,449	1,159	2,173	1,036	2,536
4,700	1,434	1,147	2,151	1,025	2,509
4,600	1,419	1,135	2,128	1,014	2,483
4,500	1,404	1,123	2,106	1,003	2,457
4,400	1,389	1,111	2,083	993	2,431
4,300	1,374	1,099	2,061	982	2,404
4,200	1,359	1,087	2,038	971	2,378
4,100	1,344	1,075	2,016	960	2,352
4,000	1,329	1,063	1,993	950	2,326
3,900	1,314	1,051	1,971	939	2,299
3,800	1,299	1,039	1,948	928	2,273
3,700	1,284	1,027	1,926	918	2,247
3,600	1,269	1,015	1,903	907	2,221
3,500	1,254	1,003	1,881	896	2,194
3,400	1,239	991	1,858	885	2,168
3,300	1,224	979	1,836	885	2,168
3,200	1,209	967	1,813	864	2,116
3,100	1,194	955	1,791	853	2,089
3,000	1,179	943	1,768	842	2,063
2,900	1,164	931	1,746	832	2,037
2,800	1,149	919	1,723	821	2,011
2,700	1,127	901	1,690	805	1,972
2,600	1,095	876	1,642	782	1,916
2,500	1,063	850	1,594	760	1,873
2,400	1,031	824	1,546	737	1,830
2,300	999	799	1,498	714	1,787
2,200	967	773	1,450	691	1,744
2,100	935	748	1,402	668	1,701
2,000	903	722	1,354	645	1,659
1,900	873	696	1,306	622	1,616
1,800	839	671	1,258	599	1,573
1,700	807	645	1,210	577	1,486
1,600	775	620	1,162	554	1,399

1. Normal retirement age for unreduced benefits.

2. Surviving spouse under age sixty must have at least one child under sixteen. Child's benefit continues to age eighteen.

Table A-11—Disability Benefits

Match nearest AIME from Tables A-8 and A-9

Disability Benefits				
AIME (Average Indexed Monthly Earning)	Disabled Worker	Disabled Worker Spouse & Children	One Child No Surviving Spouse	Spouse Age 62
4,800	1,449	2,173	724	543
4,700	1,434	2,151	717	537
4,600	1,419	2,128	709	532
4,500	1,404	2,106	702	526
4,400	1,389	2,083	694	520
4,300	1,374	2,061	687	515
4,200	1,359	2,038	679	509
4,100	1,344	2,016	672	504
4,000	1,329	1,993	664	498
3,900	1,314	1,971	657	492
3,800	1,299	1,948	649	487
3,700	1,284	1,926	642	481
3,600	1,269	1,903	634	475
3,500	1,254	1,881	627	470
3,400	1,239	1,858	619	464
3,300	1,224	1,836	612	459
3,200	1,209	1,813	604	453
3,100	1,191	1,791	597	447
3,000	1,179	1,768	589	442
2,900	1,164	1,746	582	436
2,800	1,149	1,723	574	430
2,700	1,127	1,690	563	422
2,600	1,095	1,642	547	410
2,500	1,063	1,594	531	398
2,400	1,031	1,546	515	386
2,300	999	1,498	499	374
2,200	967	1,450	483	362
2,100	935	1,402	467	350
2,000	903	1,354	451	338
1,900	871	1,306	435	326
1,800	839	1,258	419	314
1,700	807	1,210	403	302
1,600	775	1,162	387	290

Glossary

ACCRUAL METHOD OF ACCOUNTING—Income is reported when earned, whether or not received, and expenses are reported when they are incurred, whether or not they are paid. The accrual method must be used to track inventory.

ADJUSTABLE RATE MORTGAGE—A mortgage with a changing interest rate. The interest rate will rise or decline according to one of the national indexes.

ANNUAL PERCENTAGE RATE—The interest rate borrowers pay on a loan.

ANNUAL RENEWABLE TERM LIFE—Term life insurance that is renewed each year. As a person grows older, each year the cost of insurance is more expensive.

ANNUITY—A tax deferred investment account offered through an insurance company. When a person places money into an annuity account, they can receive guaranteed payments for a lifetime or for a certain time period.

ARM'S—Adjustable rate mortgages. Interest rates move up and down based on market conditions.

ASSET ALLOCATION—How money is divided among various investments, such as 30% in bonds, 30% in cash and 40% in stocks.

ASSETS—Something you own that has value, such as a home, stocks, personal property, or a savings account. An asset can also be something that is owed to you, like a note held for money to be paid in the future.

BABY-BOOMERS—Those born during the twenty-five years following World War II. During this time, the birth rate greatly increased. As these people have aged, they have affected the economy in various ways due to their sheer numbers. When the baby-boomers retire, there will be more retirees than workers.

BALANCE SHEET—A financial statement showing what you own and what you owe.

BALANCED FUNDS—A mutual fund that must keep a certain percentage of its assets in bonds or preferred stocks and the rest in common stocks. It is more conservative than a growth fund and tends to be more stable, not moving up or down very quickly.

BASIS—The amount of money a person has in an asset. This includes cash and loans. For example, the basis in a home would consist of the total purchase price, closing costs upon purchase, and all improvements made to the home. The basis for any investment is what you pay for it plus other money spent to improve or to add to the investment.

BENEFICIARY—Someone named to receive assets from another person upon their death.

BIG BOARDS—A popular term for the New York Stock Exchange and the American Stock Exchange since they are the two largest stock exchanges in the country.

BILL CONSOLIDATION LOAN—A larger loan by a second party to pay off many smaller loans.

BLUE CHIP STOCK—The stock from a well-known company. The company's products and services are widely used, and the company has established its ability to make profits and pay dividends on their stock.

BODILY INJURY LIABILITY—A term used in auto insurance for liability protection. It provides financial compensation for injury or death caused by your automobile.

BOND FUNDS—A mutual fund that invests all or most of its money in bonds.

BOND RATINGS—Moody's Investor Services and Standard & Poor's are two companies that rate bonds. Higher rated bonds have little risk, but the issuer may default on lower rated bonds and not make the promised payments.

BONDS—An I.O.U. or promissory note of a corporation, government, or municipality. The issuing party promises to pay the bondholder a certain amount of interest for a specified time period for the "loan."

BREAK-EVEN RATE OF RETURN—What you must earn on your money to stay even with taxes and inflation.

BROKERAGE ACCOUNT—Your personal account with a brokerage firm.

BROKERAGE FIRM—A company that deals with taking orders from the public to buy and sell securities. The firm charges a commission for this service.

CASH FLOW STATEMENT—A financial statement that shows how much money a person or company brings in and how much they spend. It compares income to expenses.

CASH METHOD OF ACCOUNTING—Income is reported when it is received and expenses are reported when they are paid.

CERTIFICATE OF DEPOSIT (CD)—A type of savings account issued by a financial institution. The institution promises to pay a set interest rate for a certain time period. At the end of the time period, the agreement ends.

CLOSED-END FUNDS—A mutual fund that offers a fixed number of shares. Once the specified number of shares are sold, new investors are allowed into the fund only by buying someone else's shares.

CLOSING COSTS—The many costs and fees associated with closing escrow on a home or other real estate purchase. These include recording fees, title insurance (to protect the lender), points or loan origination fees, title search, surveys and appraisals, preparation of documents, credit reports, attorney fees, and other costs.

COBRA—The Consolidated Omnibus Budget Reconciliation Act of 1985. It provides the right for people to buy health insurance from their former employer for a minimum of eighteen months.

CODICIL—An addition to a will to change or explain some of the will's provisions or to add new provisions.

COINSURANCE—A term often used with medical insurance. It is the amount the insured pays for each claim, (often 20%) once they have met their deductible.

COLLISION INSURANCE—The part of automobile insurance that covers physical damage done to an automobile regardless of responsibility.

COMMERCIAL PAPER—A short-term note (from one to 270 days) issued by a corporation. The time period is fixed, but the interest rate fluctuates daily with the current market. The minimum investment is usually $25,000.

Commercial paper is used by corporations to finance their short-term working capital.

COMMON STOCK—Securities representing part ownership in a company.

COMMUNITY PROPERTY—All property acquired during marriage, except gifts and inheritances, becomes community property. Each spouse owns 50% and is entitled to 50% when death or divorce occurs. Community property states are: AZ, CA, ID, LA, NV, NM, TX, WA, and WI.

COMPOUND INTEREST—Interest compounds when it is added to the principal on deposit with a financial institution. At the end of a certain time period (daily, monthly, quarterly, or annually), the interest is added to the principal, then the combined sum compounds to earn interest for the next time period. (See Rule of 72).

COMPREHENSIVE INSURANCE—A type of automobile insurance that protects a person against physical damage done to their car. It covers a wide variety of perils not covered through collision or liability insurance. Some of these perils could be glass breakage, theft, fire, or flying objects.

CONSUMER PRICE INDEX (CPI)—Statistics gathered by the U.S. Department of Labor, Bureau of Labor Statistics to show the change over time of prices in goods and services. It measures what a sample of goods and services cost today compared to some time in the past. Since the CPI is an index of the rising cost of goods and services, it measures inflation.

CREDIT REPORT—A report issued by one of the many credit bureaus showing a person's payment history on credit cards and other installment debt. These reports are used by lending institutions to determine if the person has been diligent in meeting their obligations.

DEDUCTIBLE—An insurance term used in automobile, homeowner's, and medical policies stating the amount the insured agrees to pay before their policy starts paying. Medical policies have a deductible that is met each year; the other policies have a deductible that is paid for each claim filed. For all policies, the higher the deductible, the lower the cost of insurance.

DEFINED BENEFIT PLAN—A traditional pension plan that pays a retiree a fixed monthly check based on salary, years of service, and age at retirement.

DISABILITY INCOME PROTECTION—Insurance that protects the insured against lost wages should they become either permanently or totally disabled and unable to work.

DIVERSIFICATION—Spreading investment dollars among many different investments or many different companies. Diversification is automatic with mutual funds since ownership in one fund represents ownership in hundreds of companies.

DIVIDENDS—Payments to stockholders from the issuing corporation. Dividends come from the company's current profits or sometimes past earnings. They are paid equally for each share of stock owned although amounts vary for common and preferred stock.

DOLLAR COST AVERAGING—A system of buying stocks or mutual funds at regular intervals to balance the highs and lows associated with market fluctuations.

EDUCATION IRA—An education fund, not an IRA. All contributions are non-deductible and limited to $500 each year. The beneficiary must be under age eighteen. Money must be taken out by age thirty. Contributions are subject to income limitations.

EMERGENCY FUND SAVINGS—A term used in financial planning for a savings account designated to cover unforeseen family emergencies.

ENROLLMENT PERIOD—A term used in group insurance contracts that are offered by employers. During the enrollment period, all members of the group are admitted for an amount of health or life insurance (determined by the employer) regardless of insurability or prior health conditions.

EQUITY—The value of property beyond the total amount owed on it. This equity is an asset.

ESTATE PLANNING—The process of planning for the disposition of assets accumulated during a person's lifetime. A good estate plan will minimize taxes and provide for the passing of assets to heirs in a timely manner.

ESTATE TAX—A federal tax levied upon property transferred at death. Currently, a taxpayer has a $600,000 exemption, so no taxes are due on estates worth less than the exemption amount.

EXCHANGE PRIVILEGES—A term used by mutual fund companies that allow money to be transferred from one or more funds within their family to other funds within their family.

FEDERAL DEFICIT—When the government spends more than it takes in, the result is a deficit. Each year that the government has deficit spending, an amount is added to the public debt. The cost of the public debt is shared by all taxpayers.

FEDERAL DEPOSIT INSURANCE CORPORATION (FDIC)—Insurance offered by the federal government to cover deposits in member banks and credit unions. Each account is covered for a maximum of $100,000.

FEDERAL RESERVE—Responsible for the monetary policy of the country. Their concerns are full employment, steady growth, and stable prices. The Federal Reserve Board controls the amount of money in circulation. When more money is in circulation, prices and interest rates begin to rise.

FINAL EXPENSES—A life insurance term for the money used to pay burial and funeral expenses.

FIXED EXPENSES—An expense that is the same amount each month. This term is used in budgets and financial statements.

FIXED INCOME—Income that is the same each month. It can come from interest earnings on a savings account, from a fixed pension, or from bonds, mortgages, and notes.

FIXED INTEREST MORTGAGE—A mortgage having the same payments and same interest rate for the term of the mortgage, normally fifteen or thirty years.

FIXING-UP EXPENSES—Used in figuring the profit from the sale of a principal residence. Fixing-up expenses are made to make the home more salable and are incurred ninety days prior to signing the contract

GENERAL PARTNER—The managing agent of a limited partnership who generally purchases the investment and assumes responsibility for prudent, daily management.

GIFTING—A term used in estate planning. It is a method of giving assets to heirs early, thereby removing them from the donor's taxable estate. Currently, each person is allowed to gift up to $10,000 each year with no gift tax due. The beneficiary only pays taxes on the earnings from the gift. The gift itself has no taxes due.

GLOBAL FUNDS—Mutual funds that invest in stocks and bonds worldwide.

GOVERNMENT SECURITIES—Treasury Notes, Treasury Bills, and Treasury Bonds issued by the federal government. The earnings from these securities are exempt from state income taxes.

GRACE PERIOD—Most state laws require that life insurance carry a thirty-day grace period to make a past due premium payment before the company cancels the policy. Automobile insurance and homeowner's insurance are not required to have grace periods. When premiums are not received on time, the company automatically cancels the policy.

GROUP LIFE INSURANCE—An insurance plan offered by an employer for the employees. Group plans allow life insurance coverage to decrease with age so the employer can pay the same premium for all employees. Therefore, older employees have less insurance coverage than younger employees.

GROWTH AND INCOME FUNDS—Mutual funds that have a dual purpose: growth and income.

GROWTH FUNDS—Mutual funds that invest primarily in growth stock.

GROWTH STOCK—Stock issued by an emerging company that has shown a rapid increase in earnings.

HARD ASSETS—Investments in gold, silver, and other precious metals.

HEALTH INSURANCE—Insurance to cover illness and accidents. Policies are sold with an annual deductible, usually $100 to $250. After the deductible is met, the insurance will pay a percentage of all covered medical costs, the standard is 80% (see coinsurance). After reaching the stop loss clause, the policy pays 100% of all charges up to the policy limits.

HEALTH MAINTENANCE ORGANIZATIONS—A new concept for providing total health care under one roof. FHP and Kaiser Permanente are two examples. Doctors and other health care employees work set hours. Lab work, x-rays, and other diagnostic work is performed in the same complex as the examining physician.

HOME EQUITY LINE OF CREDIT—Similar to a home equity loan, except instead of receiving cash for the equity, the owner receives a line of credit with the institution. The owner can then write checks up to the amount of the credit. Once the balance is paid down, or paid off, the credit can be reused.

HOME EQUITY LOAN—Lending institutions usually offer these loans to those who have more than 20% equity in their home. They will take a second trust deed on the property to secure the loan. Some institutions will offer a loan up to 90% of the appraised value of the home.

HYBRID METHOD OF ACCOUNTING—A combination of the cash and accrual methods.

INCOME MUTUAL FUNDS—Mutual funds that have the goal of providing a steady dividend. They will usually invest in government securities, corporate bonds, or certificates of deposit.

INDEPENDENT CONTRACTOR—An independent contractor is a person who works for others. He or she has their own tools and needs no training or supervision. They are hired to do a job and usually invoice their customers.

INFLATION—A rise in the cost of goods and services as measured by the Consumer Price Index.

INFLATION HEDGE—An investment that will increase in value over the years and stay ahead of the combined increases paid for goods and services.

INSTALLMENT DEBT—Credit cards and bank loans that are paid off in monthly installments.

INSURANCE COMMISSIONER—A state official who regulates the insurance industry within that state. The commissioner enforces the state insurance code, making certain that companies and agents comply with the code.

INSURED—The party who owns insurance as a form of protection against unknown losses.

INSURER—The insurance company who provides a certain type of insurance for a set premium.

INVESTMENT COMPANIES—The name given to companies that offer and manage mutal funds.

JOINT TENANCY WITH RIGHT OF SURVIVORSHIP—An asset owned by two parties that passes to the surviving party or parties when one dies.

JUNK BONDS—Low-grade bonds with a substandard rating. They carry more risk and pay higher interest than higher rated bonds.

KEOGH PLAN—A retirement plan for small business owners or self-employed people. All contributions are tax deductible.

LEVERAGE—Using borrowed money to make money.

LIABILITIES—Claims against a corporation or an individual. They include money owed for taxes, wages, bank loans, and other debts.

LIABILITY INSURANCE—In a homeowner's policy, liability covers medical payments to others if they are injured on the insured's property. It also covers physical damage to the property of others that occurs on the insured's premises.

LIFE INSURANCE—Insurance to cover the loss of life of the primary wage earners of a family. Available policies fall within two categories: whole life (a savings portion is attached) or term (pure insurance). Both concepts come in many varieties.

LIMITED PARTNER—An investor in a limited partnership.

LIMITED PARTNERSHIPS—An investment vehicle managed by a general partner for the benefit of a specified number of limited partners. The limited partners put up the money and participate in their pro rata share of income distributions from the partnership. The general partner assumes responsibility for management.

LIQUID ASSETS—Assets such as bank account savings that can be readily converted to cash.

LIVING TRUST—A legal document drafted for the benefit of a person who often names themselves as the beneficiary. It can also pass property to heirs upon the trust holder's death, avoiding the cost and time of probate.

LOAN ORIGINATION FEE—A charge by a financial institution for a new mortgage loan. In reality, it is the commission paid to the institution and/or the loan officer. It is commonly referred to as "points."

MEDICAID—A health insurance program for people with low income and limited assets. It is usually run by state welfare or social service agencies.

MEDICAL SAVINGS PLANS (MSP)—A tax-deferred, tax-deductible savings plan that can be used to pay for medical expenses for the self-employed or some small employers. To participate, you must have a high deductible health insurance policy.

MEDICARE—A federal insurance program for people age sixty-five and older and other people with qualifying disabilities.

MEDIGAP—Private insurance policies designed to cover the portion of medical expenses not covered by Medicare.

MONEY MARKET FUNDS—A mutual fund that invests in short-term money investments such as certificates of deposit and corporate commercial paper. Some funds invest solely in government obligations. The interest rate changes daily and compounds daily.

MOODY'S INVESTOR SERVICES—A service that rates bonds according to their volatility. From highest to lowest, bonds are rated: Aaa, Aa, A-1, A, Baa-1, Baa, BA, B, Caa. The highest rated bonds are considered prime, while the lowest are considered speculative.

MORTALITY TABLES—A base for calculating the cost per thousand for a life insurance policy. The mortality tables show how many people died during a certain time at each age.

MORTGAGE INSURANCE—Decreasing term insurance often sold to cover a mortgage. The insurance declines each year as the mortgage decreases.

MUTUAL FUNDS—Investments in stocks, bonds, and cash accounts that are diversified over thousands of different investments to meet a stated objective of the fund, such as growth, growth and income, or income (many variations exist within each of these objectives). All funds will have an objective, and the fund manager selects the investments to meet that objective. New shares are continuously offered to the public, and current shares can be redeemed on demand.

NASDAQ—An acronym for National Association of Securities Dealers Automated Quotations. An information network that provides brokers and dealers with price quotations for trading on the over-the-counter market.

NATIONAL ASSOCIATION OF SECURITIES DEALERS (NASD)—A branch of the Securities and Exchange Commission that oversees the selling of securities by brokers and dealers. The NASD is committed to enforcing their rules of fair practice, to preventing fraudulent acts, and to seeing that investors receive full disclosure via a prospectus or offering circular. All persons selling securities to the public must be licensed and registered with the NASD.

NET ASSET VALUE (NAV)—A term used by mutual fund companies to show what each share of the fund is worth. NAV is calculated daily by subtracting the fund's liabilities from the market value of the shares, then dividing the balance by the number of shares outstanding.

NET SALES PRICE—A tax term used for the sale of real estate and other assets. The net sales price is the contract sales price minus the selling costs.

NET WORTH—On a net worth statement, net worth is assets minus liabilities. It shows what a person or company owns free and clear after all debts are paid.

NET WORTH STATEMENT—A financial statement that lists the assets and liabilities of a person or a business. The bottom line is the net worth; what is left after all debts are paid.

NO LOAD FUNDS—Mutual funds that are sold through fund advertising rather than through broker-dealers and registered representatives. The investor pays no sales charge.

NONFORFEITURE OPTIONS—A life insurance term. If the owner stops making payments on a permanent policy, the life insurance company must give to the owner the cash value of the policy, or insurance benefits equivalent to the cash value. The cash value and the equivalent benefits are referred to as nonforfeiture options.

OPEN-END FUNDS—Mutual funds that continuously offer new shares to the public and will redeem current shares upon request of the shareholder.

OVER-THE-COUNTER MARKET—Securities traded by securities dealers for their clients. The securities sold are from smaller companies that do not qualify to have their stock listed on one of the exchanges.

PERSONAL PROPERTY INSURANCE—Insurance used to cover personal belongings, such as appliances, furniture, and jewelry. Homeowner's policies usually automatically cover personal property for one-half of the dwelling coverage. Renters must buy a separate renters policy to cover their belongings.

POINTS—A type of prepaid interest on a mortgage loan (loan discount), or a loan origination fee, which is a service fee paid to the lender.

POLICY LIMITS—The limit or cap that an insurer will pay per individual for major medical insurance.

PREFERRED STOCK—A class of stock that has a claim on the company's stock before common stockholders are paid. If the company liquidates, preferred stockholders have priority over common stockholders.

PREMIUM—1) When the market price for bonds and preferred stock rise above the original purchase price, they sell for more than their par value and are said to be selling for a premium. 2) Dollars paid in exchange for insurance coverage. Insurance can protect a persons income or value of work performed, a home, personal belongings, automobiles, illness, accidents, and disability.

PRIVATE MORTGAGE INSURANCE—An insurance policy written to protect the lender of a mortgage from declining prices when they have more than 80% invested in the property.

PRIVATE PLACEMENT—A type of limited partnership that raises smaller amounts of money and is not required to be registered with the SEC. There can be no more than thirty-five limited partners.

PROBATE—The legal process of passing ownership of property from a deceased person to others. If there is no will, probate will pass the property to heirs according to state law.

PROSPECTUS—A document required by the Securities Act of 1933 that discloses pertinent information about an investment. Registered representatives are required to give a prospective investor a prospectus before accepting money and filling out an application.

REDUCED PAID-UP INSURANCE—A nonforfeiture option for permanent life insurance policies. The cash value purchases a reduced, paid-up policy.

REFINANCING—Refinancing occurs when a mortgage holder takes out a new loan on their home or other real property. People usually refinance when interest rates drop 2% or more below their original mortgage, or when property values rise, giving them more equity in their home.

REGISTERED REPRESENTATIVES—A reference to those who sell securities. They are required to be registered with the NASD (National Association of Securities Dealers), the branch of the Securities and Exchange Commission that regulates brokers and their representatives.

REIT'S—Real Estate Investment Trusts. A type of mutual fund that owns real estate investments instead of stocks and bonds. REITS are traded on the stock exchanges.

RENTER'S INSURANCE—An insurance policy offered to renters to protect their personal belongings against theft, and destruction from certain perils.

RIDERS—An addendum to an insurance policy that gives additional coverage for an additional premium.

ROTH IRA—A new IRA available in 1998. The contributions are not deductible, but all money taken out of the plan are tax free. More people can contribute to a Roth IRA because the income eligibility limits are higher than the traditional IRA.

RULE OF 72—A rule used to easily calculate how many years it will take for a given sum to double at a specified interest rate. Dividing the interest rate into 72, tells how many years it will take for the principal to double. $1,000 earning 6% will double in twelve years (72 ÷ 6 = 12).

SABOTEUR—One who causes loss, damage, or destruction.

SECOND TRUST DEED—A mortgage on a piece of real estate that is in second position to the first lien holder.

SECURITIES—Investments such as stocks, bonds, mutual funds, and limited partnerships that have no guarantee for their performance. They must be purchased through a securities dealer that is registered with the Securities and Exchange Commission.

SECURITIES AND EXCHANGE COMMISSION (SEC)—The Securities and Exchange Commission was established by Congress to help protect investors.

SECURITIES INVESTOR PROTECTION ACT (SIPC)—Congress passed the Securities Investor Protection Act in 1970 to protect investors from loss if a brokerage firm fails. Each member firm pays an amount to the SIPC fund. If a member firm fails, the SIPC fund covers the liabilities owed by the broker.

SELF-EMPLOYMENT—Self-employed persons work for themselves. They may or may not have employees. Their form of doing business is a sole-proprietorship, and they report their income and expenses on Schedule C when they file their personal tax return (Form 1040).

SELF-EMPLOYMENT TAX—FICA and Medicare tax due from all sole proprietors who have a profit on their business. Since they are the owner and the employee, they pay both taxes for the employee and the employer. The current rate is 15.3%.

SELF-INSURANCE—An amount you determine that you can afford to pay for a certain loss. If you self-insure, you reduce the premiums you will pay to an insurance company.

SEP IRA—A retirement plan for the self-employed. They can contribute 13.04% of net earnings from self-employment to this plan. All contributions are tax deductible.

SERIES EE BONDS—A U.S. Government bond sold in denominations ranging from $25 to $5,000. The interest earned can be tax free if used for education.

SETTLEMENT STATEMENT—A final statement given to persons who have purchased a personal residence or other real estate. It lists the price paid for the property and all amounts dispersed from the escrow account to pay for expenses.

SIMPLE INTEREST—Interest that is not added to the principal at the end of the compounding period.

SIMPLE IRA—A retirement plan for small employers who have one hundred or fewer employees.

SMALL BUSINESS ADMINISTRATION (SBA)—A branch of the federal government designed to help small business owners. They offer advice and provide loans for small businesses.

SOLE PROPRIETOR—A person who is self-employed or runs their own unincorporated business.

SPECIALTY FUNDS—A mutual fund that invests in a particular product or has a special emphasis. Some examples are gold funds, environmental funds, health care funds, and overseas funds.

STANDARD AND POOR'S—A company that rates bonds. From highest or prime grade to lowest or very speculative bonds, their ratings are: AAA, AA, A, BBB, BB, B, CCC

STANDARD RISKS—A person considered to be an average risk according to their age and current health condition or their current driving record.

STATE INSURANCE CODE—The law that regulates insurance companies within that state. It is enforced by the insurance commissioner.

STEPPED-UP BASIS—When an investment passes to an heir at its market value as of the date of death, rather than the original purchase price, it is said to have a stepped-up basis.

STOCKS—Ownership of shares in a corporation.

STOP LOSS CLAUSE—A feature of major medical insurance that relieves the insured from paying any more once a certain limit is reached, such as $5,000 or $10,000.

SUBCONTRACTOR—An independent contractor who works for others. He or she has their own tools and needs no training or supervision. They are hired to do a job and usually invoice their customers.

SUBSTANDARD RISKS—A person considered to be an above average risk for health, life, or automobile insurance.

TAKING TITLE—The many ways that real estate or other property can be owned by one or more persons. Some examples are: 1) joint ownership with right of survivorship, 2) tenants in common, 3) tenants in the entirety, 4) separate property, and 5) community property.

TAX BRACKET—The percentage paid in federal and state income taxes once income reaches a certain level.

TAX SHELTERED ANNUITY—A contract with an insurance company, usually under section 403(b) of the IRS code, where the participant pays in a monthly sum that comes from payroll deduction. The contribution is tax deferred until withdrawal. The amount paid reduces gross wages dollar for dollar.

TENANTS BY THE ENTIRETY—A way to hold title on property among any number of persons that can also denote unequal ownership. Each co-owner has a separate legal title to his/her undivided interest. Upon a co-owner's death, the property passes to the other tenants. Co-owners cannot sell their portion of the property without the permission of others.

TENANTS IN COMMON—A way to hold title on property among any number of persons. It can also denote unequal ownership. Each co-owner has a separate legal title to his/her undivided interest. Co-owners can sell their share of the property without permission from the other tenants. Upon a co-owner's death, the property passes to his/her heirs according to his/her will. No right of survivorship exists among tenants.

TERM INSURANCE—A reference to life insurance contracts that have no cash value buildup. The insurance premiums pay for the cost of pure insurance and will not be returned to the insured.

TERM RIDER—An addition made to a life insurance policy that provides for additional term coverage for additional premiums paid.

TESTAMENTARY TRUST—Created as part of a will. It can be canceled or changed before the will maker dies. It comes into existence upon the death of the will maker.

TITLE INSURANCE—Required by lenders to protect their ownership in the property. The insurance will pay the lender if title to the property is contested by the courts and the lender loses their investment.

TITLE SEARCH—Research done by an escrow company to make sure the ownership of the property is as stated.

TREASURY BILLS—Short-term debt securities offered by the U.S. Government. Minimum investment starts at $10,000. The holding period can be three months, six months, or one year. The interest earned is exempt from state income taxes. New issues are sold through a Federal Reserve Bank; outstanding issues are traded on the over-the-counter market.

TREASURY BONDS—Bonds with holding periods of ten years or longer that are offered by the U.S. Government. The interest earned is not taxable to the states.

TREASURY NOTES—Short-term investments, ranging from two to ten years, that are offered by the U.S. Government. Interest earned is not taxable to the states.

TRUST DEED—On pieces of real property, a trust deed is taken by the lender to secure their interest in the property. Should the mortgagee not make the payments as promised, the lender can repossess the property.

TRUSTS—Used in estate planning to minimize estate taxes, avoid probate, and pass assets on to heirs in the most efficient manner.

UMBRELLA POLICY—An umbrella liability policy can be an insurance rider to a homeowner's policy that gives liability protection for incidents such as lawsuits or unusual accidents that are not covered by other insurance.

UNDERWRITING—A procedure used by life insurance companies to approve a party for insurance. Underwriting determines if the company will insure the amount applied for. They may order medical records from doctors and hospitals and require urine or blood specimens.

U.S. GOVERNMENT SECURITIES—Used to refer to U.S. Treasury Bonds, U.S. Treasury Bills, and U.S. Treasury Notes.

VARIABLE EXPENSES—Used in budgeting or in preparing financial statements. For individuals, they are expenses that vary month to month. They are usually expenditures for items like food, clothing, and recreation.

WILLS—A will determines how property will be distributed to heirs upon the maker's death. Wills also name guardians for minor children and appoint executors for the estate.

ZERO COUPON BONDS—These bonds are sold at a discount and at maturity are worth their face value. Although interest is not paid annually, it is taxable annually.

Index